# National Trust Guide
# Seattle

# National Trust Guide
# Seattle

America's Guide for Architecture
and History Travelers

## WALT CROWLEY
with
Paul Dorpat
Photography Editor

PRESERVATION
PRESS

## John Wiley & Sons, Inc.
New York • Chichester • Weinheim • Brisbane • Singapore • Toronto

A cooperative publication with the National Trust for Historic Preservation, Washington, D.C., chartered by Congress in 1949 to encourage the preservation of sites, buildings, and communities significant in American history and culture.

This text is printed on acid-free paper.

*Library of Congress Cataloging in Publication Data:*
Crowley, Walt
    National trust guide, Seattle: America's guide for architecture and history travelers / Walt Crowley.
        XXX p.   XXX cm.
        "A cooperative publication with the National Trust for Historic Preservation, Washington, D.C." — T.p. verso.
        Includes index.
        ISBN  0-471-18044-0 (pbk. : alk. paper)
    1. Historic buildings — Washington (State) — Seattle — Guidebooks.
    2. Architecture—Washington (State) — Seattle — Guidebooks.
    3. Seattle (Wash.) — Buildings, structures, etc. — Guidebooks.
    4. Seattle (Wash.) — Guidebooks.    I. National Trust for Historic Preservation in the United States.    II. Title
FB99.S43C76   1998
979.7'78 — dc21                                    97-34627

Printed in the United States of America
10 9 8 7 6 5 4 3 2 1

# Contents

# Preface

Welcome to my city, Seattle. I have to confess my affection for this place, in part because I hated it upon my arrival as a teenager in 1961.

When my parents informed me that we were relocating from our home in Ridgefield, Connecticut, to a place called Seattle, I looked it up in the atlas and found it uncomfortably close to Alaska and remote from any city of significance. I imagined a frontier backwater of perpetual rain, sullen, mud-caked locals, and a cultural life consisting chiefly of totem pole carving and clog dancing.

I wasn't far from the mark, but Seattle was already changing when we arrived. The 1962 "Century 21" world's fair ushered in a new era that energized the city's movements for the arts, urban design, and progressive reform. Battles over the preservation of historic landmarks such as the Pike Place Market and Pioneer Square were defining moments in this process of democratic change and social renewal. It is no exaggeration to say that Seattle reclaimed its soul as well as its history in the preservation struggles of the late 1960s and 1970s, and this is a war that is far from over.

In writing this guide, I have tried to do more than just catalog the physical vestiges of Seattle's past. My hope is that the reader will come away with an understanding of the kinds of people, events, and dynamics that shaped the city's personality. More than monuments or curiosities, the structures and places described here are part of the architecture of Seattle's civic psyche, and, like subconscious memories, they represent forces that are still very much alive.

## How to Use This Book

The physical evidence of Seattle's history is arrayed like the concentric growth rings of a fallen cedar. Pioneer Square stands at the center, and its 1890s architecture survives largely intact, thanks to the vagaries of urban development and later preservation. Move outward from the Square in any direction and, with a few exceptions such as West Seattle, you move forward in time.

Thus, this book begins with Pioneer Square and focuses on Seattle's downtown districts because they contain most of its significant historic structures. A vicinity map, geographical orientation, and historical overview precede the narrative guide to each downtown district's attractions. As appropriate, actual walking or motor tours are offered.

The rest of Seattle is divided into six major sectors: North of Downtown, East of Downtown, Northwest Seattle, Northeast, Southeast, and West Seattle. Each sector is then subdivided into discrete districts or neighborhoods with their own orientations, histories, and narrative guides. A brief sampling of nearby historical attractions outside Seattle is also provided.

A consolidated register of official national, state, and city landmarks brings up the rear, along with a listing of major historical agencies and groups, a bibliography, and a general index.

## Advice to the Visitor

**WEATHER:** It rains in Seattle—no more than it does in New York City according to the rain gauge—but rainfall is spread out over more days of the year. Which brings us to the mythical phenomenon of a Seattle summer. It does not begin typically until mid-July, but it lasts into October; lately, September has been Seattle's most reliable month for summer weather. Winters are mild and wet, and snowfall within the city limits is rare. Late January and early February have, in recent years, offered a pleasant "thaw" of several weeks.

**SECURITY:** Seattle is by and large a clean, safe, and friendly city. Except as noted otherwise, you should feel comfortable on its streets most hours of the day and evening. Crimes against tourists are rare, but visitors should use common sense.

**JAYWALKING:** Seattle is one of the few places in the civilized world where you can get a ticket (and a healthy fine) for jaywalking. This is one souvenir you can do without.

**ALCOHOL AND OTHER VICES:** Washington State enacted Prohibition nearly four years before the rest of the country, and its laws retain a few Temperance twitches. "Taverns" may serve only beer and wine, while restaurants and hotels may also serve hard liquor. Minors are not permitted in taverns or cocktail lounges, and all bars must close between 2:00 and 6:00 A.M. Beer and wine may be purchased at most grocery stores, but hard liquor is available by the bottle only from state liquor stores. Public drinking is prohibited unless you're sitting in a sidewalk cafe, and laws against driving under the influence are enforced aggressively. Legal gambling is mostly limited to the state Lotto. Smokers should beware that the self-appointed Carrie Nations of tobacco prohibition are very busy here, although how this city can drink all that coffee without lighting up is beyond me. It might account for Seattle's growing edginess.

**TRANSPORTATION:** The city recently strengthened regulations governing taxi-cabs, and the overall quality of service is beginning to improve (I recommend Orange Cab and Red Top). Rates are set by law and posted in each cab. Metro offers good bus service throughout the city, and you may hop on any bus within the downtown core for no charge during the day (see "Downtown Orientation"). Downtown parking charges shock the locals but will probably strike visitors from larger cities as reasonable.

**PRIVATE PROPERTY:** Most properties listed in this book are public or commercial buildings open to visitors. Some, however, are private residences, and visitors should respect their owners' rights.

## Acknowledgments

I am deeply indebted to the knowledge, skills, and comradeship of Paul Dorpat, who supplied virtually all of the historical and original photography for this book. Mary Randlett and John Stamets also contributed key images, and I am grateful to the University of Washington Northwest Collection, the Museum of History and Industry, the Washington State Historical Museum, and other archives for permission to use many historic photographs. Special thanks are also due the University of Washington Press for use of its map art.

The text relies heavily on the work of other historians and architectural critics (please see the bibliography). I strongly recommend the writings of Murray Morgan, Roger Sale, Jeffrey Ochsner, and Lawrence Kreisman to visitors seeking a deeper understanding of Seattle's development. This book would not have been possible without the support and patient assistance of Karen Gordon and her staff in the Seattle Urban Conservation Division, as well as the staff of the State Office of Archeology and Historic Preservation.

Finally, I want to thank preservation consultant Shirley Courtois for reviewing and correcting the final manuscript, but I take full responsibility for any errors of commission or omission.

*Walt Crowley*
August 1997

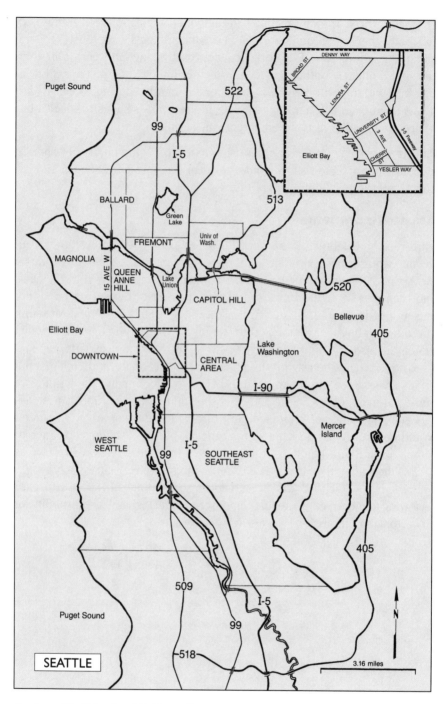

Courtesy of the University of Washington Press, copyright 1992.

# National Trust Guide
# Seattle

# Introduction

## THE SHAPING OF SEATTLE

*(More detailed local histories are provided in each section of this book. The following discussion offers a general survey of the events and forces that shaped Seattle and created the artifacts described in this book.)*

First there was fire—the ongoing tectonic collision that built up the Olympics and Cascades along the the eastern Pacific Ocean's "Rim of Fire" tens of millions of years ago and continues to rattle the region with earthquakes and volcanic eruptions. Then the ice came in waves of glacial advance and retreat until 14,000 years ago, when the shrinking Vashon Glacier gouged out Puget Sound and sculpted Seattle's hills and valleys. A great frozen dam then burst, and the Pacific rushed in and filled the vast estuary.

The first humans arrived across the Bering Strait land bridge 5,000 years later, although the oldest remains suggest that they belonged to a vanished caucasoid race predating the migration of the Asiatic ancestors of today's Native Americans. For at least 2,000 years, Seattle and its environs were populated by humans sharing the language and culture of the Lushootseed, or Puget Sound Salish.

Among them were the Duwamish, more a clan than a tribe, who lived lightly on the land in villages and longhouses along the shoreline of Elliott Bay and the meandering Duwamish River and its tributaries. Related bands and tribes populated north Seattle and the hills east of Lake Washington. Village middens and occasional brush fires, set to expose deer and other game, barely altered the environment, and the inhabitants' peaceful, culturally rich lives were disturbed only by raucus *potlatch* festivals and the occasional raiding party from more aggressive North Coast tribes.

1

Duwamish Chief Seattle welcomed the whites who arrived in 1851 and was repaid with exile to the Suquamish reservation, where he died 15 years later. *(Seattle Public Library)*

Although Spanish explorers had ventured as near as the San Juan Islands in 1790, the first European eyes to gaze upon this little Eden belonged to Captain George Vancouver and the crew of the British sloop-of-war *Discovery.* While filling in the blanks from Captain Cook's earlier North Pacific cruise in search of the fabled Northwest Passage to the Atlantic, Vancouver anchored off Bainbridge Island on May 19, 1792, within sight of Alki Point. The next day, he directed Second Lieutenant Peter Puget to take several longboats south into the inland waters that now bear his name.

Puget sailed west of Vashon Island and thus missed Seattle proper. Upon the survey party's return a week later, Vancouver steered the *Discovery* along the east channel but deemed the future site of Seattle unworthy of a visit. The

British sailors were ultimately welcomed by the Salish residents of "Puget's Sound," but, in a nice reversal of roles, only after the whites convinced the natives that they were not cannibals. The visitors soon left the area to press their search for the elusive Northwest Passage.

Whites did not return to Puget Sound until 1824, when a party of Hudson's Bay Company explorers blazed a trading route north from Fort George (old Astoria) on the Columbia River. Nine years later, the Company established Fort Nisqually on the sound, north of present-day Olympia, and encouraged settlement by American farmers. Notwithstanding this local coexistence, Britain and the United States pushed competing claims to the vast region between the Columbia River and the southern boundary of "Russian America" at 54 degrees 40 minutes north latitude.

The spat over sovereignty intensified after Lieutenant Charles Wilkes surveyed Puget Sound for the U.S. Navy in 1841 and filed detailed reports on the area's natural harbors, including Elliott Bay, which he named in honor of expedition chaplain  Rev. J. L. Elliott. Despite jingoistic chants of "54-40 or Fight!" the United States signed the compromise Oregon Treaty of July 15, 1846, which drew British Columbia's southern boundary along the 49th parallel. Old Glory now flew undisputed over the future states of Washington and Idaho (but for a brief military standoff on San Juan Island in 1859, which claimed the lives of a British pig and several American potatoes).

By 1850, Isaac Ebey and other refugees of the California gold rush had begun to scout upper Puget Sound. In 1850, John Holgate canoed into Elliott Bay and up the Duwamish, marveling at the fertile valley. He staked a claim (but neglected the paperwork) and returned to his native Iowa to round up his family. When he returned two years later, he discovered that Luther Collins and others had already homesteaded the same Duwamish bottomland.

When these homesteaders arrived overland from Olympia with their cattle, they already had neighbors. Lee Terry and David Denny were at work helping John Low build a log cabin at Alki Point. They were the vanguard of a party of settlers from Illinois led by David Denny's older brother Arthur, who had trekked west along the Oregon Trail to Portland. The rest of the settlers arrived on November 13, 1851, aboard the schooner *Exact*.

A dozen adults and as many children huddled in a roofless cabin, pelted by a bitter wintry rain, and, we are told, the women wept. Theirs were not tears of joy. Undaunted, the men boasted that this was the beginning of a second "New York," and they named the claim after Terry's home town. Skeptics soon appended the native word *Alki* (pronounced al-KEE by purists and al-KEYE by everyone else) meaning "by and by," and so New York-Alki was named.

The first cabin was finally finished and others begun when, in December, the brig *Leonesa* called at Alki and contracted for a load of timber piles. New York-Alki was in business. Meanwhile, Carson Boren, William Bell, and Arthur Denny explored Elliott Bay. On February 15, 1852, they decided that the little beach and island below present-day Washington Street was a much better location on which to realize their dream of a great metropolis to come, but they picked the unfortunate name "Duwamps." Merchant and physician Dr. David Maynard arrived from Olympia soon after and suggested a better name, Seattle, for the Duwamish chief who had welcomed the whites into his people's midst.

The town's fortunes received a tremendous boost that summer when Henry Yesler chose the new town of Seattle as the location for the first steam-powered sawmill on the Sound. Seattle's hills were quickly stripped of timber to feed the mill, and wood waste and ship ballast were used to begin to fill in the lagoons and mud flats that are now covered by Pioneer Square.

Not everything went smoothly. A squabble between Arthur Denny and "Doc" Maynard led to the mismatched platting of downtown streets along Skid Road (Yesler Way). Denny hoped to secure the capital of the new Washington Territory in 1854, but it went to Olympia. Relations with the

David "Doc" Maynard was one of early Seattle's most aggressive boosters, but he lost faith and sold his claim to most of present-day Pioneer Square. *(Museum of History and Industry)*

Railroads, "Mosquito Fleet" steamers, and trans-Pacific clippers had established Seattle's economic dominance of Puget Sound by the early 1880s. (A. Curtis, University of Washington Library Special Collections Neg. 32738)

The Territorial University (center) opened in 1861 atop Denny's Knoll, roughly where the Four Seasons Olympic Hotel stands today. (Seattle Public Library)

Indians soured following the signing of unfair pacts such as the Point Elliott (Mukilteo) Treaty of 1855, which denied the Duwamish their own reservation, and Seattle was attacked during a brief uprising in 1856.

The Territorial University was launched in a building atop Denny Knoll in 1861. Seattle incorporated four years later, but a taxpayer revolt repealed the charter and it had to be redrawn in 1869. The town was hit hardest by the decision of the Northern Pacific Railroad to locate its western terminus at the tiny village of Tacoma in 1873, but the line was not finished for another decade.

Seattle's citizens rallied by trying to build their own railroad across Snoqualmie Pass. The locally financed Seattle & Walla Walla never reached

5

its goal, but it did earn a profit hauling coal from newly discovered fields near Renton. The Northern Pacific (NP) finally arrived in Tacoma in 1883 and built a spur to Seattle the following year. Judge Thomas Burke arranged generous concessions that gave the NP control of Seattle's waterfront and later created "Railroad Avenue" (now Alaskan Way).

The employment of some 350 Chinese immigrants aggrieved Seattle's "Knights of Labor" and precipitated the forced expulsion of most Chinese early in 1886. At the same time, women briefly gained the vote and launched a campaign against saloons and vice. Despite these tensions, the town was booming on June 6,1889, when its wood-frame downtown burned to the ground. It quickly rebuilt with stone and brick, and most of these structures survive in Pioneer Square. The effort also created new opportunities for Seattle engineers and architects such as George Cotterill and Elmer Fisher to redefine the urban landscape.

When Washington gained statehood on November 11, 1889, Seattle was its dominant city. Some 43,000 residents were pushing Seattle outward from its original center, and new cable car and streetcar lines opened up "suburbs" such as First Hill, Queen Anne, and Lake Union to development. Swarms of "Mosquito Fleet" steamships linked Seattle with the rest of Puget Sound, and the Great Northern Railway gave Seattle its first direct transcontinental service in 1893. Not long after, the "Panic" of that year sent the national and local economies into a depression.

Economic growth resumed with the Klondike gold rush of 1897–98, and Seattle boosters and merchants positioned the city as the "Gateway to Alaska." In 1900, agents of the giant Stone & Webster utility cartel consolidated control of the city's streetcar system and hoped to monopolize electric service, and the railroads ruled the waterfront with an iron hand. This fueled a Progressive response that created City Light and, later, the Port of Seattle, and led to ambitious public works and plans such as City Engineer R.H. Thomson's crusade to flatten Denny Hill and every other topographical irregularity.

In 1903 the city hired the Olmsted brothers to lay out a comprehensive park system. The Olmsteds returned in 1908 to expand their plan after Seattle had annexed Ballard, West Seattle, and most of Southeast Seattle. They also helped to plan Seattle's first world's fair, the Alaska Yukon Pacific (AYP) Exposition, which was held in 1909 on the new (and present) campus of the University of Washington. The AYP celebrated and formalized Seattle's graduation from frontier boomtown to major Pacific Rim port city.

The following year, Seattle numbered more than 237,000 residents—marking more than a fivefold increase in just 20 years. Many of these new residents were recent arrivals from China, Japan, the Philippines, Scandinavia, Germany, and Italy (or their first generation children) and they created dis-

Seattle's original downtown was consumed by fire on June 6, 1889, but it was quickly rebuilt and now survives as Pioneer Square. *(Seattle Public Library)*

Few of the eager miners who crowded Seattle's docks during the Klondike gold rush of 1897–98 struck it rich, but they made millions for local merchants and ship owners. *(Asahel Curtis, Washington State Historical Museum)*

The Smith Tower's steel skeleton rose in 1914 to claim the prize of being the "tallest building west of the Mississippi." *(Ivar's)*

tinctive neighborhood cultures in the International District, Ballard, Georgetown, and Rainier Valley. The Pike Place Public Market, established in 1907, became the city's unofficial melting pot and cultural general assembly.

By 1911, the Union Pacific and Milwaukee Road had arrived to give Seattle a total of four transcontinental rail lines. That year Olmsted protégé Virgil Bogue unveiled his ambitious comprehensive plan for the city, but voters rejected it in 1912. The town was too hot to submit to the cool logic of planned growth, a fact symbolized by the erection of the Smith Tower in 1914, which reigned as the "tallest building west of the Mississippi" until 1968 (when it was displaced by Seattle's Seafirst Building).

The city bought Stone & Webster's street rail system in 1918 and brought reliability to its services (although it also shouldered a debt that ultimately crushed the system). More development followed completion of interurban lines to Tacoma and Everett and the opening of the long awaited Ship Canal, which connected Lakes Washington and Union with Puget Sound in 1917. The Canal and World War I created new opportunities for commerce and industry, among them amateur aviator William E. Boeing. He built his first airplanes on Lake Union in 1916 and, later, on the Duwamish River, where he began organizing what would become the city's largest company and employer.

By then, Seattle's downtown commercial center had moved north from Pioneer Square to the "Metropolitan Tract" formerly occupied by the University of Washington. The area provided a blank canvas for the visions of talented architects such as John Graham Sr., Henry Bittman, Harlan Thomas, Carl Gould, Charles Bebb, Robert Reamer, and Abraham Albertson.

Seattle's nouveau riche demanded homes of corresponding grandeur and style, and Kirtland Cutter, Ellsworth Storey, Arthur Loveless, and Andrew Willatsen were happy to meet their needs. The city's burgeoning middle and working classes occupied spacious bungalows and inexpensive builder's cottages in thriving "streetcar neighborhoods," while Frederick Anhalt created charming apartment courts for those who hungered for a little romance.

Seattle's children were educated by a crusading public school superintendent, Frank Cooper, in stylish and efficient buildings designed over the years by John Parkinson, James Stephen, Edgar Blair, and Floyd Naramore, among others. On Saturdays, the kids could escape to watch movies and serials in one of B. Marcus Priteca's fantastic theaters.

Viewed through vaseline lens of nostalgia, the first decades of the twentieth century seem idyllic, but not all were contented. Rapacious capitalists spawned a correspondingly militant labor movement, led by "Wobblies" and radicals such as Anna Louise Strong, a charismatic Marxist and school board member. Seattle was idled in 1919 by the nation's first general strike, and labor strife deepened during the Depression as Teamster boss Dave Beck's teamsters battled Harry Bridge's

Radicals such as Anna Louise Strong led the nation's first general strike in 1919 and gave the city a lasting reputation for political and social activism. (*Seattle Public Library*)

Thousands of unemployed and homeless men camped in Seattle's "Hooverville," south of Pioneer Square, during the Depression.

longshoremen for control of the Seattle waterfront. They at least had jobs; thousands of unemployed and homeless men camped in a vast "Hooverville" south of Pioneer Square, and the original name of Yesler Way gave the nation a new synonym for urban decay, "Skid Road."

In 1940, Seattle traded in its bankrupt streetcar system for buses, and the state opened the first floating bridge across Lake Washington. World War II boosted ship construction and Boeing's output of B-17s and other aircraft. The war also changed Seattle's cultural mix as the West Coast's second largest Japanese American community was banished to inland internment camps. Thousands of African-Americans arrived to work in the city's factories but found themselves confined to its "central area" neighborhoods. This de facto segregation persisted largely unchallenged for another 20 years.

Seattle dozed contentedly through much of the 1950s. Only a few malcontents organized in groups such as the Municipal League and Allied Arts

City engineers literally moved mountains while regrading Denny Hill and downtown's steeper ridges.

A traffic officer at Fifth Avenue and Westlake wipes his brow on a warm afternoon sometime in the early 1900s. *(Old Seattle Paper Works)*

Boeing rolled out its "Dash-80" prototype of the 707 in Seattle on July 15, 1954, and ushered in a new era for both the world and the city.

A plan to demolish Seattle's beloved Pike Place Market galvanized the city's preservation movement, and voters saved the landmark in 1971. (John Stamets)

Today's downtown Seattle skyline, seen here from Queen Anne Hill's Kerry Park, seems to have fulfilled its founders' dream of building a "New York, by and by." (Paul Dorpat)

The survival of Seattle's physical past owes much to these five visionary architects: Ralph Anderson *(left)*, Al Bumgardner, Ibsen Nelson, Fred Bassetti, and Victor Steinbrueck. *(Mary Randlett)*

dared to challenge a smug commercial establishment. They campaigned for the arts, social justice, urban beautification, and a regional rail transit system, while highway interests walled off Seattle's waterfront with the Alaskan Way Viaduct and began digging a trench through the heart of the city for Interstate 5. The most important progressive victory came in 1958 with creation of "Metro" to clean up Lake Washington's foul soup of raw sewage and industrial waste.

A new, more imaginative generation of business and political leaders made their mark by planning the Century 21 Exposition of 1962. Seattle's second world's fair galvanized the community and reopened its doors to the world. It also left behind a legacy of civic facilities at Seattle Center and gave the town a new totem, the Space Needle.

The 1962 fair truly marks the boundary between "historic" and "modern" Seattle. Postfair plans to raze historic treasures such as the Pike Place Public Market and Pioneer Square also energized the preservation movement. Visions of a new Seattle collided with veneration of the old in a series of crucial political battles during the late 1960s and 1970s.

Neither side won completely (indeed, the result can be rightly called a draw), but it produced Seattle's singular amalgam of economic dynamism, environmental sensitivity, progressive populism, cultural diversity—and enough historic preservation to justify this little book.

# 1

# Downtown Seattle

## INTRODUCING DOWNTOWN SEATTLE

### Orientation

Seattle's several distinctive downtown districts are enclosed by Mercer Street on the north, Dearborn on the south, Interstate 5 and Eighth Avenue on the east, and Elliott Bay on the west. This remarkably compact area measures only about four square miles (10 square kilometers), and most of Seattle's significant historical attractions are concentrated within easy walking distance of its best hotels, restaurants, and stores.

Following general custom, this guide divides the downtown into six districts as follows, moving roughly from south to north:

**PIONEER SQUARE:** Yesler Way on the north, King Street on the south, Fourth Avenue on the east, Elliott Bay on the west. This guide defines "Lower" Downtown as the area between Madison on the north and Yesler on the south.

**CHINATOWN/INTERNATIONAL DISTRICT:** Yesler Way on the north, Dearborn on the south, Interstate 5 on the east, Fourth Avenue on the west.

**CENTRAL WATERFRONT:** Broad Street on the north, Jackson on the south, Elliott and First Avenues on the east, and Elliott Bay on the west.

**PIKE PLACE MARKET:** Virginia Street on the north, Union Street on the south, First Avenue on the east, and Western Avenue on the west.

Opposite: Today's Occidental Square features new totem poles and carved figures. *(Mary Randlett)*

**CENTRAL BUSINESS DISTRICT:** Virginia Street on the north, Madison on the south, Interstate 5 on the east, and First Avenue on the west.

**BELLTOWN, DENNY REGRADE, AND SEATTLE CENTER:** Mercer Street on the north, Virginia Street on the south, Eighth Avenue on the east, and Western Avenue on the west. The grounds of Seattle Center are contained within a notched triangle roughly bounded by Mercer Street on the north, Broad Street on the south, Denny Way on southeast diagonal, and First Avenue North on the west.

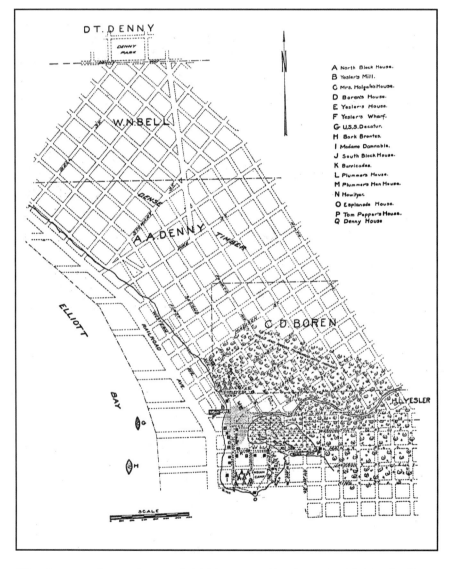

A North Block House.
B Yesler's Mill.
C Mrs. Holgate's House.
D Boren's House.
E Yesler's House.
F Yesler's Wharf.
G U.S.S. Decatur.
H Bark Brontes.
I Madame Damnable.
J South Block House.
K Barricades.
L Plummer's House.
M Plummer's Men House.
N Howitzer.
O Esplanade House.
P Tom Pepper's House.
Q Denny House

This early map superimposes downtown Seattle's later street grid on the town's original shoreline. Pioneer Square now stands on the lower "Piners Point" and the tidal lagoon behind it. *(Seattle Public Library)*

# HISTORICAL OVERVIEW

*(Detailed histories are provided for each of the downtown districts in the sections that follow. This essay is offered as a general introduction to the downtown's pattern of settlement and development.)*

Before the arrival of whites, Elliott Bay and its environs were the exclusive realm of the Duwamish and Suguamish, small clans belonging to the community of Puget Sound Salish, or Lushootseed. They regularly camped near the mouth of the Duwamish and called it *Zechalalitch,* or the "place to cross over," because the area offered a convenient route between the bay and Lake Washington. Except for occasional raids by warriors and slavers from North Coast tribes, they lived a peaceful and culturally rich existence blessed with abundant fish and game and a mild, if damp, climate.

The first European eyes to gaze on the site of the future city of Seattle belonged to Captain George Vancouver and his crew. In 1792 they surveyed the local waters and named the "Sound" for Lieutenant Peter Puget, before continuing on their quest for the Northwest Passage. White trappers returned to the area after 1824, when the Hudson's Bay Company established Fort Nisqually near the present-day town of Dupont, but they did not linger.

Like the natives, but for different reasons, the area's first white residents were attracted by the delta of the Duwamish. John Holgate scouted the area for a farm in 1850, and other settlers arrived the next year to till the Duwamish Valley's rich soil.

Arthur Denny and his party of two dozen Midwesterners arrived in November 1851. Being city builders, not farmers, their scouts chose the exposed western shore of Alki Point as a good anchorage for passing ships, but a wet winter persuaded most to relocate to Elliott Bay by April 1852. They settled on a small patch of level land and a nearby island in the middle of what is now Pioneer Square. Henry Yesler's decision later that year to build the Sound's first steam-powered sawmill in the new village of Seattle secured its economic future.

Arthur Denny led most of Seattle's original settlers from Alki Point to the site of Pioneer Square in April 1852. *(Seattle Public Library)*

Seattle's original symbol was stolen from a native village by drunken city fathers and erected in Pioneer Place in 1899. *(Museum of History and Industry)*

Brisk maritime trade in lumber and salmon sustained the village through the 1860s, and in the 1870s it vied with other Puget Sound towns for the coveted terminus of the Northern Pacific Railroad. In 1873 the town was shocked when this honor went to Tacoma, so it started building its own "transcontinental" railroad. This got only as far as the newly discovered coal fields near Renton, but the ore made Seattle rich while Tacoma waited another decade for its train to come in.

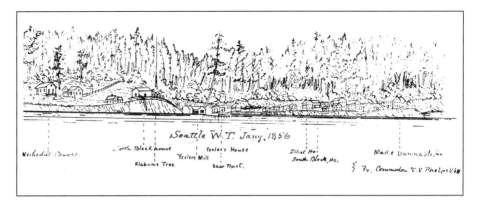

*Seattle W.T. Jany, 1856*

Methodist Church.   South Block house   Yesler's House   Elliot Ho   Madc Damnable.in
Klakum Tree   Yesler Mill   South Block, Ho,
Saw Dust.   By. Commodore U.S. Phelps USN

T. S. Phelps drew this sketch of early Seattle from the Navy warship *Decatur* during the 1856 native uprising. *(Seattle Public Library)*

Seattle's original downtown lay in smoldering ruins on the morning after the June 6, 1889, fire. *(Michael Maslan)*

Railroad service expanded during the 1880s, and Seattle's population increased twelvefold to more than 40,000. A handsome downtown rose in present-day Pioneer Square, then burned to the ground within hours on June 6, 1889. The city was quickly rebuilt, but with stone and brick instead of wood. Seattle prospered until the national economic downturn of the Panic of '93, but the Klondike gold rush revived its growth four years later.

By the early 1900s the city was served by cable railroads and electric streetcars. A "Mosquito Fleet" of ferries and high-speed interurban railways linked Seattle to neighboring cities. Fast steamships established trade with the Pacific Rim, and no fewer than four transcontinental railroads rolled in and out of town daily.

The sidewheeler *Alida* navigates among log booms in this 1860s view of Seattle's future downtown dominated by the Territorial University at present-day Fifth and University. *(A. Curtis. University of Washington Library Special Collections. Neg. 25117)*

The pattern of downtown Seattle's early growth was largely determined by the topographical corset formed by Elliott Bay on the west and the steep eastern slopes of First and Capitol Hills on the east. The resulting "wasp waist" tended to push progressive expansions outward from the original center at Pioneer Square into the hilly "bosom" surrounding Lake Union and south into the "hips" of the Duwamish delta. In her youth Seattle was a model "Gibson Girl," although her middle later spread, thanks to repeated regrades and landfills.

As the city's commercial enterprises expanded northward out of Pioneer Square along First and Second Avenues, city engineers went to

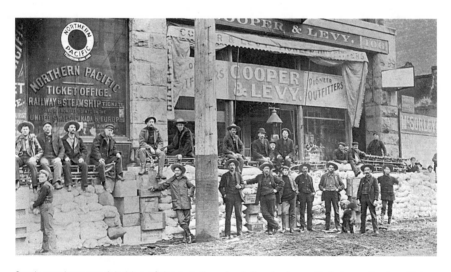

Seattle merchants struck it rich outfitting eager "sourdoughs," posing here with their supplies along First Avenue South before heading north to the Klondike in 1898. *(A. Curtis, Washington State Historical Society. Neg. 26368)*

Second Avenue's "canyons" frame the 1911 Golden Potlatch Parade as marchers proceed south past Spring Street. The Empire Building and gingerbread "New York Kitchen Block" on the right have long since fallen for new office towers. *(Schoenfelds Furniture)*

work leveling steep grades and hills. Their most formidable challenge was towering Denny Hill, north of Pine Street, and it took nearly three decades before the last of it was dumped into Elliott Bay. Meanwhile, the relocation of the original University of Washington from Denny's Knoll, centered at Fourth and University, to its present-day campus allowed for the planned development of a new central business district. Construction continued until the stock market crash of 1929 dried up development capital.

Meanwhile, Pioneer Square slid into decline and gave the nation the term "Skid Road" (sometimes misstated as "Skid Row") to describe a blighted community. The relative prosperity of the town's Chinatown/International District was shattered by World War II and the internment of thousands of Japanese-Americans. The war was kinder to ship and plane builders and their workers, but the postwar slump hit the town hard. By the late 1950s, Boeing's success had helped to lift Seattle's economy and spirits, and in 1962 the town undertook the audacious task of hosting a World's Fair. This event left the Seattle Center as a permanent legacy. The new Interstate 5 freeway had a different impact, a year later, by severing the downtown from its Capitol and First Hill neighborhoods.

Such misguided planning and the threat of "urban renewal" led citizens such as visionary architect Victor Steinbrueck to champion historic preservation. They saved Pioneer Square and the Pike Place Market from redevelopment in the early 1970s, and although they did not win every battle, their victories secured preservation of scores of individual structures.

## Navigating Downtown

Seattle's street grid is fairly easy to master. As a rule, "Avenues" run north-south, "Streets" run east-west, and "Ways" wander around willy-nilly. Within the downtown, Alaskan Way is the westernmost avenue, followed by Elliott (north of Virginia), Western, and, finally, First Avenue, Second Avenue, and so on, as you move inland. North of Denny Way, avenues have the word "North" appended—for example, First Avenue North. Similarly, avenues south of Yesler Way are followed by "South"—for instance, First Avenue South. Avenues between Denny and Yesler dispense with these notations.

Alaskan Way, Western (south of Virginia), First, and Third Avenues carry both north- and southbound traffic; Elliott, Second, Fifth, and Seventh Avenues carry only southbound traffic; Western (north of Virginia), Fourth, and Eighth Avenues carry northbound traffic. Sixth Avenue is schizoid: northbound north of Marion, southbound south of Marion.

East-west street names are less logical, but long ago an anonymous wag came up with a mnemonic for central downtown above Yesler Way: **J**esus **C**hrist **M**ade **S**eattle **U**nder **P**rotest. While we cannot verify the theological or historical accuracy of this statement, the first letter of each word does correspond to the first letter of each couplet of downtown street names from south to north: **J**efferson/**J**ames, **C**herry/**C**olumbia, **M**arion/**M**adison, **S**pring/**S**eneca, **U**niversity/**U**nion, and **P**ike/**P**ine. Almost all east-west downtown streets are one-way between James and Denny.

Streets south of Yesler Way bear the prefix "South"—for example, South Jackson Street. Just to make things interesting, avenues lying north of Denny Way are denoted "North" unless west of Queen Anne Avenue North, in which case they are "West." Streets lying east of Queen Anne Avenue and north of Denny Way bear no compass notation. Got it? Compass notations for areas outside the downtown are explained as best we can elsewhere.

Addresses on the west and south sides of streets and avenues are odd numbers; addresses on the east and north sides are even.

## Getting There

**BY AUTOMOBILE:** Southbound on Interstate 5, take any of several exits beginning with Stewart Street. Northbound, the Seneca Street exit ("Exit Only" lane on your left) will put you in the heart of the central business district.

Southbound on Aurora Avenue/Highway 99, the best exits are the Broad Street and Denny Way ramps north of the Battery Street Tunnel, and the First Avenue South exit (left lane) near the Kingdome. Northbound on the Viaduct, take the Seneca Street exit (a hard right turn) or the Western Avenue ramp north of Pike Place Market (right lane).

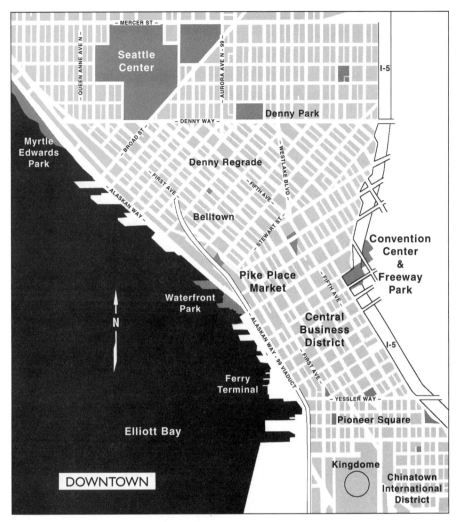

Seattle
Center

Myrtle
Edwards
Park

Denny Park

Denny Regrade

Belltown

Pike Place
Market

Waterfront
Park

N

Convention
Center
&
Freeway
Park

Central
Business
District

Ferry
Terminal

Elliott Bay

Pioneer Square

Kingdome

Chinatown
International
District

DOWNTOWN

Based on City of Seattle Geographic Information System data, copyright 1997.

Westbound on Interstate 90, just follow the ramp around to your right and then take a left onto northbound Fourth Avenue at the light.

Westbound on State Route 520 (Evergreen Point Bridge), the merge with southbound Interstate 5 can be tricky since you enter I-5 from the left and just north of the downtown exits, which are on the far right. For a slower but safer route, take the Roanoke Street exit, turn left (west), and then turn left (south) on Boylston. Follow this around under I-5 (Boylston becomes Lakeview and affords a nice vista of Lake Union, Queen Anne Hill, and the downtown) and continue to the stop sign at East Roy Street above I-5. Turn right and take the ramp down to Eastlake. Turn right (west) on Stewart, which leads into the retail core.

Parking is generally available in downtown's numerous garages, but rates can run as high as $15 per day. Metered on-street parking is available, espe-

Destruction of the Seattle Hotel *(center)*, shown here soon after the Smith Tower's completion in 1914, and its replacement by the "Sinking Ship Garage" in 1963 galvanized Seattle's historic preservation movement into action. *(Lawton Gowey)*

cially north of Virginia Street, but parking is prohibited throughout most of downtown during morning and afternoon peak hours (7:00 to 9:00 A.M., 3:00 to 6:00 P.M.). A good idea on most days is to park near Seattle Center and take the monorail to Westlake Center.

Beware that major events at Seattle Center on the north or at the Kingdome and other sports stadiums on the south end of downtown can quickly fill up nearby parking lots.

**TRANSIT:** As a result of the area's topography and history, most city bus lines run through downtown Seattle regardless of their origin or ultimate destination, so access via transit is especially good. You can find route maps and schedules posted at most downtown bus stops, or call Metro Transit at 553-3000.

Seattle established a "Ride Free Zone" within the downtown back in 1973. Free service has since been limited to the hours between 6:00 A.M. and 7:00 P.M. within the area bounded by Battery Street on the north, Jackson Street on the south, Sixth Avenue on the east, and Alaskan Way on the west. (Fares are charged within this zone for the Monorail and the Waterfront Streetcar.)

Looking northeast from Colman Dock, today's downtown skyline is dominated by new skyscrapers such as the Washington Mutual Tower *(center)*, but much of the city's past survives in their shadows. *(Paul Dorpat)*

The Ride Free policy also applies to buses using the Downtown Transit Tunnel, which has provided a sheltered crosstown route on weekdays since 1990. All buses in the tunnel stop at all stations (from north to south): Convention Center/Ninth Avenue, Westlake Center, University Street, Pioneer Square, and International District/Union Station. The architecture and extensive artworks of these stations are worth a tour in their own right. Note that the tunnel is closed after 7:00 P.M. on weekdays, 6:00 P.M. on Saturdays, and all day on Sundays. The new Regional Transit Authority hopes to begin running rapid-rail trains in the tunnel by early 2005.

The Monorail offers frequent service between Westlake Center, in the heart of the retail core, and Seattle Center seven days a week and most evenings.

The Waterfront Streetcar also offers frequent weekday and weekend service between Broad Street on the north and the International District/Union Station on the south, with intervening stops along Alaskan Way at Vine Street, Bell Street Pier, Pike Street (serving both the Seattle Aquarium and the Pike Street Market), University Street, Madison Street, Washington Street, and South Main Street at Occidental Avenue South in Pioneer Square.

**ON FOOT OR BIKE:** Downtown is a pedestrian's paradise — except for the stiff fines issued for jaywalking and some steep east-west grades between Union Street and Yesler Way. The latter may be negotiated via elevators and escalators noted in the walking tours. Heavy traffic makes bicycling somewhat perilous unless you're a bike courier, in which case everybody else had better watch out!

## Seasonal Events

**FEBRUARY:** Chinese New Year celebration in the International District and "Fat Tuesday" in Pioneer Square

**MAY:** Maritime Week events along the waterfront

**MEMORIAL DAY WEEKEND:** Pike Place Market Street Fair, and Folklife Festival at Seattle Center

**JUNE–SEPTEMBER:** Outdoor concerts and special events throughout the downtown

**EARLY JUNE:** Fire Festival in Pioneer Square, marking the Great Fire of June 6, 1889

**JULY:** Bon Odori celebration in the International District

**AUGUST:** Seafair Parade on Fourth Avenue

**LABOR DAY WEEKEND:** Bumbershoot Arts Festival at Seattle Center

**DECEMBER:** Holiday carousel, menorah and Christmas tree lighting at Westlake Park

## Personal Safety

Crimes against tourists are rare in downtown Seattle, but more skittish visitors may want to avoid the following areas after dark: Occidental Park and vicinity in Pioneer Square; Freeway Park east of the retail core; Pike Street between the Public Market and Third Avenue; and the Denny Regrade area around Third and Bell.

Like any big city, Seattle has its share of homeless and "street people." Merchants ask that you politely decline appeals from panhandlers. Notable exceptions are licensed peddlers of *Real Change*, a "street rag" published by and for the homeless, and the Public Market's semipermanent cast of street musicians and assorted buskers.

# PIONEER SQUARE AND LOWER DOWNTOWN

## Orientation

We begin our tour of historic Seattle where the city itself began, in Pioneer Square. After a brief sojourn on Alki Point, Seattle's founders relocated to this area and built the city's original downtown. A lively shopping and entertainment precinct is now contained within a 20-block historic district—one of the first and largest to be listed on the National Register—bracketed

Yesler's Wharf was Seattle's first gateway to the world. It is seen here in 1882, piled with lumber and flanked by cross-sound stern-wheelers. *(Seattle Public Library)*

between the present-day financial district and the Kingdome (due to be replaced by a new stadium in 2001).

The Pioneer Square area is bounded roughly by Cherry Street on the north, King Street on the south, Alaskan Way on the west, and Fourth Avenue South on the east (streets and avenues are marked "South" below Yesler Way). "Lower Downtown" is defined here as the business district lying between Columbia Street on the north and Yesler on the South and includes the complex of city and county buildings clustered around Fourth and James.

Most destinations of interest to visitors are concentrated west of Second Avenue South. Pioneer Square is a few blocks northwest of the International District/Chinatown and south of the Waterfront Place neighborhood, and it is served by the Waterfront Streetcar and Downtown Transit Tunnel. This makes it a perfect home base for an extended exploration of several historic areas.

## Seasonal Attractions

Since 1978 area restaurants and taverns have sponsored a "Fat Tuesday" week of Mardi Gras events roughly coinciding with Shrove Tuesday in February. Merchants also sponsor an annual "Fire Festival" on or about June 6 to mark the anniversary of the Great Seattle Fire of 1889. The area's many fine art galleries typically unveil their new shows on the first Thursday of each month, and specialty shops offer a wide array of unique gifts for holiday shoppers.

## History

After weathering a winter at Alki Point, most of the original Denny party opted on February 15, 1852, to resettle on the more sheltered eastern shore of Elliott Bay. They landed on an expanse of relatively level land at the foot of present-day Washington Street. This shore was framed by steep, wooded slopes to the east and north. A low, oblong island lay to the south, separated from the mainland by a narrow tidal stream that fed a marshy lagoon (lying between present-day I-5 and Occidental Street). This basin immediately began filling with trash and debris as the settlers set about building their city-to-be.

The land on which Seattle would rise was allocated initially among three settlers: William Bell took the north stretch, Carson Boren the south, and Arthur Denny the middle. This first subdivision seems arrogant, since the land was already occupied by others, but the local Duwamish tribe and its leader, Chief Sealth (as crude a transliteration of the original phonetics as *Seattle*), did not object to the intrusion.

Indeed, Sealth and his tribesmen were already regular consumers of the wares offered by the larger settlement in Olympia. Sealth is credited with persuading "Doc" David Maynard to relocate his general store from Olympia to the new village and thereby eliminate native shoppers' long commute by canoe. Maynard arrived in April and convinced his new neighbors to name the town "Seattle" in honor of the chief. The new name certainly beat "Duwamps," the village's informal moniker.

Another entrepreneur followed that fall—Henry Yesler. He had scouted Puget Sound for the best place to build the region's first steam-powered sawmill, which made him very popular in every would-be metropolis. Yesler chose Seattle after Denny and Bell donated forest land on the ridge east of town, as well as a slice of Boren's waterfront (he was out of town at the moment) where the new mill could load lumber directly onto ships. They also threw in a narrow east-west strip so logs could be dragged from the forest to the mill. This rutted, muddy path became known as "Skid Road," then Mill Street, and now bears Yesler's name.

Yesler's cook house was built in late summer 1852 on the

Henry Yesler's decision to locate Puget Sound's first steam-powered lumber mill launched Seattle's economy in 1852. (*Seattle Public Library*)

Yesler's Mill belches smoke at the foot of a muddy, littered "Skid Road" in this photo from the 1870s. *(Seattle Public Library)*

site of the Mutual Life Building (First Avenue at Yesler) and became the town's first community center. The cook house was also the site of the town's first religious service, a Catholic mass celebrated on August 22, 1852, by a traveling prelate, Bishop Modeste Demers, at the request of Arthur Denny, who, although he was not Catholic, but a Protestant, was desperate to lift the village's spiritual level. Seattle had few white Catholics, but peripatetic priests had converted many natives, including Chief Sealth himself. This fact greatly annoyed the Rev. David Blaine, a Methodist missionary, who arrived in 1853 and built Seattle's first church two years later at Second and Columbia.

The mill was finished at the foot of Skid Road in the spring of 1853, and its logs and lumber soon found buyers as far away as San Francisco and Hawaii. The settlement's success seemed assured by May, when Denny, Boren, and Maynard met to formally plat their claims and lay streets for the future city.

Denny later recalled that Maynard, "stimulated" with liquor, decided that "he was not only monarch of all he surveyed, but what Boren and I surveyed too." Maynard insisted on a grid of streets dictated by the compass south of Skid Road, while Denny and Boren preferred their streets to parallel the shoreline on the north. The dispute extended even to names: First Avenue was originally called "Front Street" north of Yesler, and "Commercial Street" on the south. Their disagreement is preserved in the tangle of Pioneer Square's streets where they meet—and often miss—each other at Yesler Way.

Despite the success of the mill, Seattle grew slowly at first. Most of the population could fit inside two small blockhouses (at First and Marion and at

This view north on Commercial Street (First Avenue South) reveals Seattle as a rough-hewn frontier town in the 1870s. A magazine artist depicted a more genteel scene a decade later. *(Seattle Public Library)*

Occidental and Main) when the village was attacked on January 28, 1856, during a brief Indian uprising. The "Battle of Seattle" was ended by cannon fire from the USS. *Decatur* anchored in Elliott Bay, and in the battle's aftermath the government hanged Chief Leschi—unjustly, in the opinion of many whites and Native Americans.

Beyond Yesler's mill stretched a long pier, which was the young city's main gateway to the world. Here, on May 16, 1864, 11 "maidens" recruited by Asa Mercer from Lowell, Massachusetts, debarked to be wooed by eager bachelors (the story of Mercer's maidens inspired a 1960s television series, *Here Come the Brides*, almost as fanciful as its theme song proclaiming that the "bluest skies you'll ever see are in Seattle"). Those men not lucky enough or disinclined to marry could find solace in the Illahee, John Pennell's "bawdy house" a few blocks south of Skid Road.

When not trying to lure women to join the mostly male populace, the town fathers courted the railroads for the favor of becoming a transcontinental terminus, but the latter played even harder to get. Much to Seattle's dismay, the (then) village of Tacoma won the hand of the Northern Pacific (NP) in 1873, but the marriage of rails was not consummated for another decade. Rather than wait for a spur to the NP, local business leaders tried to lay track across the Cascades with volunteer labor. This effort failed, but the Seattle & Walla Walla Railroad and, later, the locally financed Seattle, Lake Shore and Eastern, made money hauling coal from nearby mines.

Even without direct transcontinental rail service (the NP opened a spur in 1884 with intermittent service), Seattle's population spurted a dozenfold during the 1880s. A handsome downtown rose on the original settlement and spread north, providing homes and jobs for some 35,000 souls. Many crowded

A Northern Pacific train pauses on Railroad Avenue at Yesler Wharf. In 1884 the NP grudgingly ran a line up to Seattle from its main terminus in Tacoma. *(Kurt Jackson)*

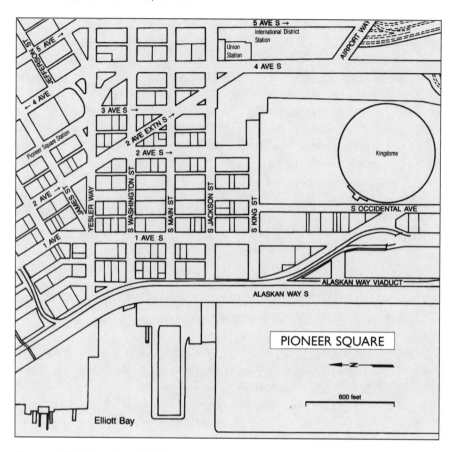

Courtesy of the University of Washington Press, copyright 1992.

aboard the region's first horse-drawn streetcar system, built by Frank Osgood along Second Avenue in 1884. Operation of the first electric generator plant west of the Rockies followed in 1886, and Osgood used the new energy source to power his streetcars three years later. Meanwhile, in 1887, J. M. Thompson borrowed an idea from San Francisco and built a cable car line that climbed Yesler's steep grade from Occidental Street to reach the far shore of Lake Washington and returned via Jackson Street.

Seattle's future seemed as bright as the summer sun on June 6, 1889. Then, at 2:40 in the afternoon, a pot of glue boiled over on the wood stove in Victor Clairmont's cabinet shop (John McGough has been falsely accused for over a century) near the corner of First and Madison (site of the "old" Federal Office Building). Burning glue fell to the floor and ignited shavings; fire then quickly engulfed the wooden building. Despite the efforts of firemen and volunteers, a brisk wind spread the flames south toward the heart of the downtown. As more hoses tapped into the city's wooden (and privately owned) water mains, the flow slowed to a trickle. By sunset, 64 acres—from the waterfront to Fourth Avenue and from Union Street to Jackson—lay in smoldering ruins.

The clouds of smoke rising from Seattle held a silver lining for developers and a cadre of young architects, led by Elmer Fisher—who alone received some 50 postfire commissions. The city council wisely mandated the use of stone and brick for the downtown's phoenixlike resurrection. It also chose this opportunity to address the downtown's chronic and odoriferous flooding and sanitation problems by raising the streets a full story above their original level.

The Occidental Hotel at First and Yesler is shown here before and after the Great Fire of June 6, 1889. It was rebuilt as the Seattle Hotel in 1890 and stood another 73 years until demolished for a parking garage. *(Seattle Public Library)*

This view north along First Avenue from Main Street dates from about 1900. Most of the structures, including the Grand Central in the right foreground, still stand today. *(University of Washington Library Special Collections)*

Many private property owners did not wait for the city road crews and built their new structures with two street levels stacked one on the other. As the new, higher streets were completed, some merchants on the original ground floors struggled to lure customers down sidewalk stairwells to their shops. Inevitably, they failed, and access to the old storefronts was paved over, sometimes with glass inlays to illuminate the chambers below the new sidewalk. This created a labyrinth of subterranean passages, which the late Bill Speidel helped to reopen in 1964 with his famous tours of "Underground Seattle" (exaggerated ad absurdum in the 1970s TV movie *The Night Strangler*).

Seattle's renewed growth stalled during the economic downturn of the Panic of '93. Prosperity returned with a vengeance on July 17, 1897, when a steamer pulled into Seattle bearing more than two tons of gold and 68 suddenly wealthy prospectors. They were fresh from the banks of the Klondike River in Canada's Yukon Territory, which was best reached via Alaska. The news set off the multiyear Klondike gold rush, depicted at the National Historical Park on South Main near Occidental. Seattle loudly declared herself the "Gateway to Alaska" and the gold fields beyond, while merchants advised prospectors to lay in at least a ton of supplies. Few "stampeders" struck it rich in the frozen north, but the cost of their provisions more than warmed Seattle's economy and established the city's dominance among Pacific Northwest ports.

As the downtown recovered, it also gradually expanded northward along First and Second Avenues. When typewriter magnate L. C. Smith built his 42-story office tower at Second and Yesler in 1914, most new construction was already happening uptown. Pioneer Square stagnated, and with the Depression, began to slide precipitously. Transients took over the catacombs beneath the sidewalks, and thousands of homeless, unemployed men erected a ramshackle "Hooverville" near the waterfront south of the Square.

Pioneer Square was already down on its luck on April 13, 1949, when a 7.1 magnitude earthquake rumbled through Seattle and killed eight people. In the Square, aging turrets and ornate cornices crashed to the streets, and most of those that survived were removed for public safety. Offices and hotels that had been the pride of Seattle were taken over by flophouses and bordellos. Most of Seattle forgot Pioneer Square until the early 1960s, but this had the accidental effect of sealing some 40 blocks of Victorian-era architecture in a virtual time capsule.

In 1962, Seattle hosted its "Century 21" world's fair, but a few fretted that "Century 19" was about to be sacrificed on the altar of modernity. That same year, architect Victor Steinbrueck's sketchbook *Seattle Cityscape* celebrated the Square's "rich and flavorsome old buildings" in drawings and prose and urged "sympathetic restoration." Such was not the fate of the once-grand Seattle Hotel (the former Occidental Hotel; Donald McKay, 1884), which was demolished in 1963 to make way for the infamous "Sinking Ship" garage at Second and Yesler. The shock of the new and the ache of losing the old set groups such Allied Arts of Seattle, a federation of architects, artists, and urban visionaries, to sound the first alarms about the potential obliteration of Seattle's physical history.

Preservationists' worst fears were confirmed on August 10, 1966, when Mayor Dorm Braman and leaders of the Central Association (now the much more progressive Downtown Seattle Association) announced an "urban renewal" plan to flatten most of Pioneer Square and erect giant parking garages. The charge to save the Square was led by Allied Arts of Seattle, while local architect Ralph Anderson and gallery owner Richard White rallied the many artists, artisans, and activists who had taken up residence in the Square's low-rent apartments and lofts. Future politicians such as attorney John Miller helped present the case for preservation to a conservative and skeptical city council.

The latter's days were already numbered due to a broad insurgency by younger, more liberal candidates. The elections of 1967 and 1969 routed the council's old guard and elected a young, progressive mayor, Wes Uhlman. The City Planning Commission conducted a survey of Pioneer Square in 1968, and an application to list the entire district on the National Register was approved the following year. In May the city council and the mayor created a 30-acre historic district governed by a Preservation Board that must approve any exterior alterations to private or public properties and acts as an advocate for the area's social health. A larger 40-acre "special review district" was established in 1973 in anticipation of the impacts of the Kingdome, then beginning construction.

Private developers have funded the rehabilitation of most of the Square's buildings, while the city has financed improvements such as the median strip down First Avenue, vintage lamp posts and street furniture, and conversion of two blocks of Occidental into a park and pedestrian mall. Goverment has also spent millions on the Waterfront Streetcar and on efforts to stabilize the Square's ancient streets. The numerous properties owned by the late Sam Israel were untouched by such investments, but his refusal to make more than minimal improvements also kept his rents low and thereby preserved some of the neighborhood's bohemian character (his heirs, the Samis Foundation, appear to have very different plans).

Many of Pioneer Square's older population of pensioners and low-income workers were inevitably displaced as gentrification took its toll on former boarding houses and single-room-occupancy hotels. These effects compounded the loss of nearly 15,000 downtown housing units due to freeway construction and the closing of scores of flophouses following the disastrous Ozark Hotel fire of 1972. Thus was spawned a permanent corps of homeless men and women, whose ranks have since swelled with the emptying of mental institutions and the growing economic inequities of recent decades.

The result can be seen on the streets of Pioneer Square and in the swirl of its urban motley of earnest young professionals and staggering winos, carefree shoppers and ragged beggars, cheering sports fans and shadowy bag ladies. It is a heady and volatile mixture of humanity, framed by the ornate and stately facades of buildings now entering their second century of useful life.

## Walking Tour

The following tour includes a quick loop south on First Avenue South from Yesler Way to South Jackson Street and back along Occidental South. It should take no more than an hour, barring the suggested side trips and numerous temptations to browse.

### ■ At First and Yesler

Seattle's first intersection was dubbed **Pioneer Place** in the late 1800s, with construction of a small triangular park and, later, the erection of a Tlingit totem. The original pole was espied on the shore of a village near Fort Tongass by some of Seattle's leading citizens while returning from a "goodwill mis-sion" to Alaska. Crewmen rowed ashore from the steamship *City of Seattle*, hacked down the pole, and loaded it aboard the steamer for transport to Pioneer Place, where it was trimphantly unveiled on the afternoon of October 18, 1899. Unfortunately, these pole poachers neglected to ask permission of the totem's owners for any of this and

Pioneer Place's original totem pole towers over the Pergola in this early twentieth-century view. Thanks to preservationists, all of the structures in this photo survive today except the totem, which was replaced in 1938 after an arsonist set it afire. *(Lawton Gowey)*

The ornate **Pergola,** designed by Julian F. Everett in 1909 to shelter passengers waiting for streetcars and cable cars, stands on top of an underground "comfort station." This "Queen Mary of Johns" closed long ago, but you might notice its ventilator grates still concealed in the upper portion of the light standards. Nearby stands a drinking fountain designed to refresh both horse and man, topped by James A. Wehn's bronze bust of **Chief Seattle**. Pioneer Place and its furnishings were carefully restored in 1973 thanks to a generous grant from United Parcel Service, whose founder, James Casey, had started out in Seattle carrying messages for businesses and the area's many houses of ill repute.

The park's abutting buildings have their own stories to tell, beginning with the **Lowman** at the corner of Cherry Street and First Avenue. It rises from the site of Yesler's second Hall (or Pavilion; see Yesler Building, described later), which served until the 1860s as Seattle's main entertainment and social center. The Lowman was designed in 1900 by Emil DeNeuf and Augustus Heide, and its French Renaissance Eclectic style announces its relative youth. The adjacent **Lowman and Hanford** (1899) and the **Howard** (1890) Buildings are more typical of the Richardsonian Romanesque style favored by Elmer Fisher and other postfire architects.

The **Pioneer Building** came to symbolize the city's rise from the ashes of the 1889 fire, and it stands on the site of Henry Yesler's original Seattle home. Designed by Elmer Fisher, the six-story block was hailed by the American Institute of Architects as "the finest building west of Chicago" upon completion in 1892. Its western facade was once crowned by a peaked tower, but this did not survive the 1949 earthquake. Ralph Anderson directed a sensitive rehabilitation in 1975, which recreated its original open-cage elevators—Seattle's first. The building now houses the offices of the popular

ended up paying a fine, but the pole remained standing in Seattle until 1938.

At this point the record and folklore diverge. The former says that the pole was torched on the night of October 22, during a wave of arson fires, and removed for repair. After restorers discovered extensive dry rot, the U.S. Forest Service generously agreed to commission Charles Brown and his father, William, to carve a replica at federal expense. Legend holds that chastened city fathers sent a $5,000 check to the Tlingit craftsmen for a replacement. The endorsed check came back with a memo, "Thanks for finally paying for the first one. A new pole will cost you another $5,000." I prefer the legend.

Commuters dangle from the Lake Washington Cable Car as it rumbles up Yesler from Second Avenue in this view ca. 1915. (A.Curtis, Washington State Historical Society. Neg. 21780)

Underground Tour, which leads visitors through the catacombs created when the Square's sidewalks and streets were raised a full story during reconstruction following the 1889 fire.

### ■ At the Corner of First South and Yesler Way

Directly opposite First from the Pergola stands the **Mutual Life Building**, begun in 1890 by Fisher and finished in 1897 by Robert L. Robertson and James E. Blackwell. This building occupies the site of Yesler's original cook house. It faces south onto the dark stone facade of the **Yesler Building** (Fisher, 1890), which stands on the site of the first "Yesler's Hall." Benjamin Harrison, the second U.S. president to visit Seattle, briefly addressed a damp but patriotic throng from the new building's balcony during a pouring rain on May 6, 1891.

The southeast corner of First and Yesler is occupied by the **Olympic Block**, one of the Square's rare new buildings. Designed by the partnership of Hewitt/Walker/Olson/Daly/Isley in 1985, it replaced the original Olympic Block, which had collapsed 13 years

earlier when workers mistakenly removed supporting walls during a remodel. Farther up Yesler, the **Merchants Cafe** and **Korn Building** were erected shortly after the 1889 fire. Historian Esther Mumford believes that Seattle's original African-American resident, Manuel Lopes, established the town's first barber shop in this vicinity shortly after his arrival in 1852.

### ■ South Along First South

Walking along First South, you will notice the planted median strip, dating from the early 1970s. Like everything else in Pioneer Square, this was the object of heated debate, and it was built over the objections of visionaries who championed reconstruction of a First Avenue streetcar line between the Square and Pike Place Market. Nearly two decades passed before the Waterfront Streetcar proved the feasibility of such "retrotransit."

The two buildings on the west side of First South are monuments to the Klondike gold rush. The **Schwabacher** (Fisher, 1890) housed a prominent outfitter managed by Bailey Gatzert,

Seattle's first Jewish mayor, and the **Northern Hotel** (Charles W. Saunders, 1889) was built by Seattle founders Charles Terry and Arthur Denny. The west side of the block ends triumphantly with the **Maynard Building** (Albert Wickersham, 1892), on the site of Dexter Horton's original store and Seattle's first bank, which was a box under the floorboards. Dexter Horton later spotted an ad for a very inexpensive safe and ordered it. When it arrived, he realized why it was so cheap: it had no back. He discreetly shoved it against a brick wall, and thus was born what became the state's largest bank, Seafirst. The Maynard was rehabilitated in 1975 under the direction of Olson/Walker architects.

The east side of First South is lined by the **Lippy** (E. W. Houghton, 1902) and **City Club** (unknown, 1897; 1905) Buildings. The latter's Art Nouveau facade at first advertised a gentlemen's club and then a posh restaurant. The south end of the block is anchored by the **Delmar Building**, really two buildings, the Terry and the Kittinger, designed by Hermann Steinmann in 1889 with matching facades and later renamed the **State Hotel.**

## ■ Side Trip West on South Washington

A stroll down this street leads you past the restored **St. Charles Building** (1889) on the south side and the **Washington Park Building** (1890), former home of one of Seattle's first printing presses, on the northwest corner. This street was once the terminus of the West Seattle Streetcar, which followed the shoreline south and then crossed the Duwamish mud flats via an elevated track.

The street terminates at Alaskan Way with a Waterfront Streetcar stop. Across Alaskan Way stands the **Washington Street Boat Landing** (D. R. Huntington), built in 1920 to house Seattle's harbor master and shelter foreign seamen passing to and from their ships. Previously, this site was a popular landing for canoes of Native Americans bearing salmon and crafts for sale to the settlers and returning to the Suguamish and other reservations with manufactured wares. The structure was rehabilitated in the 1970s with a grant from the Committee of 33, a civic philanthropy supported by leading women in Seattle, and now provides short-term moorage for pleasure boats.

## ■ South on First South from Washington South

The west side of the block comprises less distinguished but no less durable structures dating from the postfire boom. The **J & M** has been a bar and card room (as the law permitted) since the gold rush. A few doors down, the **Central Tavern** bills itself as Seattle's "oldest second-class tavern" and once served as an employment agency for patrons sober enough to do odd jobs. The **New England Hotel Building** (1889), at the south end of the block, stands on the site of Doc Maynard's first Seattle home and the town's second log cabin.

The sad building on the southeast corner of First and Washington bears the scars of crude modifications made after the 1949 earthquake. In contrast, restaurateurs François and Julia Kissel commissioned James Daly Architects to undertake a sensitive rehabilitation of the adjacent **City Loan Building** in 1975. The rest of the block is occupied by **Grand Central on the Park,** which led the way in proving the feasibility of adaptive reuse and rehabilitation of Pioneer Square's "derelict" buildings.

Designed by Nelson Comstock and Carl Troetsche, the Grand Central was christened the **"Squire-Latimer Block"** when it opened in 1889. The southern portion of the building occupies the site of Watson C. Squire's Opera House, which opened in 1879 as Seattle's first formal entertainment venue and perished in the Great Fire. The Squire-Latimer housed the Grand Central Hotel during the gold rush and then declined with the rest of the neighborhood. Richard White, Alan Black, and architect Ralph Anderson acquired and rehabilitated the building in 1971 for retail and office use (don't miss the labyrinthine retail mall on the lower level of the central arcade). The building's central two-story arcade opens onto the cobblestoned **Occidental Park**, designed by Jones & Jones architects, on the building's east side. This harmonious blend of office, retail, and park improvements convinced skeptics that you could teach old buildings new tricks—without destroying their historic character.

### ■ South on First South from South Main

The Bread of Life Mission occupies the **Matilda Winehill Block** (1889) on the southwest corner of South Main and First South. This former hotel sits on the site of Doc Maynard's original general store in Seattle. The adjacent **Maud** was also built in 1889, and the **Squire** (Charles H. Bebb) and **Smith** Buildings (Max Umbrecht) were completed in

1900. All have been rehabilitated for retail and office tenants.

The former **Globe Hotel** (William E. Boone, 1890) on the southeast corner is now the home of the **Elliott Bay Book Company**, one of Seattle's largest independent booksellers, a basement cafe, and professional offices. The building once housed Seattle's first hospital, run by Doc Maynard, and was restored in 1965 by Ralph Anderson. The nearby street clock was relocated from Fourth and Pike in 1984 and dedicated to honor Earl D. Layman, Seattle's first historic preservation officer.

A brief side trip east on South Main will bring you to the **Klondike Gold Rush National Historical Park**, a compact museum and interpretive center operated by the National Park Service. Other units of this unique historical "park" are located in Skagway, Alaska, and at Dawson and Whitehorse in Canada's Yukon Territory.

Returning to First South, the **Nord Hotel** (1890) and the **Seattle Quilt Building** (Boone & Corner, 1904) were rehabilitated respectively by Stickney & Murphy and Charles Bergman in the early 1980s for a variety of retail, office,

Here, a Pioneer Square survivor is shown when still new: the Mutual Life Building at First and Yesler. *(Lawton Gowey)*

Captain Felker built Seattle's first house made of milled lumber near First South and South Jackson Street, and "Madam Damnable" turned it into the town's first brothel. *(Seattle Public Library)*

and residential uses. The **Jackson Building** (1901) on the south end of the block once housed the **Capitol Brewing Co.** and was the first structure rehabilitated in Pioneer Square (Ralph Anderson, 1963).

### ■ At First South and South Jackson

For the visitor pausing at the corner of South Jackson, the view down First South reveals several handsome commercial buildings. The **Wax & Raine Building** (1904) on the southeast corner was remodeled in 1982 by Naramore Bain Brady & Johanson (NBBJ) architects for the firm's headquarters (it also houses the Northwest Fine Woodworks Gallery). The first building to rise on the southwest corner was a hotel built by Captain Leonard Felker in 1853. This two-story colonial house was Seattle's first building constructed with milled lumber, and it was also the village's finest bordello. The proprietress, Mary Conklin, kept order with a wicked Irish tongue that earned her the nickname "Madam Damnable" and even cowed a squad of Marines sent to occupy her property during the 1856 "Battle of Seattle."

The site of the **Felker House** is now occupied by the **Pacific Marine Schwabacher Building** (Bebb & Mendel, 1905), which echoes the style of Louis M. Sullivan and is a monument to the enduring prosperity created by the gold rush. It is part of the 1984 block-long **Merrill Place** rehabilitation designed by Olson/Walker and NBBJ, also comprising the **Seller Building** (A. Warren Gould, 1906) and the **Hambrack Building** (Saunders & Lawton, 1913). One of Seattle's few "flat iron" buildings stands one block farther south. The original **Triangle Hotel** (C. A. Breitung, 1910) offered guests a choice of just eight rooms, making it the smallest hostelry on the West Coast.

Before you turn east on South Jackson, you might consider a short walk west down the south side to the **Pioneer Square Post Office**, which houses a small museum of artifacts from the early days of postal service.

### ■ East on South Jackson

Walking east past the Wax & Raine Building, you will immediately notice the **Fisher Building** (1900) and how its Art Deco details, added in 1928, contrast with its Victorian neighbors. From

41

the corner of South Jackson and Occidental South, the view south is currently dominated by the **Kingdome**, a concrete carbuncle which first erupted on the Square's backside in 1976. This monument to testosterone, tractor pulls, and lowest-bid construction has already been declared obsolete by the Seattle Seahawks and the Mariners, both of which are building new stadiums of their own. While the "Doomed Stadium" is marked for demolition in A.D. 2000, its frame of fin de siècle warehouses and commercial buildings will likely survive another century. Most of these house offices and restaurants, such as the popular **F.X. McRory's Steak House** on the northwest corner of Occidental South and South King. Looking east from this corner, you might ask how the campanile from Venice's St. Mark's Square got here. This faithful copy is the tower of the **King Street Station**, which is described in detail in the Chinatown-International District section. We return now to South Jackson.

### ■ South Jackson at Second South

Looking south of Jackson, you will see the west side of Second South occupied

by one of the Square's more imaginative rehabs. The **Court in the Square** links two buildings, the **Fuller** (William Boone and James Cormer, 1901) and the **Crane** (Saunders and Lawton, 1907), with a soaring arcade over a former alley and rail spur. Looking north up Second South, your attention may be drawn to the model of a horse suspended over the entrance to the **Duncan & Sons Building** (1900), a replica of the sign by which the original occupant advertised equestrian and outdoors gear (it is still in business at 541 First South). We return west to Occidental South to resume our tour.

### ■ North on Occidental South

Turning north on Occidental South places you on one of Seattle's few pedestrian malls, from which cars were banished in 1972. The flanking buildings date from the early 1890s and now house a variety of retailers, galleries, and cafes. Among the best-preserved structures is the **State Building** (Elmer Fisher, 1890) on the southeast corner of South Main. This site was occupied in the 1850s by the southern blockhouse of the Seattle stockade. Note the island

The Alaska Building towers over the former Seattle (Occidental) Hotel in this early twentieth-century view north on Occidental Way. (*Lawton Gowey*)

This 1880s magazine etching shows the elegant hotels and retailers that once lined the west side of First Avenue between Columbia and Cherry.

shelter for the Waterfront Streetcar just west of Occidental.

### ■ Side Trip East on South Main

A quick jaunt east on South Main brings you to **Fire Station No. 10** (1929), a dignified concrete structure with corner niches for vertical search-lights and home of one of the area's few public "comfort stations." Directly across South Main is the somewhat incongruous **Waterfall Garden**, a privately managed pocket park built by the Annie E. Casey Foundation. Designed by Masao Kinoshita and com-pleted in 1977, the park stands on the 1907 birthplace of United Parcel Service (also see the earlier discussion of Pioneer Place), not far from the for-mer bordellos and saloons that consti-tuted part of James Casey's original clientele. Now return to Occidental and enter the cobblestoned park.

### ■ North through Occidental Park

The modern pergola was erected in 1972 as part of the new **Occidental Park**, dominated by the east face of the Grand Central Building. The dramatic ensemble of totem poles and carvings standing farther north was donated by Richard White and installed in 1987 and 1988, and all of the pieces were carved by Duane Pasco. The tallest totem, *Sun and Raven*, tells of the raven's theft of the moon and was created for the 1974 Spokane World's Fair. The nearby *Man Riding on Tail of Whale* was carved in 1971. The westernmost of the two facing figures is *Tsonoqua*, a mythological giantess and "nightmare bringer" invoked by exasperated North Coast mothers to frighten their children into obedience. She faces a slightly less fear-some *Bear*.

### ■ At Occidental South and South Washington

Looking east from this intersection, you may notice the incongruous Chinese-style balcony of the building on the northeast corner of Second South and South Washington. This is the former home of the **Wah Chong Company** and one of the first brick buildings completed after the 1889 fire, and it marks the center of Seattle's original Chinatown (see the International District section for more detail).

The site of Seattle's first Catholic church, **Our Lady of Good Hope**, lies a block farther east. It was erected in 1870 by Father Francis X. Prefontaine and was razed in 1904 for completion of the downtown railroad tunnel leading to King Street Station. The neighboring **Washington Court Building** (1890), which still stands, once housed madam Lou Graham's popular bordello. Pioneer deveoloper Henry Broderick used to marvel at the coexistence of "piety and prostitution on the same corner."

### ■ North on Occidental South to Yesler Way

This block's notable structure stands on the southeast corner of Yesler Way. The **Interurban Building** was designed in 1890 by John Parkinson, who left many marks on the Seattle cityscape before establishing his more famous practice in Los Angeles. The building housed the offices of the city's first interurban railway, an elec-

tric line started in 1889 to connect with the then-independent town of Georgetown. It took nearly four years to lay as many miles of track, and then its investors went bankrupt. The line was taken over in 1902 and extended to Tacoma by the Puget Sound Electric Railway. (The Washington State Ferries sign on the building's southern face is not original, by the way; the state did not take over the ferries until 1951, and the sign was painted in the 1970s.)

You now face the infamous **"Sinking Ship" garage**, whose construction in place of the Seattle Hotel galvanized the city's historic preservation movement in 1963.

### ■ East on Yesler Way

By the time the 42-story, terra-cotta-clad **Smith Tower** (Gaggin & Gaggin) was finished in 1914, downtown development had already broken out of Pioneer Square and was racing north on Second and Third Avenues. Typewriter magnate L. C. Smith thought his new building would reverse this trend, but it failed to do so. Although it

This postcard shows the Frye Hotel, Smith Tower, Morrison Hotel, and early King County Courthouse ca. 1920.

was Seattle's first fireproof structure, and for decades the tallest west of the Mississippi, the tower became a marginal business address until the rediscovery of Pioneer Square renewed its appeal.

In the mid-1980s, famed Seattle restaurateur Ivar Haglund acquired and rehabilitated the Tower, including its bank of eight brass-caged, attendant-operated elevators and its elaborate "Chinese Room" observation hall. The view is worth the trip; getting there in the express elevator is half the fun. The Smith Tower is now owned by the Samis Foundation, which is planning further remodeling at this writing.

Walking up Yesler will lead you past Garth Edwards' whimsical gate to the **Downtown Transit Tunnel's Pioneer Square Station**, designed by architect Jerry McDevitt. The lower levels feature the work of Kate Erickson and other artists and a drive wheel that once powered the Yesler Way cable car. A little farther east on Yesler Way is **Prefontaine Place**, built in the triangle once formed by Jefferson Street and Yesler Way. Designed by Carl. F. Gould in 1926, the fountain commemorates Father Francis Xavier Prefontaine, who had become Seattle's first resident Catholic priest 59 years earlier.

## ■ At Yesler Way and Third Avenue

Across Third is the lawn of **City Hall Park**. This was once occupied by the seat of municipal government, an accretion of buildings and add-ons whose external appearance and internal high jinks earned it the nickname "Katzenjammer Castle." The park once faced the formal entrance of the **King County Courthouse** (formerly the City-County Building), which stands on the site of Henry Yesler's second Seattle home and the city's first public library. Augustus Warren Gould's original design called for a 22-story edifice, but only 6 floors were finished when the build-

City government was once directed from "Katzenjammer Castle" at Third and Jefferson, while the county occupied its original courthouse (with Victorian belvedere) on Profanity Hill until 1914. *(Old Seattle Paper Works)*

ing opened in 1916. Henry Bittman and John L. McCauley topped off the building with 6 more stories in 1930, and the top-story jail was recently converted (appropriately, in the minds of many) into new chambers for the Metropolitan King County Council. Planners hope to reopen the courthouse's southern entry as part of a future remodel.

On the south side of Yesler rises the **Frye Apartment Hotel** (Bebb & Mendel, 1906–1911), which was one of Seattle's first and tallest steel frame buildings upon completion. Once one of the city's grandest hotels, the Frye now houses low-income tenants.

The **Yesler Bridge** over Fourth Avenue was built in 1909 as one element in the city's endless regrades. It is easy to understand why citizens and office holders trudging up to the old County Courthouse, where Harborview Hospital now stands, dubbed this grade "Profanity Hill" before the cable car offered a welcome lift.

The **Old Public Safety Building** (Clayton D. Wilson) has another flat iron floor plan designed to fill the triangle formed by Yesler and Terrace Street. It replaced Katzenjammer Castle as City Hall in 1909 and was later abandoned. In 1977, Richard Mayo & Associates remodeled it to house a new generation of municipal agencies. Legend has it that the marble partitions from the old jail's urinals were salvaged and "recycled" in the 1960s as tables for a coffee house in the University District.

Turn around at this point, and gratefully descend Yesler to return to Pioneer Place, where this tour began, or hop any of the numerous buses on Third or in the Transit Tunnel to travel uptown.

## MINI-TOUR OF LOWER DOWNTOWN

This short tour of Seattle's "second downtown" will take you on a zigzag walk north from Pioneer Place on First Avenue to Marion Street, back south on Second to Yesler. The steep east-west grades may be conquered via elevators or escalators as indicated.

## ■ North on First from Pioneer Place

The simple but diginified **110 Cherry Building** on the northeast corner of First has endured since 1890. The next major historical structure on First is the **Colman Building,** filling the western side of the street from Columbia to Marion. Before landfills pushed the shoreline westward from First Avenue in the late 1880s, the building's eponymous developer, James Colman, laid claim to the site by beaching a ship there. Note that the walkway on the Colman's Marion Street side is connected to the State Ferry Terminal (originally "Colman Dock") via a pedestrian bridge over Western Avenue and Alaskan Way.

Construction of Stephen J. Meany's original Romanesque Revival design began in 1889, but only two stories were finished when Colman's capital temporarily fled in the Panic of '93. The building was completed in 1904 under the direction of August Tidemand, who introduced a Chicago School flavor, and Arthur B. Loveless added Art Deco flourishes such as the street canopy in 1930. Thus, the

This 1913 panorama from the then-unfinished Smith Tower shows the "Commission District" and waterfront, dominated by the Colman Building *(center)*.

The "Moderne mountain" of the "old" Federal Office Building fronts First Avenue between Cherry and Madison. It is is shown here during construction of the Jackson Federal Office Building in the 1970s. *(Frank O. Shaw)*

Colman offers a snapshot of evolving architectural tastes over four decades. The Colman faces the Norton and Exchange Buildings, which we will save for a little later in this tour.

The block north of the Colman is filled by the miniature Moderne mountain of the **"Old" Federal Office Building**, completed in 1933 under the supervision of James A. Whetmore. The Great Seattle Fire of 1889 began in a cabinet shop on this site near the corner of First and Madison. The "Old" faces the "New," across First Avenue, in the form of the **Henry M. Jackson Federal Office Building**, designed in 1974 by Fred Bassetti and renamed in memory of the late U.S. Senator ten years later. This was the site of Arthur Denny's second Seattle home (his first cabin stood at the corner of First and Battery), which doubled as the town's original post office. In 1884, the **Frye Opera House** opened here, as the city's largest and finest theater, with 1,400 seats. The curtain was brought down by the Great Fire of 1889.

We will visit First Avenue's other historic buildings during the Waterfront, Pike Place Market, and Central Business District tours.

### ■ Ascending Marion to Second Avenue

Now climb the Jackson's dramatic "Florentine Steps" to Second Avenue (or take the elevator in the Exchange Building at First and Marion). The plaza on Second Avenue retains a sandstone archway from the former **Burke Building** (Elmer Fisher, 1891), demolished in 1973 for the new tower.

### ■ South Along Second from Marion

Turning back south on Second Avenue leads you across Marion Street. The southeast corner is occupied by the **Marion Building** (1916), a former stock brokerage integrated by Ralph Anderson and T. William Booth with its neighbors and a new, low-rise structure on Third to create **Seattle Trust Court** in 1977.

John Graham Sr.'s. Exchange Building at Second and Marion opened in 1930 as one of Seattle's last and most stylish Art Deco skyscrapers.

The southern side of Marion between First and Second is commanded by the **Exchange Building**, one of John Graham Sr.'s Art Deco masterworks. Completed just as the Depression was being felt in 1931, the building has been praised by many critics for its spare and sophisticated ornamentation and dramatic Second Avenue lobby (compromised, alas, to accommodate offices of Metro Transit). The Exchange Building's elevators also offer a quick shortcut in ascending the steep grade between First and Second Avenues.

John Graham Sr. also designed the tiny bank immediately south of the Exchange Building. This Classic Revival temple to finance was built in 1916 to house the **Bank of California**. The arrival of the Modern Era was proudly

announced by the neighboring **Norton Building** (Bindon & Wright with Skidmore, Owings & Merrill) in 1959. One of Seattle's first "international-style" curtain-wall buildings, the Norton features one of the city's longest escalators, linking Second and First Avenues.

The southeast corner of Columbia and Second was the site of Seattle's first house of worship, the Rev. David Blaine's Methodist Episcopalian Church, better known by its paint as the **"White Church."** Glancing east up Columbia, you will notice the charming Italian Romanesque-inspired facade of the **Chamber of Commerce's former headquarters**. Designed by Schack, Young & Meyers and completed in 1924, it was remodeled and occupied by that firm's distant heir, TRA, in 1970. The eastern panel of the exterior bas relief frieze was sculpted by Morgan Padelford to celebrate native life, and Mildred Stumer depicted more modern activities on the western panel.

### ■ At Second and Cherry

The northwest corner of Cherry and Second was the site of Carson Boren's cabin, built in April 1852 and the first structure erected after settlers relocated from Alki. The original *Seattle Post-Intelligencer* later published from a building on this corner, which today is anchored by the **Hoge Building**, an elegant shaft topped by an elaborate cornice in the Beaux Arts style. Upon completion in 1911, the Hoge reigned briefly as Seattle's tallest building. It was also one of Charles Bebb and Louis Mendel's last major commissions before they ended their partnership in 1914 and Bebb joined with Carl Gould.

Across Second, the Hoge faces the terra-cotta facade of the **Dexter Horton Building** (1921–1924), designed in an "E" plan by John Graham Sr. to maximize natural light. Detroiters may notice a resemblance to

Looking southwest from just above Cherry Street, Second Avenue bustles with street-cars, autos, and pedestrians. The Alaska Building *(center)* became Seattle's first steel-frame skyscraper in 1904. It was joined and superseded by the Smith Tower 10 years later. *(Lawton Gowey)*

the General Motors Building; this may not be accidental since Graham numbered Henry Ford among his clients and was probably very familiar with "Motor City" architecture.

The 14-story **Alaska Building** (Eames & Young, 1904), which rises from the southeast corner of Second and Cherry, holds the title as Seattle's first "skyscraper" of steel-frame construction. It takes its name from the Alaska Club, a sodality of that territory's residents and entrepreneurs that once convened in the building's penthouse. Looking east up Cherry from Second, you will notice the midblock **Cherry Street Garage**. This building once echoed to the applause of patrons of **John Cort's Grand Opera House** (Edwin W. Houghton, 1898).

The southwest corner is anchored by the **Broderick Building** (originally the Bailey Block, 1889–1891), designed by Saunders and Lawton. This was the office of pioneering real estate developer Henry Broderick for many decades; its interior was recently remodeled.

### ■ South Along Second to James

The **Corona Hotel** (Bebb & Mendel, 1903) stands immediately south of the Alaska Building on the east side of Second Avenue. It is another example of Louis Sullivan's influence on the expanding downtown, and the first Seattle building to make significant use of terra cotta.

The northeast corner of Second and James is occupied by the **Hartford Building** (1929), designed by John

Graham Sr. during his Art Deco period. Back in 1882 several sturdy maples stood on this corner. A "vigilance committee" employed their limbs on January 17 to hang two suspected "footpads" who had murdered a popular citizen, George Reynolds, during a robbery. Emboldened, the mob of 500 also seized a third man being held in the town jail for killing policeman David Sire a month earlier and lynched him too for good measure. The frayed scantlings were left dangling for many years as a warning to would-be villains and scofflaws.

The northwest corner of Second and James is filled by the **Butler Block** (John Parkinson, 1890), which briefly served as City Hall during postfire reconstruction. Once a major hotel, it lost several upper stories and most of its guests are now automobiles.

### ■ South to the Smith Tower

The **Collins Block** on the southeast corner of Second and James is another Sullivanesque building dating from 1893. The adjacent **Palace Theater** survived as one of the city's last operating burlesque houses until the late 1970s, and was briefly occupied by the now-defunct Pioneer Square Theater, which gave the world the musical "Angry Housewives." Rounding the corner of the **Smith Tower** (see the Pioneer Square tour) brings you to the Pioneer Square station of the Downtown Transit Tunnel, or you can head west back to Pioneer Place.

### HISTORIC BUILDINGS ON LOWER THIRD AVENUE

Most of the west side of Third between Jefferson and James is occupied by the **Morrison Hotel** (Schack & Huntington, 1908). Originally the upscale Seward Hotel and first home of the Arctic Club, the Morrison is now operated as an emergency shelter for transients and homeless people. (The

west side of Third is filled by the King County Courthouse, described in the Pioneer Square tour.)

### ■ Drexel Hotel

The **Drexel Hotel** on the southwest corner of Third and James is significant because its now-drab upper stories constitute one of the few downtown structures to have survived the Great Fire of 1889. When Third Avenue was lowered in 1890, the original structure was placed atop a new foundation and ground floor credited to Timotheus Josenhans and Norris Best Allan.

### ■ Lyon Building

The **Lyon Building** on the northwest corner of James and Third was designed for French investors by John Graham Sr. and David J. Meyers in 1910. It is one of the few Seattle buildings constructed by Stone & Webster, the giant utility and engineering cartel that once controlled much of the city's street railways and electric power. It was designated as a Seattle landmark in 1996 and is currently being remodeled to house AIDS patients. John Graham Sr. also designed the **St. Charles Hotel** (originally the Hotel Rector, 1911) immediately north of the Lyon.

### ■ Arctic Building

The most significant building on Third stands on the northeast corner of Cherry and Third. The **Arctic Building** (A. Warren Gould, 1917) is immediately recognizable for its fanciful Italianate terra-cotta facade and tusked walrus heads (the original ivories were replaced with plastic for fear of skewering unlucky pedestrians below). Built to house the prestigious Arctic Club (successor to the Alaska Club), most of its former interior details have been lost in remodeling for city offices (including the Office of Urban Conservation). One architectural survivor is the Dome Room, a banquet room topped by a rococo gilt and stained-glass skylight.

Terra-cotta walruses guard the former Arctic Club at Third and Cherry, now home of the Seattle Office of Urban Conservation and other city offices. *(Paul Dorpat)*

The building was the scene of a political tragedy on August 7, 1936, when left-wing Congressman Marion Zioncheck hurled himself out of an upper-story window. Filling the resulting vacancy catapulted the late U.S. Senator Warren G. Magnuson into Congress.

### ■ Central Building

Our tour of the lower downtown ends with the **Central Building**, which fills the eastern side of Third between Columbia and Marion. The Central's "granite" facade is deceiving; it is actually sheathed in terra cotta. The building was completed in 1907 without the soaring clock tower originally proposed by architect C. R. Aldrich to mark it as the downtown's new center. Over time, development on the blocks north eclipsed the Central Building's grand ambitions, but it remains a respectable office address.

# CHINATOWN-INTERNATIONAL DISTRICT

## Orientation

This compact and lively multiethnic neighborhood is concentrated between I-5 on the east and Fifth Avenue South on the west, and between Dearborn on the south and Jackson Street on the north. It is a short eastward walk on South Jackson Street from Pioneer Square. The Waterfront Streetcar and Downtown Transit Tunnel both terminate near Union Station at the main gateway to the International District.

## History

Historians believe that Seattle's first Chinese resident was Chin Chun Hock, who arrived around 1860. He was the vanguard of hundreds of Chinese immigrants lured by the Northwest's "Golden Mountain" and the jobs to be had there—digging mines, laying railroad tracks, and canning salmon.

Initially, Seattle's whites welcomed the aid of Chinese labor, but this attitude soured during the hard times of the 1870s and led to passage of the

This decaying storefront at First South and South Main still showed traces of Seattle's original "Chinatown" long after the Asian community had relocated southeast to the International District. *(Frank O. Shaw)*

national Chinese Exclusion Act in 1882. White workers (including Seattle's many recent German and Scandinavian immigrants) came to view the low-paid Chinese as unfair competitors for scant jobs during the depression of the mid-1880s, and local organizers of the Knights of Labor and other early unions excoriated them as potential strikebreakers.

The anti-Chinese agitation on the West Coast reached fever pitch in 1885–1886, and the Territorial Legislature passed a law barring Chinese ownership of property. Populist agitators demanded the expulsion of the 350 or so immigrants already living in Seattle, mostly in the first Chinatown east of the "Lava Beds," Pioneer Square's red-light district. The town's "better element," led by Judge Thomas Burke and Mayor Henry Yesler, tried to cool passions, but they also agreed that the Chinese had to go, albeit by orderly and legal means.

This approach proved too slow for socialist firebrand Mary Kenworthy, utopianist George Venable Smith, who later founded the Puget Sound Co-Operative Colony at Port Angeles, and their allies. On February 7, 1886, a throng of workers rounded up every Chinese in Seattle and herded them to the "ocean dock" at the foot of Main Street for passage out of town on a waiting steamer. The mob and its frightened charges were met at the pier by police and a contingent of the volunteer Home Guard, and a stalemate ensued when territorial governor Watson Squire prevented the ship from leaving.

The following morning, nearly 200 Chinese embarked for San Francisco, stranding another 150 on shore to await the next boat, due in six days. When police and deputies tried to escort these people back to their homes, the mob rioted. The deputies fired into the crowd, and five agitators fell. One died of his wounds, and the mob demanded Judge Burke's neck in retribution. Governor Squire and President Cleveland declared martial law, and passions gradually cooled in Seattle and elsewhere as all but a few Chinese departed. Congress ultimately paid $276,619.15 to the Chinese government in compensation for the West Coast rioting—but the actual victims never saw a dime.

By 1889, Seattle's Chinese-born population had rebounded to its preexpulsion level. Chin Gee Hee built one of the first brick structures to rise from the ashes of the Seattle Fire, at 208–210 South Washington Street, and his Quong Tuck Co. supplied workers for railroads and mines while selling goods to local Chinese residents. Although prejudice persisted, the growing importance of Asian trade to Seattle was celebrated by the Alaska-Yukon-Pacific Exposition of 1909. This did not assure that the racist violence of the 1880s would not be repeated against the Chinese and the growing numbers of Japanese and Filipino immigrants.

Completion of the Jackson Street regrade in 1909 and the opening of Union Station (for the Union Pacific and Milwaukee railroad lines) in 1911 created new opportunities for Chinese entrepreneurs. Goon Dip, a leading merchant and consul for the Chinese government, built the Milwaukee Hotel in 1911. The Northern Pacific Hotel followed in 1914 and, under ownership of Niroku Frank Shitamae, became the anchor for an emerging Nihon Machi, or "Japan Town," along Yesler Way. Hundreds of Japanese truck farmers settled in Rainier Valley and became the mainstays of the Pike Place Public Market, despite xenophobic state laws barring land ownership.

Early Chinese merchants such as Chin Gee Hee, shown in his store at Second and Washington, supplied labor for Seattle enterprises while selling goods and protection to immigrants. *(Wing Luke Asian Museum)*

This contemporary sketch depicts Seattle's Home Guard battling Anti-Chinese rioters on Seattle's Pioneer Square waterfront on February 8, 1886.

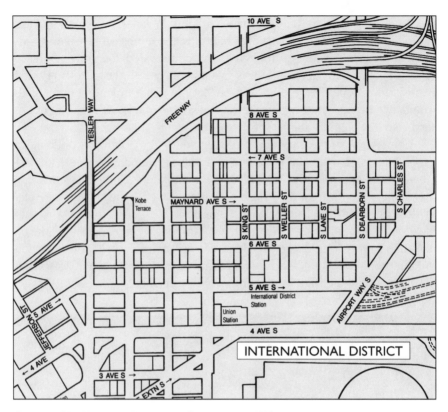

Courtesy of the University of Washington Press, copyright 1992.

By the late 1920s, when construction of the Second Avenue Extension uprooted much of the original Chinatown, a thriving neighborhood of Chinese, Japanese, and Filipino families and their American-born descendants was already blooming to the southeast. When the Seattle Buddhist Church (designed by Yoshio Arai and still open at 1427 South Main) welcomed its first worshipers in 1941, Japanese-Americans constituted Seattle's largest ethnic minority and the second largest such community on the West Coast.

Then the attack on Pearl Harbor rekindled old prejudices and led to a new "expulsion." In the spring of 1942, Presidential Order 9066 forcibly relocated all West Coast Japanese-Americans to inland internment camps regardless of their citizenship or loyalty. Seven thousand Seattle residents disappeared virtually overnight—with barely a word of protest from their neighbors.

As if salting the earth on which they had lived, the city quickly demolished much of Japan Town and built a public housing project, Yesler Terrace, in its place. Thousands of African-Americans, chiefly attracted to Seattle by defense jobs, moved into the area and established Jackson Street as the city's hub for jazz, swing, and rhythm and blues. They also inherited the unfair burden of bigotry and de facto segregation.

The International District survived, thanks to the Chinese (the Exclusion Act was repealed in 1943, but the national quota limited Chinese immigrants to 105 annually) and growing numbers of Filipinos, employed chiefly in fisheries, but the Japanese-American community never recovered its prewar size or vitality. Despite the efforts of the new Jackson Street Community Council, the city's first neighborhood advocacy group, the state constructed I-5 through the heart of the International District in the early 1960s.

Asian-Americans remained effectively segregated south of Yesler Way, but an important breakthrough occurred in March 1962 when business leader and civic activist Wing Luke was elected to the Seattle City Council and became the first Chinese-American to win a major elected office in the continental United States. He would likely have risen to higher office but for his death in an airplane accident in 1965. Ironically, restrictive immigration quotas were liberalized for Chinese and other Asians that same year.

Since the 1960s, growing numbers of Koreans and Pacific Islanders have also moved into Seattle, but their arrival did not slow the decline of the

Internment during World War II devastated Seattle's Japanese-American community, then the second largest on the West Coast. The family shown here has just arrived at an inland camp. (H. Clifford, University of Washington Library Special Collections. Neg. UW526)

Wing Luke celebrates his 1962 election to the Seattle City Council with his family. He became the first Chinese-American elected to a major office in the continental United States. (Seattle Times)

Seattle's influx of Southeast Asians has led to establishment of a new commercial district at South Jackson Street and Twelfth South, dubbed "Little Saigon." *(John Stamets)*

International District. Construction of the nearby Kingdome posed a direct threat by clogging streets with game traffic, driving up land values, and diluting the District's cultural character. This prompted creation of a Special Review Board in 1973 to protect the area's historical and cultural assets, and the area was listed on the National Register. The Seattle Chinatown-International District Public Development Authority was established in 1975 to fund housing, services, and neighborhood improvements. (Although the Kingdome is now slated for demolition, development of new football and baseball stadiums pose similar challenges for the area.)

In the 1980s, the Seattle area welcomed thousands of new immigrants from Vietnam, Laos, and Cambodia. After acclimation in Tacoma, many followed tradition and settled in Rainier Valley. Southeast Asian merchants established their own thriving commercial center, dubbed "Little Saigon," around the intersection of Jackson and Twelfth Avenue on the International District's eastern margin.

Meanwhile, current and former Seattle citizens (such as Gordon Hirabayashi) pressed successful campaigns to win Japanese-Americans a federal apology and restitution for the World War II internment. And in 1996, Washington voters elected Gary Locke, grandson of Chinese immigrants, as the first Asian-American governor of a state other than Hawaii. Thus, the influence of Seattle's Asian-American community extends far beyond the confines of its "hometown" in the International District.

## Walking Tour

We start at the **International District Station of the Downtown Transit Tunnel,** which opened in 1990 and was designed by architect Gary Hartnett in collaboration with artists Sonya Ishii and Alice Adams. We pause here to view Seattle's two major railroad terminals, Union and King Street Stations.

**Union Station** was designed by Daniel J. Patterson and opened in 1911. It served passengers on the Union Pacific and Milwaukee Railroads for 60 years until Amtrak service began using King Street Station to the west in 1971.

James J. Hill built **King Street Station** with some reluctance because he opposed the expense of a "fancy depot." His Great Northern Railroad came into Seattle from the north, and after he gained control of the Northern Pacific, he relegated passengers on both lines to the cramped terminal at Marion Street and present-day Alaskan Way. City Engineer R. H. Thomson persuaded Hill to dig a tunnel under downtown Seattle from Virginia to Washington Streets in order to provide relief for overcrowded Railroad Avenue (see the Waterfront section).

Charles A. Reed and Allen H. Stem (who helped to design New York's Grand Central Station) created King Street Station two blocks south of the tunnel's mouth and topped it with a faithful rendition of the campanile of Venice's Piazza San Marco. The station opened in 1906 amid the Jackson Street regrade that leveled the land for the future International District. Although altered over time, most of the original building survives, and plans are now underway for its use as part of an intermodal transportation center. Now we'll loop around the central blocks of Seattle's most diverse and interesting business district. With so many nooks and crannies to explore, don't be surprised if you end up spending hours in this neighborhood.

### ■ Heading East on South Jackson Street

The southeast corner of Fifth Avenue South is dominated by the **Buty Building**, built in 1901 and expanded in 1920 for the **Idaho Hotel** under direction of architect James Stephen. Most of the north side of Jackson is lined by the delicate terra-cotta facade of the **Governor Apartments**,

The King Street Station (with campanile) and Union Station are still new in this 1914 view from the Smith Tower, as is the "New Chinatown" district on the east. *(Webster & Stevens, Photographers; Museum of History and Industry)*

designed by J. L. McCauley and built in 1926, now home of the **Mikado Restaurant** and other businesses.

### ■ Up Sixth Avenue South

Turn left and head north up Sixth South. Past the Governor, on your left, you will find the former **Main Street School Annex**, dating from around 1910 and now used for professional offices. The east side of the street is dominated by the **NP Hotel**, designed by John Graham Sr. in 1914 and restored by Robert Kovalenko in 1995 for low-income housing. Like its northern neighbor, the **Panama Hotel** (1910), and the Ticino Apartments farther up Sixth, the NP was a major center for Seattle's original **Japan Town.** Pressing north up the steep hill between Main and Washington will lead you past two newer public housing towers. A right turn on South Washington Street brings you to the **Nippon Kan** (Japanese Hall) theater in the original **Astor Hotel**. It was built in 1909 and designed by the father-and-son team of Charles L. and C. Bennet Thompson,

who were responsible for many of the International District's important buildings. The Nippon Kan served as the cultural center of Seattle's Japanese community from 1909 until the mass internment of 1942, then resumed its original function after rehabilitation in 1978. The lobby features a nice display of historical photos celebrating the theater's prewar heyday.

The nearby **Kobe Terrace Park** was designed by William Teufel and dedicated in 1975. The park's large Yuki Midoro ("snow viewing lantern") and cherry trees were donated by residents of Kobe, Japan, a sister city of Seattle. From the Terrace, you have an excellent view of the **Pacific Medical Center** on the far slope of **Beacon Hill**, which rises south of the District. This superb Art Deco tower was designed by John Graham Sr. for the former U.S. Marine Hospital, and it has survived several attempted closures as well as numerous additions since completion in 1934. The lower path through the park leads you above the terraced beds of the **Danny Woo International District**

Japan's visiting Keio baseball team poses in front of the NP Hotel in "Japan Town" in this photo from the 1930s. *(Wing Luke Asian Museum)*

**Community Garden**, named in honor of the restaurateur who donated the site. You exit Kobe Terrace at the intersection of South Main Street and Seventh South, which offers a panoramic view of the entire district.

## ■ Down Seventh South and West on Jackson South

The **Jackson Hotel** on the northwest corner of Seventh and Jackson dates from 1917 and was rehabilitated by Ing and Associates for housing in 1984. The **Viet Hoa Market** was one of the District's first retailers to cater to the city's growing Southeast Asian population.

Heading west along the north side of Jackson leads you past another of J. L. McCauley's terra-cotta facades. Built for the **Rainier Heat and Power Company** in 1917, this building became the first home of the national Japanese-American Citizens League in 1930 and once housed the Japanese Chamber of Commerce.

Crossing South Maynard puts you in front of the **Far East Building**, designed as the **Havana Hotel** by Thompson & Thompson and built in stages between 1900 and 1908. It was restored and altered in 1984, under the direction of Robert Kovalenko, for retail space and low-income apartments.

West of the Far East Building is the **Higo Variety Store**. Higo was the orginal name of Japan's Kumamato Prefecture, birthplace of Sanzo Murakami, who founded the store in the early 1900s. The store opened at 602 South Jackson in 1932 and is now managed by Murakami's daughters. It was one of the District's few Japanese-American businesses to return to its prewar location. Now cross South Jackson at Sixth and head east along the south side of the street.

## ■ Back East on South Jackson

The **United Savings & Loan Bank** became the nation's first Asian-American-owned savings and loan association in 1960. The present building was designed in 1972 by Woo and Par architects, and the entryway mural of "The Eight Immortals" was painted by Fay Chong.

The former **Bush Hotel**, now the **Bush-Asia Center**, dominates the south side of Jackson. Designed by J. M. McCauley and built in 1915, the dilapidated hotel was refurbished in 1981 by Arai/Jackson architects for the Chinatown-International District Preservation and Development Authority and includes more than 170 units of low-income housing.

George Tsutakawa's sculpture, Heaven, Man and Earth, was installed on the southeast corner of South Jackson and Maynard South in 1978. The adjacent **Evergreen Apartments** was built as the **Tokiwa Hotel** in 1916, designed by the ubiquitous team of Thompson & Thompson.

## ■ South on Seventh South, Sibilantly

A right turn at Seventh Avenue South brings you to the door of the **Wing Luke Asian Museum** (407 Seventh Avenue South), housed in a former garage dating from 1915. The museum's exhibits offer an excellent introduction to the International District and the history of its numerous ethnic groups. The **Theater off Jackson** next door features live drama and readings drawn from many cultures.

The **Milwaukee Hotel** fills the rest of the block, but we will return to it a little later. The opposite side of Seventh is anchored by the ornate **Republic Hotel**, formerly the **Lyn Yuen Apartments**, built in 1920 to house transient workers and newly arrived immigrants. The **Linyen Restaurant** on the northeast corner of Seventh and South King occupies the former **New American Hotel** (Thompson & Thompson, 1916). This building houses

The Wing Luke Asian Museum's exhibits at Seventh South and South Jackson retell the histories of Seattle's diverse Asian communities and honor the memory of the late Seattle City Council member Wing Luke. *(Paul Dorpat)*

The New American Hotel's ceremonial balcony facing South King Street between Seventh and Eighth Avenues South marks the hall of the Bing Kung Association. *(Paul Dorpat)*

the **Bing Kung Association**, an early tong (fraternal organization) offering immigrants protection and social benefits. Cross South King and look back at the New American's elaborate top-story balcony.

### ■ Continuing Along Seventh South to South Weller

The southeast corner of Seventh South and South King is dominated by the **Kong Yick Apartments** (Thompson & Thompson, 1910), one of the District's first and largest Chinese hotels and home of the **Yick Fung Company** since 1913. The **Luck Ngi Musical Club** at 512 Seventh South was established in 1938 to promote Chinese opera, which was once performed next door in a hall designed by Andrew Willatsen in 1924 for impresario Charlie Louie. In 1929, Louie converted the space into a popular nightclub, the Chinese Garden, and it now houses the **China Gate Restaurant** (which serves great dim sum).

The hall of the **Chong Wa Benevolent Association** at 522

Seventh South also dates from 1929. This organization was established in the early 1900s to advocate the interests of all Chinese-Americans in the state and to help resolve community conflicts. A side trip one block farther down Seventh to South Lane Street will take you to the **International Children's Park** (Joey Ing, 1981).

### ■ Heading Back North on Seventh South

The northwest corner of Seventh and South Weller is filled by the former **Eclipse Hotel** (1908) and a slightly older hotel, which were taken over by the **Gee How Oak Tin Family Association** in 1921 (note the ceremonial balcony on the top story). The state's largest such group, the association was founded in 1900 to serve members of the extended Chin, Woo, and Yuen families. North of this location you will find the **Chinese Community Bulletin Board**, a neighborhood media mainstay since the 1960s, against the wall of the adjacent **Louisa Hotel** (1909). Now take a right turn on South King.

### ■ West on South King

The **Milwaukee Hotel** fills the northwest corner of Seventh South and South King. Built by Chinese Consul Goon Dip (note the inscription above the main entrance) in 1911, it long reigned as the largest and most important building in "New Chinatown." The adjacent **Atlas Hotel** opened in 1920.

The southern side of South King between Seventh South and Maynard South is divided by **Maynard Alley**, which is worth a peek for **Liem's Pet Shop**, a menagerie of exotic fish, birds, mammals, and reptiles. The **Rex Hotel** west of the alley was designed by F. H. Perkins in 1909 and was remodeled in 1997. The nearby **Tai Tung Restaurant**, at 655 South King, dates from 1935 and is the oldest continously operating eatery in the neighborhood.

Crossing South Maynard brings you to the **Alps Hotel**, designed by Graham and Myers in 1910. Opposite this is **Hing Hay Park**, dedicated in 1975. The elaborate pavilion was built in Taipei, Taiwan, and John Woo painted the mural on the back wall of the Bush-Asia

Members of the Chong Wa Benevolent Association, based in this building, have worked for the rights of Chinese immigrants since the early 1900s. *(Paul Dorpat)*

Center. A memorial also honors local Chinese-Americans who fell in World War II. The park is a focal point for casual conversation among residents and for community events such as the celebration of Chinese New Year and the International District Summer Festival.

### ■ Heading West Across Maynard South

J. L. McCauley designed the **Hotel Publix** (1927) on the northwest corner. The south side of King is taken up by the parking lot and Minka-style architecture of **Uwajimaya's**, an Asian-American supermarket established in 1970. Its founder, Fujimatsu Moriguchi, started out in 1928 running a fish market in Tacoma; his son Tomio now runs the region's largest Asian retail store. The rest of the block is filled by another McCauley design, the **American Hotel**, built in 1925.

You are now back at the International District Station, leaving you free to delve deeper into the District or to hop a bus or trolley to your next destination.

Hing Hay Park stands behind the Bush Hotel Asian Center. The ornate pavilion was a gift from the people of Taiwan. *(Paul Dorpat)*

Uwajimaya is one of the largest Asian-American retailers on the West Coast. *(Paul Dorpat)*

# CENTRAL WATERFRONT

## Orientation

Seattle's central waterfront extends from the foot of Broad Street and Pier 70 on the north roughly 2 miles (3.2 km) to the foot of South Main Street and Pier 48. Enough structures survive to conjure up Seattle's days as a young, brawling port and to evoke the enormous transformative power of steam in driving trains, ships, and "progress" at the turn of the nineteenth century. We will rely on a suitably venerable form of transportation, the Waterfront Streetcar—it is actually an anachronistic transplant—for most of our tour.

## History

During Seattle's first century, its waterfront was shaped not by wind or waves but by steam—first by Henry Yesler's sawmill, then by titanic contests between competing railways, and finally by the "Mosquito Fleet" of cross-Sound ferries and the steamships that linked Seattle to the Pacific Rim.

As noted in the introductory history, Elliott Bay was not named and surveyed by whites until 1841, when Lieutenant Charles Wilkes led a U.S. Navy expedition into Puget Sound. Wilkes named the body of water in honor of the Rev. J. L. Elliott, chaplain aboard his flagship *Vincennes*, but it received no other particular attention in his log.

Wilkes's report, combined with news of the Hudson's Bay Company's expanding settlements on Puget Sound and a missionary urge, inspired Asa Whitney, a New York–based merchant with dealings in the Far East. In 1845 he proposed that Congress

This 1892 drawing from *Harper's Weekly* shows native canoes and a camp at the foot of present-day Washington Street South. The inset portrait depicts Chief Seattle's aging daughter Angeline.

finance a transcontinental railroad from Lake Superior to Puget Sound as a "grand highway to civilize and Christianize all mankind." Whitney's idea was no less audacious, or absurd, than that of firing a rocket to the moon a century later, but his persistence and eloquence persuaded Congress to dispatch survey teams, led by future General George B. McClellan and future Washington territorial governor Isaac Stevens, to scout rail routes across the Cascades in the mid-1850s.

Meanwhile, the first white farmers were drawn, like the natives before them, to the delta of the Duwamish rather than to the steep ridges surrounding Elliott Bay. The original scouts for the Denny party also ignored Elliott Bay, preferring to settle in 1851 at Alki Point on the weather side of West Seattle, which offered an anchorage for passing ships. But after a wet winter on the exposed beach at Alki, most of the town's founders decided to resettle in present-day Pioneer Square (see the West Seattle and Pioneer Square sections for details).

In February 1852, Arthur Denny, William Bell, and Carson Boren explored the bay, and Denny took soundings with a horseshoe tied to his wife's clothesline. Steep, heavily forested ridges and hills met the water north of present-day Yesler Way. Level shoreland was confined to the foot of Skid Road, where Henry Yesler built Puget Sound's first steam-powered sawmill in 1852–53, and Doc Maynard's "point" on the south, which became an island at high tide. This fronted a marshy lagoon (where the Kingdome now stands) that opened south on the Duwamish River's vast and murky delta. Low tide revealed hundreds of acres of gooey but clam-rich mud flats bracketed between the ridges of Beacon Hill and West Seattle.

In short, Elliott Bay's anchorage was the town's only natural asset, but it was enough. As the settlers cleared Seattle's heavily wooded slopes for cabins, gardens, stores, and entertainment halls, they also tampered with the original topography. The lagoon behind Maynard's Point quickly filled with chips from Yesler's Mill, and ballast dumped by ships before loading lumber and, later, coal created an island off Pioneer Square's shore. It was the first of the waterfront's many landfills.

Yesler's wharf extended 900 feet into the bay, and it was the town's front door for many years. Other piers were extended over the mud flats north and south of Yesler, but extensive waterfront development did not begin until the 1870s. The driving force was anticipation of a transcontinental connection, which Congress had finally approved in the closing days of the Civil War. Although Congress adopted Whitney's idea of funding the Northern Pacific Railroad with a 60-mile-wide "land grant" along the route, it was financier Jay Cooke who started laying track west from Duluth in July 1870. Asa Whitney himself died penniless two years later and more than a decade before his dream was actually realized.

During the bitter winter of 1880, ice floes blew north from the mouth of the Duwamish River and blockaded the Seattle waterfront. *(Greg Lang)*

The planked expanse of Railroad Avenue, shown here ca. 1915, was filled to create Alaskan Way in the mid-1930s. *(Lawton Gowey)*

The privilege of being the Northern Pacific's Puget Sound terminus set off fierce competition among the region's numerous budding metropolises. As a fledgling city of 2,000, Seattle fully expected to win. Thus, it was bitterly disappointed when Tacoma, a village a tenth its size, won Cooke's nod in 1873, but this turned out to be a blessing in disguise for the loser.

Cooke's capital evaporated in a national depression that same year, effectively putting development of the "City of Destiny" on hold for a decade. Seattle's business leaders decided to fund and build their own railroad to the east, and volunteers rallied on May 1, 1874, to lay track across Snoqualmie Pass. They soon wearied, and the 21-mile, narrow-gauge "Seattle & Walla Walla

Railroad" never came near the ampersand in its name, let alone Walla Walla, but a Scottish engineer named James Colman redirected the track to newly discovered coal fields near Renton. The trains reached the waterfront from the south via a curved, spindly trestle dubbed the "ram's horn" and delivered coal directly to docked ships bound for fuel-hungry San Francisco and other coastal cities. As new piers were built north of Yesler, the tracks were gradually extended along a planked viaduct called Railroad Avenue (since filled and renamed Alaskan Way).

This activity impressed Henry Villard, who had taken control of Ben Holladay's Oregon Railway and Navigation Company and was now closing in on the moribund Northern Pacific. He bought the Seattle & Walla Walla in 1880 and quickly consolidated control over Seattle's waterfront. The following year, Villard's famous financial "blind pool" gobbled up the NP, and on September 8, 1883, he presided over the driving of the gold spike linking the western and eastern arms of the Northern Pacific at Gold Creek, Montana. Villard also built a spur north from Tacoma to serve his Seattle holdings, giving the city its first transcontinental connection in 1884.

Thus, Villard's triumph was shared by Seattle, but it was all too brief. Cost overruns, a sour national economy, and personal illness forced Villard out in 1884. New Northern Pacific directors, led by Charles Wright, saw no reason to aid Seattle at the expense of their Tacoma interests and provided only intermittent rail service. The NP also faced fresh competition from Jay Gould, who had taken charge of the Union Pacific and proposed to push north from Portland, as well as a renewed effort by Seattle to develop its own transcontinental link.

The latter took the form of the Seattle, Lake Shore & Eastern Railway, organized by local legal eagle Judge Thomas Burke and entrepreneur Daniel Gilman in 1885 to build a line north to connect with the new Canadian Pacific Railroad at Sumas on the British Columbia-Washington border (completed in 1891). Burke convinced the City of Seattle to award him the prime seaward 30-foot right-of-way along Railroad Avenue north of Columbia Street, and again coal hauling made the line instantly profitable. Northern Pacific responded to this threat by laying track through Stampede Pass to create a shortcut to Puget Sound from its Columbia River line.

Judge Thomas Burke helped define modern Seattle by negotiating the entry of the Northern Pacific and Great Northern Railways. (Seattle Public Library)

These investments were not enough to revive a stagnant local economy, and high unemployment set the stage for violence against Seattle's Chinese population in the winter of 1885–86. On February 7 and 8, 1886, a mob herded 350 Chinese workers and family members to the "ocean dock" at the foot of Main Street and forced most to board a steamer bound for San Francisco (see the International District history for more detail).

Recovery came within a year, and despite the fire of 1889, Seattle's population reached nearly 43,000 in 1890, a twelvefold increase in just one decade. Northern Pacific wisely abandoned its strategy to beat Seattle and joined it by purchasing the Seattle Lake Shore & Eastern in 1892. Judge Burke and local capitalists had by then begun courting a new rail tycoon, James Jerome Hill, whose Great Northern Railroad was preparing to cross the North Cascades at Stevens Pass.

The Northern Pacific's control of Railroad Avenue limited Hill's access to the downtown waterfront, so he based his Puget Sound terminus at Smith Cove (now piers 90–91) at the foot of Magnolia Hill. The first Great Northern trains arrived in 1893, just in time for the onset of another national depression, which persisted in Seattle until the kick start of the Klondike gold rush in 1897.

The long battle with Northern Pacific ended in 1901 when James J. Hill bought control of the railroad and gained control of Railroad Avenue, which was now clogged with trains and wagon traffic. To help relieve the congestion on the waterfront, City Engineer R. H. Thomson persuaded Hill to dig a rail tunnel beneath downtown from the foot of Virginia Street to a new passenger terminal near Pioneer Square, which opened in 1906. Workers joked that this was the world's longest tunnel since it extended from "Virginia to Washington" — streets, that is. Seattle's final transcontinental links were forged in 1909 with the arrival of the Union Pacific and Milwaukee railroads, which shared Union Station after its opening in 1911.

While railroad capitalists battled each other on land, their steamship subsidiaries vied for dominance on the Sound and beyond. The Hudson's Bay Company introduced the region's first steamer in 1836. The intrepid little *Beaver* puffed up and down Puget Sound until 1888, when she met her end on a rock at the mouth of Vancouver's harbor.

The *Beaver* was joined over the years by stern-wheelers, many of which were transferred from duty on the Columbia River. Smaller shallow-draft steamers were perfect for navigating the Duwamish and adjoining Black River slough, which offered the only route between Elliott Bay and the fresh waters of Lake Washington before the Ship Canal was completed in 1917.

In 1858, the *Eliza Anderson* arrived from Portland and established the first regular cross-Sound steamer service between Seattle and nearby cities. This side-wheeler's lucrative monopoly prompted some to comment, "No steamer went so slow or made money faster," a fact that soon attracted competition. Foremost among the newcomers was the elegant *George E. Starr*, launched in

Seattle in 1879. The following year, she bore Rutherford B. Hayes to and from Yesler's Wharf during the first presidential visit to Puget Sound.

Cross-Sound steamers were numerous enough by 1882 for James Colman to build them their own dock at the foot of Columbia Street. On Christmas Eve, 1888, the West Seattle Land and Improvement Company introduced the city's first scheduled ferry service aboard the *City of Seattle*. The little double-ender shuttled commuters and prospective West Seattle home buyers between her Marion Street dock and a landing north of the present-day Seacrest Marina for a quarter of a century, despite competition for passengers from the Northern Pacific's Seattle Terminal Railroad in 1890 and, later, electric streetcar service to West Seattle. A second ferry, the *West Seattle*, was introduced in 1907, in time to carry revelers to the new Luna Park at Duwamish Head. Developers later fell on hard times, and first the Port of Seattle and then King County took over the West Seattle ferry service.

Meanwhile, the Klondike gold rush precipitated a dramatic expansion in shipbuilding and operations—and in the wealth of savvy capitalists like Robert Moran. He had arrived in Seattle in 1875 at the age of 14, with the proverbial dime in his pocket, and had risen to establish a major shipyard at the foot of present-day Royal Brougham Way and to be elected mayor in time for the fire of 1889. Eight years later, Moran's workers built a dozen stern-wheelers in less than five months and launched them on their way to Alaska's rivers.

The gold rush was perfectly timed for Charles Peabody, who had established the Alaska Steamship Company in 1895. He joined with future banker Joshua Green to organize the Puget Sound Navigation Company in 1898. Its famed Black Ball Line steamers and ferries went on to become the dominant marine transportation system on the Sound, meeting and beating stiff competition from the Kitsap Transportation Company and White Collar Lines.

The venerable SS *Geo E. Starr* backs out of her berth near Pioneer Square in this 1890s view, dominated by the Denny Hotel atop Denny Hill. (*University of Washington Library Special Collections. Neg. 8374*)

By May 23, 1903, when President Teddy Roosevelt disembarked from the SS *Spokane* at the Arlington Dock (now pier 56), Seattle's resident flotilla of steamers and ferries had been dubbed the "Mosquito Fleet." The phrase is usually attributed to an apocryphal newspaper description — "At five o'clock in Seattle, the little commuter steamers scurry off to their destinations like a swarm of mosquitos" — but no one has ever tracked down the actual article.

The late historian Jim Faber described these sturdy little craft best: "Unregulated, financed by loans and gall, fueled by cordwood and fierce competition, they were to forge a mass transit system that for 70 years made inter-city travel on Puget Sound a delight." The end came in 1951, when exasperated commuters finally prevailed on the State of Washington to take over the Black Ball Line and establish a publicly owned ferry service.

Pacific commerce expanded along with intra-Sound shipping, thanks in large part to the efforts—and rivalry—of the Northern Pacific and Great Northern railroads, which sought high-value cargo from the Orient to fill their eastbound trains. James J. Hill personally arranged for the arrival of the first Japanese freighter in Seattle's harbor on August 31, 1896. Citizens greeted the NYK Line steamship *Miike Maru* with church bells, factory whistles, and a 21-gun salute, in stark contrast to public attitudes toward Chinese workers a decade earlier. Hill also expanded trade with China in 1905 via the modern steamships *Dakota* and *Minnesota*, which docked at Smith Cove and transferred their cargo to high-speed "Silk Trains" bound for the mills and markets of the Midwest and East Coast.

Such seamless "intermodal" connections between ships and rail were common at the turn of the century, and they served passengers as well as freight. Northern Pacific and Great Northern steamships offered unprecedented luxury in crossing the Pacific, while The Orient Limited and the Empire

The SS *Flyer* was one of the fastest steamships in the motley "Mosquito Fleet" that once swarmed across Puget Sound. *(Waterfront Awareness)*

Builder sped passengers across the continent in three days. Other railroad companies such as the Canadian Pacific and the Grand Trunk Pacific operated elegant steamers serving Seattle, Vancouver, Victoria, and other Northwest ports for many decades.

There was a downside to such economic integration: Seattle's waterfront was ruled by the masters of the railroads, and by James J. Hill in particular. An early victim of this monopoly was former territorial governor Eugene Semple, who in 1895 began digging a "South Canal" through Beacon Hill to link Lake Washington and Elliott Bay. His project alarmed both Northern Pacific and the Great Northern, which favored a North Canal via Lake Union (see the discussion of the Hiram Chittenden Locks in the Northwest Seattle section). In 1902, Hill bought Semple's company out from under him and killed the South Canal project. Semple's legacy remains, however, in the form of Harbor Island and the East and West Waterways of the Duwamish, which were built up with fill from his grand but uncompleted trench.

Such heavy-handed financial maneuvers and Hill's stranglehold on rail and shipping rates sparked a populist revolt. Railroads were placed under state regulation in 1905, and a broad alliance of merchants, labor, and trust-busting progressives convinced the voters of King County to establish the Port of Seattle on September 5, 1911. The newly elected Port Commission used its bonding and condemnation authority to bring the harbor under public ownership and control, where it remains today.

Port ownership did not extend to Railroad Avenue, whose aging piers and planks creaked beneath the weight of trains, trucks, and automobiles swarming in, out, and around waterfront piers. The City of Seattle finally began filling the area beneath present-day Alaskan Way in the late 1920s, using soil from the last round of regrades, and finished the modern seawall in 1934.

The new highway quickly filled with traffic, which still had to compete with trains serving the wharves or passing between the great railyards north and south of downtown Seattle. The city's solution was the Alaskan Way Viaduct, hailed as an "engineering masterpiece" upon its completion in 1953 and cursed as an aesthetic and urban design disaster ever since.

Seattle's waterfront fell on hard times in the late 1950s, losing trade to San Francisco and Los Angeles. Using $10 million from a bond approved by voters in 1960, port commissioners decided to gamble on a new technology called "containerization," whereby cargo is transferred in trailer-sized boxes between ships, trucks, and trains. The Port developed its first container facility at Terminal 5, on the west waterway of the Duwamish, and its success helped to revolutionize the entire shipping industry and revive the Port's own fortunes.

The loser, ironically, was the central harbor itself, whose now-obsolete pier sheds fell into disrepair. Major help did not come until the mid-1970s, when the city and private entrepreneurs began replacing or rehabilitating the sheds to create parks, shops, restaurants, and other waterfront attractions. The

Seattle's skyline towers over Fire Station No. 5 and the waterfront in this view from a ferry departing Colman Dock. *(Paul Dorpat)*

most recent developments, notably the spectacular Bell Street Pier complex, have been created by the Port of Seattle in combination with private partners.

The best new idea on the waterfont, however, was borrowed from the distant past. Former city council member George Benson began pumping for a "Waterfront Streetcar" in 1974. Given that the tracks were already in place, he thought it would be simple to operate a shuttle along Alaskan Way, but it took eight years and $3 million before the first streetcar rolled. The cars themselves were purchased from Melbourne, Australia, and lovingly restored by volunteers. The line was extended in 1990 through Pioneer Square to connect with the International District Station of the Downtown Transit Tunnel. Today, "Benson's Folly" is not only one of Seattle's most charming tourist amenities, it is an important link in the downtown's transit system.

## Streetcar Tour

The best way to enjoy Seattle's central harbor is to take the Waterfront Streetcar. The transfer you receive with your fare allows you to hop on and off the frequent cars for side trips of up to an hour. For this tour, we board the streetcar at its southern waterfront terminus at Pioneer Square.

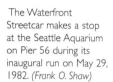
The Waterfront Streetcar makes a stop at the Seattle Aquarium on Pier 56 during its inaugural run on May 29, 1982. *(Frank O. Shaw)*

### ■ Washington Steet

In Seattle's earliest days, Puget Sound natives landed their canoes at the foot of Washington Street. The green metal **Washington Street Boat Landing** (D. R. Huntington) was built in 1920 to house Seattle's harbor master and shelter foreign seamen passing to and from their ships. The structure was rehabilitated in the 1970s and now provides short-term moorage for pleasure boats.

Just south is **Pier 48**, which was the site of Seattle's first "ocean dock." It was here on February 8, 1886, that deputies and police battled a mob that was attempting to expel 350 Chinese imigrants (see the International District). Later, Northern Pacific steamers docked here. This became the "Lower 48" base of the Alaska Marine Highway System for many decades, and it is still used intermittently by car ferries on the Victoria-Vancouver run.

Farther south, the vast expanse of container **Terminals 37–46** once housed bustling coal docks, and the Moran Brothers Shipyards once stood at the foot of Royal Brougham Way. Here, on October 8, 1904, thousands cheered the launching of the battleship USS *Nebraska*, Seattle's first major naval project, which was won with the help of

$100,000 in citizen donations. The shipyard was abandoned during the Depression, and a "Hooverville" shanty-town took its place.

### ■ At the Foot of Yesler

No trace of **Yesler's Wharf** remains today. The 900-foot pier was removed decades ago and succeeded by the docks of the Alaska Steamship Company. They too have perished, but it was here that two U.S. presidents— Rutherford Hayes in 1880 and Benjamin Harrison in 1891—first set foot in Seattle.

### ■ Colman Dock

The **Washington State Ferry Terminal at Colman Dock** still honors the name of James Colman. He built his first namesake dock here in 1882, but it perished in the great fire seven years later. He rebuilt in grand style, adding a domed waiting room and a clock tower by which commuters could mark the arrivals and departures of scores of ferries and steamers. Time stopped on the night of April 25, 1912, when the engineer of the Alaska Steamship Line's SS *Alameda* misread the captain's signal for "full speed astern" as "full speed ahead." The steel-hulled steamer sliced

This photo of crowded Colman Dock was taken not long before April 25, 1912, when a steamship rammed the pier and toppled its tower into Elliott Bay. *(Webster & Stevens, Photographers; Puget Sound Maritime Historical Society)*

The ferry *Kalakala* looked fast, but her actual performance inspired the nickname "Silver Slug." *(Jim Faber)*

through the dock, toppled the tower into the bay, and sent the waiting stern-wheeler *Telegraph* to the bottom. Astoundingly, no one died.

A new tower was erected and the dock expanded to absorb the adjacent Marion Street landing of the West Seattle Ferry. The Black Ball Line modernized the terminal in the 1930s to correspond to the new pride of its fleet, the *Kalakala*. Inspired by Norman Bel Geddes' design for an ocean liner, the sleek, streamlined "flying bird" was not all she pretended to be. The modernistic superstructure was actually built on the hull of an old (some said

jinxed) San Francisco ferry, the *Peralta*, and she rattled so horribly they had to keep her car deck doors open, which defeated any aerodynamic benefit of her design. Despite 3,000 horses worth of diesel power, she was also slow and anything but yare, earning the epithet "Silver Slug" from her passengers. But from her debut on July 2, 1935, to her retirement in 1967, the *Kalakala* looked her part and became an unofficial Seattle totem. A fund has been established to refloat the *Kalakala* at Kodiak, Alaska (where she was beached to house a cannery) and return her to her native city.

Colman Dock and the Black Ball Line were taken over by the Washington State Ferry System in 1951. The terminal was modernized anew in 1966, and the original clock is now displayed in its upper-level waiting room.

The city has docked its fireboats at **Fire Station 5**, north of Colman Dock, for nearly a century. In 1910, **Grand Trunk Pacific** (GTP) built its passenger pier next door to the south. Despite the best efforts of its neighbor, the GTP dock burned to the waterline on July 30, 1914. The rebuilt pier was taken over for expansion of Colman Dock's auto staging apron.

## ■ Pier 54

Built in 1901 by the Northern Pacific, **Pier 54** was the southernmost of three wharves, all of which survive today. Originally numbered Pier 3 and popularly known as the Galbraith Dock, Pier 54 once served the Mosquito Fleet

Ivar Haglund was a popular folksinger in the 1930s, when not serving up "Acres of Clams" at his Pier 54 restaurant. *(Ivar's)*

steamers operated by the Kitsap Transportation Company.

Since 1946 the pier has housed Ivar's Acres of Clams Restaurant. The late Ivar Haglund learned his skills from parents who once ran the Stockade Restaurant at Seattle's Alki Point birthplace, but he had his own flair for publicity. A folk singer and radio performer during the Depression, Ivar—as everyone called him—established a clam bar and Seattle's first aquarium on the pier in 1938 and invited a champion wrestler to hand-to-tentacle combat with a captive octopus. He was also a social activist and long-time supporter of historic preservation; he preached civic reform while advising one and all to "Keep Clam."

Ivar's now shares Pier 54 with Ye Olde Curiosity Shop, which was originally established at Colman Dock in 1899. It still displays many ancient (and dubious) marine oddities and artifacts along with more conventional souvenirs.

## ■ Waterfront Place

A side trip east on Madison will lead you into the heart of **Waterfront Place**, a delightful ensemble of new and restored buildings developed under the guidance of newly elected mayor, Paul Schell (former dean of architecture and urban planning at the University of Washington, and port commissioner) and Bumgardner Architects in the early 1980s.

Walking east on Madison leads you along the northern edge of the former **Commission District**, where brokers and middlemen received and disposed of local agricultural produce and goods offloaded on the waterfront (see the Pike Place Market and Lower Downtown histories). The area north of Madison between the Alaskan Way Viaduct and Western is now filled by the new **Waterfront Place Building**. It faces the rehabilitated **National**

The Alexis Hotel and upscale retailers now occupy the remodeled Globe Building at First and Madison, on the edge of the "Waterfront Place" neighborhood.

**Building**, designed in 1904 by Kingsley & Anderson.

East of Post Alley is the former **Globe Building**, one of several hotels designed in 1901 by Max Umbrecht, and remodeled in 1982 as the **Alexis Hotel**. It abuts the former **Beebe Building** and **Hotel Cecil** (Umbrecht, 1901), collectively renamed the **Arlington** in honor of the hotel that once stood two blocks north. This faces the **Holyoke Building** (Thomas G. Bird and George W. Dornbach, 1890) on the southeast corner, which once housed Seattle's first Conservatory for the Arts.

Walking north on First takes you across Spring Street to Al Bumgardner's imposing **Watermark Tower** (1982). The terra cotta and Neo-Deco massing blend nicely with the facades of James Colman's second building (Bebb and Gould, 1915) on Spring. Next along First are the rehabilitated **Grand Pacific** (1898) and **Colonial Hotel** (Umbrecht, 1901) buildings . We now turn west at Seneca and return to the waterfront.

### ■ Piers 55 and 56

These piers have been converted into stores, restaurants, and moorage for sightseeing boats. **Pier 56** was once known as the **Arlington Dock**, and it was here that President Teddy Roosevelt disembarked on May 23, 1903.

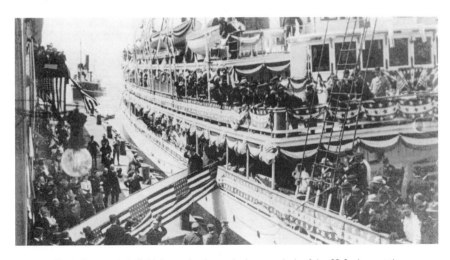

President Teddy Roosevelt doffs his hat as he descends the gangplank of the SS *Spokane* at the Arlington Dock (Pier 56) on May 23, 1903. *(Jim Faber)*

## Waterfront Park

This complex, embracing Pier 57 and the gap where Pier 58 once stood, was designed as a maritime park by the Bumgartner Partnership in 1974. Its central basin was once occupied by **Schwabacher's Wharf**, where the *Miike Maru* docked on August 31, 1896, to establish Seattle's commerce with Japan. Not quite a year later, on July 17, 1897, the SS *Portland* arrived here bearing "a ton of gold" from the Klondike. Thus, this spot marks Seattle's birthplace as a major Pacific Rim port.

A quick walk east from Pier 57 will lead you up University Street to the **Harbor Steps**. Ascending these to First Avenue brings you to the **Seattle Art Museum**. The southeast corner of First and University is occupied by the turreted **Diller Hotel** building, designed by Leonard Mendel and built in 1890.

## Seattle Aquarium

Designed by Fred Bassetti and Skip Norton with exhibit planner and founding director Doug Kemper in 1977, the **Seattle Aquarium** offers an award-winning introduction to the marine life of Puget Sound and the Pacific. It features a viewing dome submerged among native octopus, salmon, sharks, wolf eels, and chimera. Pier 59, once known as the Pike Street Wharf, now houses an OmniMax theater, restaurants, and exhibits. A hike east will lead you up the Pike Place Hillclimb to the Public Market.

## Piers 62–63

The sheds were destoyed a few years ago, and the surviving apron now hosts summer concerts. The nearby **Lenora Street** elevator and bridge offer a shortcut to the north end of **Pike Street Market**. Also note the Virginia Street entrance to the **Great Northern tunnel**, which surfaces more than a mile south near the King Street Station.

## Piers 64–65

Now just a gap in Elliott Bay's dentition of wharves, this space marks the former location of docks for the Canadian Pacific Railroad's packet liners that worked the "triangle route" linking Seattle, Vancouver, and Victoria, B.C. The last of these, the SS *Princess Marguerite*, served from 1949 until her retirement in 1975.

## Pier 66

The **Bell Street Pier** (Hewitt Isley, 1996) once housed the offices of the Port of Seattle. It was rebuilt from the pilings up to create a pleasure boat marina and moorage for cruise ships and other large vessels, and to house a functioning seafood packer, chandlery, three restaurants, the Bell Harbor International Conference Center, and the Odyssey Maritime Discovery Center. Completed in 1996, the pier is connected to the Belltown "uplands" via a pedestrian bridge, soon to be flanked by a new World Trade Center and hotel.

## Piers 67–68

The **Edgewater Hotel** was built in 1962 for the Century 21 World's Fair; it once advertised that guests could "fish from your window." The Beatles stayed here during their first Seattle tour in August 1964, and the sexual antics of another guest band were immortalized in the Frank Zappa ballad "Mud Shark."

## Pier 69

Pier 69 preserves the tradition of Seattle–British Columbia commerce as the terminus for high-speed Victoria Clipper catamarans. It also houses the spendid new headquarters of the **Port of Seattle** (Hewitt Isley, 1994). On the east side of the tracks rises the former American Can Company, remodeled by Ralph Anderson & Partners in 1976 for the Seattle International Trade Center. The "Old Spaghetti Factory" occupies the original Dunn Tin Storage Warehouse, built in 1902.

### ■ Pier 70 and Myrtle Edwards Park

The waterfront lawn and trail, north of Broad Street, Myrtle Edwards Park, was developed in 1976. It was named for an influential city councilmember after her heirs rejected the new Gas Works Park as an unsuitable memorial.

Pier 70 was built in 1901 by Dunn & Ainsworth, and it became the first shed converted to retail and entertainment uses (Barnett Schorr & Company, 1970).

This is the end of the line for the Waterfront Streetcar and for our tour of Seattle's central harbor.

# PIKE PLACE MARKET

## Orientation

The fastest way to label yourself a tourist in Seattle is to ask a native for directions to "Pike's Place Market": lose the possessive immediately. Pike Place is the bricked lane that slopes down northward from Pike Street (named for a pioneer builder, John Pike) at First to the intersection of Virginia and Western. It is the main corridor in a maze of structures that have housed a continuously operating public farmers' market and miscellaneous other merchants since 1907.

The Pike Place Market Historical District is enclosed by First Avenue on the east, Western Avenue on the west, Union Street on the south, and Virginia Street on the north. It is an easy walk from most of downtown's major hotels and its modern retail core. "The Market," as most locals simply call it, is also the seat of Seattle's soul where, in the words of architect Fred Bassetti, one can still savor a sense of "Seattle's beginnings, its lusty past, the vitality that gave it national notice long ago."

This was the scene in 1907 when shoppers and truck farmers first converged at Pike Place for an open "Public Farmers' Market" on Saturdays. *(Oregon Historical Society)*

## History

On Saturday, August 17, 1907, thousands of women, poor and rich alike, braved a summer rainstorm and converged on a newly built plank roadway fronting the Leland Hotel at First Avenue and Pike Street. They found fewer than a dozen farmer carts filled with produce and quickly stripped them bare. The first day was a "clamorous fiasco," but the seed for Seattle's Public Farmers' Market had been planted.

In the early 1900s, more than 3,000 farms supplied the city with fresh fruits and vegetables. Some lay as close as Rainier Valley and the undeveloped bottomlands of the Duwamish, Black, and White Rivers just south of the city; others were miles distant in the foothills and valleys of the Cascades and on the islands of Puget Sound.

Almost half were owned and tended by recent immigrants—Germans, Italians, Chinese, and growing numbers of Japanese and Filipinos—and all were at the mercy of the "commission houses" lining Western Avenue's "Produce Row" near Pioneer Square. Farmers sold their crops to middlemen, who then peddled them to retail grocers and restaurants for a generous markup. The system made it easy for brokers to suppress the prices paid farmers and to inflate the prices charged customers. Many suspected a collusion among commission houses to manipulate the market, and they demanded action to "bust the trust" in fresh groceries.

Frank Goodwin turned City Council member Randy Revelle's idea for a Public Farmers' Market into an urban gold mine. *(Pike Place Market Preservation and Development Authority)*

Farmers and consumers had already begun rendezvousing informally along Western Avenue, below the present-day market, when their complaints reached a receptive ear in newly elected city council member Thomas P. Revelle. A progressive Republican in the mold of Teddy Roosevelt, Revelle discovered that the city council had authorized a public farmers' market back in 1896, during the dark days of the economic panic, but had never followed through. Backed by muckraking articles and thundering editorials in *The Seattle Times*, Revelle persuaded his colleagues on August 5 to authorize the public market Monday through Saturday at Pike Place.

Real estate developer Frank Goodwin, who had recently returned from the Klondike with $50,000 in yellow ore, surveyed the soggy scene as shoppers and farmers mingled unprotected from the fall rains, and he saw gold in them thar groceries. Goodwin assembled a syndicate to build a permanent arcade (designed by his brother John,

Farmers and shoppers jam the foot of Pike Street in about 1910. The Corner Market Building, which replaced the nest of billboards in 1912, is shown here during the 1995 street fair. *(John Stamets)*

an engineer) north from the Leland, which opened on November 30, 1907. The Outlook Hotel and the Triangle Market were built the following year. Growing demand led the city to extend the shelter (dubbed "Flower Row") north to the intersection at Virginia in 1911, and the city hired John Winship as the first "Market Master" and gave him the duty of running a daily lottery for assigning stalls to competing farmers and vendors.

Retail and stall space expanded in 1910 with construction of the Sanitary Public Market (Daniel Huntington), which justified its name by barring horses from its interior. The adjacent Corner Market Building (Harlan Thomas and Clyde Grainger) followed in 1912. Two years later, Goodwin erected the vertical maze of the Fairley (Main Market) Building over the steep bluff separating Western and Pike Place and, subsequently, hired architect Andrew Willatsen to supervise improvements. He also took control of the former Bartell Building (1900) on the southwest corner of First and Pike and renamed it the Economy Market. By the Pike Place Market's 10th anniversary, its ensemble of core buildings was complete.

The Market was unfazed by Prohibition, when fruit juices became very popular, especially if they had started to ferment, but the automobile posed a different, more serious threat. Pike Place and Western Avenue became an

Streetcars, Model-Ts, and pedestrians jostle on First Avenue at Pike Street early in the twentieth century. The Liberty Theater offered to store patrons' groceries while they watched the movie. *(Lawton Gowey)*

important switchback linking the upper downtown with the waterfront, but farmers' stalls and carts made it virtually impassable. So the City Council proposed relocating the public farmer stalls to a new, underground complex at Westlake.

In 1921, ship scaler-turned-farmer Willard Soames formed the Associated Farmers of the Pike Place Market to oppose relocation. This group won by a single vote on the city council, and Frank Goodwin and his nephew Arthur developed the Municipal Market Building on the water side of Western as a new stall area, linked to the main market via a sky bridge. They also took control of part of the Pike Place sidewalk and leased it year-round to hated "middlemen."

This sparked a new controversy in 1924. Seattle's flamboyant mayor, former dentist Edwin J. "Doc" Brown, responded by dismissing Pike Place as a "narrow cow path." He proposed a giant new public market structure (complete with civic auditorium and radio station) stretching west from the base of Pike Street to the waterfront. Although John Graham Sr. drew up the design, Brown's monstrous edifice rightly repelled the public, and Brown himself lost the 1926 election to Bertha K. Landes, Seattle's first and only woman mayor to date. This was only the first of many schemes that would have effectively killed the Market in the name of "saving" it.

Around this same time, Arthur Goodwin bought out his uncle's interest in Market operations (although Frank held on to the real property). The Associated Farmers hired George Vanderveer, self-styled "Counsel for the Damned," to press their complaint that Goodwin was leasing public land to private middlemen, with the notable exception of Joe Desimone, a bona fide grower (and vice president of Goodwin's company). A judge ultimately ruled that all stalls—farmers' and middlemen's—were illegal on public sidewalks. The matter went all the way to the State Supreme Court and Legislature, but the crash of a different market in 1929 imposed a truce. As the Depression

80

deepened, Seattle needed her public market more than ever before.

The area beneath the Main
Market's neon sign and giant clock
(ca. 1930) became Seattle's answer
to London's Speaker's Corner, as
socialists, communists, evangelists,
Technocrats, and just plain crack-
pots harangued the milling crowds.
The Market's bubbling cauldron of
races, classes, and creeds was a
magnet for artist Mark Tobey when
he returned to Seattle from England
in 1938, and he dedicated much of
the next two decades to capturing it
on paper and canvas while developing his "white writing" style.

Red ink was the primary medi-
um of the Market's Depression-era
finances, despite its popularity with
cash-starved consumers. Arthur
Goodwin had to sue his uncle Frank
for unpaid property management
fees, and he gradually lost control

A pair of shoppers "meet the producer" in Pike
Place Market's Main Arcade in the 1930s. *(Pike Place
Market Preservation and Development Authority)*

of the company to Giuseppe "Joe" Desimone, a Neapolitan immigrant who
had quietly amassed a fortune farming in Seattle's South Park and selling his
produce at the Market. Although barely literate, Desimone was a savvy businessman and ingratiating politician who put his faith in real property, not
stocks or speculation. He soon owned all of Frank Goodwin's Market properties, and wrote a will prohibiting his heirs from ever selling them.

Desimone took control of the Market in 1941. The bombs that fell on
Pearl Harbor that December 7 ignited long-smoldering resentments toward
the hundreds of Japanese-born and nisei farmers who filled up to four-fifths
of the Market's stalls. Eight days later disaster struck closer to home when the
Sanitary Market burned to the ground (it was quickly rebuilt). Some mut-
tered absurdities about "Axis saboteurs" trying to starve Seattle, and thanks to
such war jitters every Japanese-American on the West Coast was headed
inland to concentration camps by April 1942. The new war and old prejudices soon echoed in scores of empty Market stalls, despite newspaper
claims that business was unaffected because "white patrons like to buy from
white farmers."

Among those who filled the void created by internment at Pike Place was
an enterprising business woman named Nellie Curtis. She catered to a differ-

NORTH

STEINBRUECK
PARK

STEWART HOUSE

NORTH
ARCADE

SKYBRIDGE ELEVATOR
FROM PUBLIC MARKET
PARKING GARAGE

TRIANGLE
BUILDING

WESTERN AVE.

ELEVATOR

FIRST AVE.  UPPER
POST ALLEY

PIKE PLACE

VIRGINIA STREET

STEWART STREET
INN AT
THE MARKET
PINE STREET

POST ALLEY
WALKWAY

FIRST AVE.

SANITARY
MARKET

MAIN
ARCADE

PIKE PLACE

CORNER
MARKET

TO DOWNTOWN SEATTLE

PIKE ST.

LOWER POST ALLEY
ENTRANCE

ECONOMY
MARKET

LASALLE HOTEL/
CLIFF HOUSE

STAIRS TO
WATERFRONT
AND AQUARIUM

TO SOUTH
ARCADE SHOPS

LOWER
POST ALLEY

PIKE PLACE MARKET

*Courtesy of the Pike Place Market Preservation and Development Authority, copyright 1997.*

ent but no less basic need than food, namely, sex. Back in 1933, she had established a bordello in the Camp Hotel at First Avenue and Virginia (destroyed), the first such house to be "tolerated" north of Yesler Way. Nine years later, she took over a Japanese-American family's lease on the Outlook Hotel at the foot of Pike Street and renamed it the "LaSalle," possibly inspired by General Motors' luxury automobile of the time. Her attempts at discretion were quickly thwarted when as many as 1,000 sailors lined up at the LaSalle's door for a "ride." Curtis kept the motor running for nearly a decade before selling the LaSalle to new Japanese-American owners who, to the disappointment of many a lonely mariner, turned it into a legitimate hotel.

Joe Desimone's benevolent dictatorship of the Market ended with his death in 1946, and his son Richard took over. The new regime faced fresh perils as suburban development and corporate agribusiness displaced truck farmers, and supermarkets and modern consumer culture turned the Market into a social and economic anachronism. For artists such as Mark Tobey and a young professor of architecture named Victor Steinbrueck, this only enhanced the Market's appeal, but in the view of the downtown establishment, the Market had become an eyesore and an obstacle to "progress."

The first hint of things to come was a plan offered in 1950 by Harlan Edwards, an engineer and husband of future city council member Myrtle Edwards. His design flattened the Market and replaced it with a giant parking garage. Nothing came of the proposal, but completion of the Alaskan Way

Viaduct in 1953 did almost as much damage by walling off the Market from the waterfront.

The Market's economic and physical decay became obvious even to its champions. In 1956, the Pike Place Market Farmers' Association was established to try to attract new vendors and customers. Its efforts secured a renewed public market lease from a skeptical City Council in 1957, but the Association suffered a setback when fire destroyed the Municipal Market Building on Western the following year.

Under the banner of the Central Association, the downtown business establishment unveiled yet another plan for the Market area in 1963. This scheme razed the old nest of buildings and alleys and replaced them with terraced garages and high-rise office and apartment buildings. By 1964, the "Pike Plaza Redevelopment Project" was integrated into Seattle's first application for federal Urban Renewal funds. Wing Luke, the first Asian-American (and, indeed, first nonwhite) elected to the City Council quietly urged attorney Robert Ashley, architect Victor Steinbrueck, and Allied Arts to organize a public effort to take over the Market before the bulldozers shifted into high gear.

In September 1964, Ashley and Steinbrueck invited 60 sympathizers to a champagne breakfast at Lowell's Cafe to defend what architect Fred Bassetti called "an honest place in a phony time." The new group called itself "Friends of the Market" and sold books, buttons, and shopping bags to raise funds. The support of influential friends such as Mark Tobey, finally famous in his hometown after his artistic triumphs in Europe, stayed the wrecking ball temporarily, but the city's 1968 demolition of the old National Guard Armory nearby on Western fed fears that the Market was next. Mayor Dorm Braman didn't calm the

Architect, teacher, and activist Victor Steinbrueck led the successful "Friends of the Market" campaign that rescued the Public Market from urban renewal in 1971. *(Mary Randlett)*

waters when he denounced the Market as "a decadent, somnolent fire-trap."

The city did scale back its urban renewal ambitions, but the concessions were trivial from the Friends' point of view. Steinbrueck engineered a master-stroke of creative "obstructionism" when he convinced the state's new Advisory Council on Historic Preservation, created by the 1966 National Historic Preservation Act, to approve a 17-acre Pike Place Market Historic District that would block use of federal funds for demolition. The establishment counterattacked by persuading the Advisory Council to shrink the District down to a mere 1.7 acres, and the Department of Housing and Urban Development gave the green light for urban renewal in May 1971.

The Friends then took to the streets with an initiative creating a 7-acre preservation zone, administered by a Market Historical Commission with broad powers for preserving not only the Market's physical structure but its social and economic character as well. In three weeks, they collected more than 25,000 signatures to qualify the initiative for the November 2, 1971, ballot. Mayor Wes Uhlman and the City Council offered an alternative for a smaller historic district and weaker enforcement, and this gained the support of some prominent Market merchants such as deli owner Pete De Laurenti, who feared that the Market would stagnate without federal aid. The campaign became a war between competing Market "saviors," but the voters sided with the Friends by 76,369 to 53,264.

The Public Market Center clock has kept time between the LaSalle and Leland Hotels at the base of Pike Street since the Depression. *(Frank O. Shaw)*

Now came the hard part. Although the city and Friends of the Market quickly made their peace, there was little agreement on what "preservation" meant in practical terms. There were also battles over plans for the larger 22-acre Urban Renewal District and the quasi-corporate Pike Place Market Public Development Authority (PDA), created in 1973 to purchase and manage public buildings in the Market and develop nearby properties. A nonprofit Market Foundation was also established to fund social services such as a senior center, a clinic, and a food bank for the area's low-income residents. Combined with the Merchants Association and the Historical Commission, the interplay of these groups and their respective constituencies has created a lively, sometimes fractious urban politics in miniature. It has also reverberated in the larger community: for example, the ongoing Market effort helped to spur King County voters to approve bonds in 1979 for the preservation of the area's rapidly dwindling farmlands.

The job of satisfying the Market's competing interests while implementing the soaring rhetoric of Steinbrueck and his allies in rehabilitating the Market fell first to supervising architect George Bartholick in 1974. The preservation and improvement effort has since cost scores of millions in public funds and private investment, and it will never really be finished.

Yet, for all the heartache and heat generated since 1971, the results are remarkably faithful to the vision expressed by Mark Tobey nearly four decades ago. The Pike Place Market is "still active, still varied, exciting and terribly important in the welter of overindustrialization."

## Walking Tour

It would be easier to herd kittens than to guide you on a linear tour through the Market and its neighborhood, but here's an hour-long reconnaissance. It will be impossible for you to resist pursuing your own detours, but don't worry about getting lost. You're supposed to, and you should really give yourself at least a whole day to explore the Market's myriad nooks and crannies.

### ■ Under the Clock

For decades, people planning to get together at the Market have only had to say, "Meet me under the clock," to pinpoint the coordinates for their rendezvous. Since 1986 the area at the **foot of Pike Street** has been graced by a second landmark: **"Rachel,"** the life-sized bronze piggy bank sculpted by Georgia Gerber. Visitors deposit as much as $8,000 a year in Rachel to support the human service programs of the Market Foundation. Proceeds from the sale of more than 46,000 personalized tiles in 1987 also aided the Foundation while repaving most of the Main Market and North Arcade.

Near Rachel stands **Pike Place Fish**, famous for its "flying fish" and raucous barkers. Heading southwest beyond this establishment takes you to the original **Outlook/LaSalle Hotel** building (1908; George Bartholick, 1977) where Nellie Curtis and her girls once tended the fleet. The aisle closest to Pike Place Fish leads you to the

Rachel, the Market Foundation's mascot piggy bank, became an instant landmark when she was installed below the Market clock in 1986. *(Paul Dorpat)*

outdoor landing of **Place Pigalle**, originally one of the Market's grittier saloons and now an upscale restaurant perched high above Western Avenue. Veering a little more to the left takes you past a spice and tea shop and down the hall to **Maximilien's Restaurant**. The LaSalle's upper floors now contain apartments. Please resist

the urge to take a hard left into the Economy Market for a moment (we'll get there later).

The stairs on the right of Pike Place Fish lead down to public rest rooms graced with tiles created in 1987 by artist Laura Sindell. A deeper descent will lead you into the caverns of the **Lower Market** (don't miss Danny Eskenazi's "Big Shoe Museum," Old Seattle Paper Works, Mr. E's Books, and the magic store). These stairs also connect to the **Hillclimb Corridor** stepping down to the waterfront, but save your urban spelunking for later.

### ■ North into the Main Market

Walking south takes you beneath the original **Leland Hotel** (unknown, 1900; Andrew Willatsen, 1939; George Bartholick, 1977) and along the ground level of the **Main Market** (former Fairley Building; John Goodwin, 1907–1914; Bartholick, 1977). On most days you will find yourself swept up in a turbulent river of humanity jostling for produce, meat, or fish at the "high" stalls, or trying to enter popular eateries such as **The Athenian Cafe** or **Lowell's** (both offering spectacular views of Elliott Bay), or just trying to navigate through to the other end.

At the foot of Pine Street, note the **City Fish Market** on your left; this was

Parked cars have replaced the wagons and crates in this view of the Market's "Lower Stalls" along Pike Place, but the farmers still come. The former Armory (since demolished) can be seen in the distance on Western Avenue. *(Pike Place Market Preservation and Development Authority)*

established during World War I to try to counteract rising prices.

The nearby ramp will lead you back south into the lower levels of the Main Market, which are populated by a potpourri of specialty shops, antique dealers, jewelers, tiny cafes, and trinket peddlers. For this tour, however, we will press on into the **North Arcade**, which is dominated by farmers and "low" stalls offering flowers, handicrafts, and souvenirs.

### ■ At Virginia Street and Western Avenue

The expanse of **Steinbrueck Park** (V. Steinbrueck and Richard Haag) has been a popular place to lunch or loll on a sunny day since its completion in 1978. The two totems, one topped by a Native American and the other by a pair of stylized farmers, were created by Quinault sculptor Marvin Oliver with the assistance of James Bender. This site, which covers a large parking garage, often hosts outdoor political rallies and speeches by visiting presidents and other dignitaries.

The stretch of Western north and south of the park is lined by newer buildings with shops, restaurants, and offices. Looking south, you will notice the **Desimone Bridge**, built in 1925 to connect the Market and the lower Municipal Market, later lost to fire. The roof of the bridge now houses an extension of the North Arcade. The bridge farther south connects with the **Hillclimb Corridor**.

### ■ South on the East Side of Pike Place

We will now walk back south along the east side of Pike Place. The **Pike and Virginia Building** (Olson/Walker, 1978) was the first entirely new building completed in the Market district. The adjacent **Champion Building** was built in 1928 for the Dollar Cab Company.

The next two buildings once housed

The "Hillclimb" combines stairs and elevators to link the Pike Place Market with the waterfront below Western Avenue. *(Frank O. Shaw)*

the **Soames Paper Company** and **Dunn's Seeds**. They were jointly remodeled in 1976 by Arne Bystrom, complete with an interior arcade in Dunn's. This opens onto a recessed courtyard with seating for **Emmett Watson's Oyster Bar** and other nearby eateries, and access into the retail level of the **Stewart House** (unknown, 1902–1911; Ibsen Nelsen, 1982) immediately south.

Crossing Stewart takes you to the door of the **Seattle Garden Center** (W. C. Geary, 1908; Arne Bystrom, 1980), painted in distinctive "Bystrom Green" after the name of the architect who remodeled it in 1980. The **Silver Oakum Building**, which rises on the opposite side of Pine Street, operated as a seamen's hotel from 1910 until 1970. It was remodeled for retail and condominiums by Fred Bassetti in 1977. The adjacent **Triangle Market** (Thompson & Thompson, 1908) originally housed the South Park Poultry Company.

The southern apex of the Triangle Market points into the ground-level

arcade of the **Sanitary Market**
(D. Huntington, 1910; McClelland &
Jones, 1942; Bassetti/Norton/Metler,
1981), an enticing rabbit warren of shops
and stalls, new and old. For example,
The Three Girls Bakery has occupied its
site since 1912. Stairs lead up through
an interior atrium to First Avenue.

## ■ North on Post Alley

A hairpin left turn at the entrance to the
Sanitary Market will head you north up
**Post Alley** past several cafes and stores
in the **Post Alley Market**, which is part
of the new **First and Pine Building**
(Bassetti/Norton/Metler, 1983). The
alley bisects the triangle formed by
Pine and Stewart. The eastern side is
occupied by the **Inn at the Market**,
designed by Ibsen Nelsen and opened
in 1985. Continuing north on Post Alley
takes you across Stewart Street. The **J.P.
Jones Building** (1925), on the east side
of the alley at Stewart, is now home to a
glass art gallery and other shops. The
**Stewart Hotel** (unknown, 1903) was
adapted to low-income housing by
Ibsen Nelson & Associates in 1982.

Farther north along **Post Alley** you
will walk past a stairway descending
into the **Soames-Dunn courtyard** and
two popular restaurants, the **Pink Door**
on the west and **Kell's** on the east. At
Virginia, head up the steep grade to
First (if this is too intimidating, back up
a few yards and take the public stairs
through the **Baker Building**).

## ■ At First and Virginia

The **Livingston Apartments** have
occupied the southwest corner of First
and Virginia since 1901. The ground
floor has served as a bar or tavern for
just as long, and the **Virginia Inn** itself
dates from 1908. The Livingston was
rehabilitated by Harader & Mebust in
1977. The adjacent **Baker Apartments**
were constructed at the same time on
the site of Nellie Curtis's original bordello in the Camp Hotel.

The **Terminal Sales Building** was
designed by Henry Bittman and has
dominated the southeast corner since
1923. The stepped wedge of **Market
Place North** (Bumgardner Partnership
and Ralph Anderson, 1981) on the
northwest corner was developed by
Bruce Lorig and was the first and most
architecturally sensitive of the new condominiums permitted under the revised
urban renewal plan for the Market
neighborhood. Unfortunately, later
buildings such as the new tower on the
northeast corner stand outside the control of Market regulators and tend to
overshadow their humble neighbors.

## ■ South Along First

The next building south of the Baker is
the **Smith Block**, built in 1923. The
adjacent **Butterworth** opened as a
mortuary in 1903. It was also the first
commercial building designed by John
Graham Sr. and anything but a dead
end for his career.

The adjacent **Alaska Trade
Building** (J. O. Taft) dates from 1915.
One of its original tenants was the
*Union Record*, which became the
nation's only labor-owned daily newspaper in 1918. A year later, on
February 4, 1919, the *Union Record*
published Anna Louise Strong's stirring
appeal to Seattle workers to launch
America's first general strike. The strike,
which grew out of a waterfront wage
dispute, paralyzed Seattle for a week
before fizzling into confusion and a
disordered retreat.

The Smith, Butterworth, and Alaska
Trade Buildings were jointly remodeled
by Ralph Anderson and Partners in
1977, along with the **Fairmount Hotel**
(W. E. Dwyer, 1914) on the northwest
corner of Stewart and First. Among their
current tenants is the **Seattle Chapter
of the American Institute of
Architects**. Seattle's best architectural
books dealer, Peter Miller, is located
across the street.

Except for the addition of distant office and condo towers, this view north along Pike Place has changed little in 70 years. *(Paul Dorpat)*

Crossing Stewart leads you past the First Avenue entrance to the **Inn at the Market**. The **First and Pine Building** anchors its eponymous intersection and is abutted on the south by the **Sanitary Market**. The block ends with the **Corner Market Building**, designed in 1912 by Harlan Thomas and rehabilitated in 1975 by Karlis Rekevics. Its three levels house several restaurants, including the distinguished **Chez Shea,** and the **Pike Place Bar and Grill**, **Left Bank Books**, **Patti Summers'** jazz cabaret, and scores of produce and retail stalls.

### ■ At First and Pike

Crossing Pike puts you at the corner of the **Economy Market** and almost back where you started. The "girlie show" and erotica boutique on the east side of First that occupy the terra-cotta-clad **York Lunch** (J. Lister Holmes, 1924) and the former **Broderick Building** (John Graham Sr., 1922) are dim echoes of the bawdy entertainments that once lined Seattle's "tenderloin" and supplied the backdrop for the film *Cinderella Liberty.*

Note that the signals at First and Pike halt traffic on both streets simultaneously, allowing pedestrians to cross freely in any direction on the "Walk" sign. The descending roadway just south of Pike Street's kiosk and bulletin board leads to **Lower Post Alley's** several restaurants, including the popular **Il Bistro**, the offices of the **Pike**

**Place Market PDA**, and the **Pike Place Theater**.

The southwest corner of First and Pike is usually filled with patrons of the **Read All About It** newsstand and **De Laurenti's Italian Market**. Pushing south along First takes you past several storefronts of the **Economy Market**. The old structure abuts the new **98 Union/South Arcade** complex, designed by Olson/Walker in 1985.

### ■ Returning North Through the South Arcade

Instead of continuing south on First, which would lead you to the **Seattle** Art Museum and **Harbor Steps** complex, make a hairpin turn to your right at Union Street. This takes you back north into the **South Arcade**, which houses numerous shops and the **Pike Place Brewing Company** and pub. Continuing north leads you into the **Economy Market** (unknown, 1900; A. Willatsen, 1916), whose airy atrium was designed by George Bartholick in 1978. Ascending a short flight of stairs puts you in a hallway leading back to the Main Market. A jog left and then right will bring you to **Rachel**, under the clock where you began a few hours ago. Now you're on your own.

## CENTRAL BUSINESS DISTRICT

### Orientation

Seattle's core downtown business and shopping district is roughly bounded by Interstate 5 on the east, Second Avenue on the west, Virginia Street on the north, and Madison on the south. Here most of the city's major hotels, restaurants, and retail store attractions are concentrated in 40 blocks along with some of its finest buildings.

### History

The late nineteenth and early twentieth centuries were shaped by men who viewed nature as something to subdue and conquer. In Seattle this impulse translated into an almost pathological aversion to the town's original hills and ridges. These "obstacles to progress" attracted clever and determined engineers such as George Cotterill and Reginald H. Thomson, who regarded any grade over 5 percent as a personal insult.

The city's first regrade was begun in 1876 along First Avenue, then "Front Street," north of Yesler. This required bridging and later filling Seneca, then a deep ravine. The work of regrading the future downtown's streets and avenues progressed virtually uninterrupted over the next forty years. However, the march of progress stalled before two natural redoubts of resistance, both owned, ironically, by Arthur Denny, who was an indefatigable champion of development.

The first obstruction was Denny's Knoll, a hillock roughly bounded by present-day Third and Fifth Avenues and by Union and Seneca Streets. Denny

Seattle's first regrade straightened and leveled Front Street (First Avenue) north of Yesler Way in 1876. *(Old Seattle Paper Works)*

had hoped to lure the territorial capital from Olympia to this plot, but the Rev. Daniel Bagley, newly arrived pastor of the Episcopal-Protestant "Brown Church" at Second and Madison, persuaded him to settle for the territorial university instead. Denny deeded a 10-acre tract (with slivers donated by Charles and Mary Terry and Edward Lander) to the territorial government, and John Pike designed a handsome two-story schoolhouse with an imposing porch supported by four Doric columns. As president, Bagley hired Asa Mercer as the university's "principal" and greeted his first 16 students on November 4, 1861. Classes continued on this site until 1895, when the University of Washington (and, later, the original four columns) were relocated to a new 160-acre land grant north of Portage Bay.

An even more daunting obstruction was presented by Denny Hill, which rose steeply north of Pine Street between First and Seventh Avenues and tapered off into Belltown. Denny Hill might still dominate Seattle's downtown but for City Engineer R. H. Thomson, who finally vanquished his topographical foe in 1911 (see Belltown and the Denny Regrade history in a later section).

As the downtown began to outgrow Pioneer Square, the steep western slope of First Hill and Denny's two bumps in the road squeezed development northward first along First Avenue and then along Second, but these remained muddy tracks before the Great Fire. Horses, wagons, and pedestrians still had to dodge lake-sized pot holes; only the hardiest could master the east-west grades.

Beginning in 1884, the downtown's expansion was propelled literally by street railways. The first such system was proposed in 1879 for First Avenue, but merchants feared that the rattling horse-drawn trams would frighten away

High upon its Denny Hill perch, The Washington (Denny) Hotel loomed over downtown from 1890 until 1905. It is seen here looking north along Third Avenue from University Street. *(Michael Maslan)*

shoppers and the line was never built. Frank Osgood had better luck five years later when he secured a city franchise for a line on Second Avenue from Pioneer Square to Pine Street. The nickel-a-fare service on the Seattle Street Railway was an instant success when it commenced on September 23, 1884.

Eighteen months later, agents of Thomas Edison fired up Seattle's first electrical generator, and in 1887, Francis Sprague demonstrated the first electric streetcar in Richmond, Virginia. Osgood was quick to make the connection and announced that he would replace his "hay burners" with "electric traction." Skeptics scoffed that the streetcars could never climb Seattle's hills, and local Chicken Littles warned that Osgood's contraptions would magnetize pocket watches and zap pedestrians with runaway lightning bolts. Osgood gave the honor of proving them all wrong to a woman, Addie Burns, who rode in Seattle's first electric streetcar on March 30, 1889. Service was not interrupted even as the downtown burned three months later.

Electric traction had a competitor well suited to the downtown topography. In 1887, J. M. Thompson borrowed a leaf from San Francisco's book and introduced Seattle's first cable railway on Yesler Way (see Pioneer Square history). He added cable service on First and Second Avenues the following year, and the transportation revolution helped to establish Second Avenue as Seattle's premier address after the fire, attracting the city's first "skyscrapers" (see the Lower Downtown tour) and "uptown" department stores such as the Bon Marché and Frederick & Nelson. In 1890, L. H. Griffith took just five days to lay track along Westlake Avenue to connect the future city center with Lake Union and, later, Fremont and the North End. Before long, cable and electric railways were crisscrossing the city as real estate developers sought to lure buyers to outlying home and office sites with the promise of "rapid transit."

The fact that street railways made modern cities possible was recognized early on by Stone & Webster, a national engineering and utility cartel. Their local agent, banker Jacob Furth, quietly bought up Seattle's street railways and fledgling interurban lines at the turn of the century and consolidated control in the Puget Sound Power, Traction and Light Company, predecessor of Washington Energy, which remains the state's largest private utility. This precipitated a long "power struggle" with advocates of public ownership, who established City Light in 1902 and convinced voters to purchase the city's street rail lines in 1918, albeit at an inflated price that ultimately bankrupted the system.

Meanwhile, the relocation of the University of Washington in 1895 created a dramatic new opportunity by freeing up 10 virgin acres for commercial development. The regents had hoped to sell the tract, but the sour post-Panic economy dashed that plan. The area languished until 1900, when the regents decided to lease the tract and use rent income to help improve the new campus.

The first taker, J. C. Levold, was able to complete only one building, a new home for the *Seattle Post-Intelligencer* (where the Washington Building now stands), and the cash-starved regents sold the southeast corner of Third and Union to the federal government for a new post office in 1901. R. H. Thomson finally got his hands on Denny's Knoll in 1904 and pushed Fourth Avenue through the site as part of a larger downtown regrade. That same year, the regents signed a new 50-year lease for development with James A. Moore, but he had no better luck raising capital than his predecessor.

Moore's lease was bought in 1907 by the Metropolitan Building Company,

The intersection of Fourth Avenue and Westlake Boulevard swarms with traffic and pedestrians in this World War I view, and it still does, although virtually all of the buildings shown here have been demolished. *(University of Washington Library Special Collections. Neg. UW5315)*

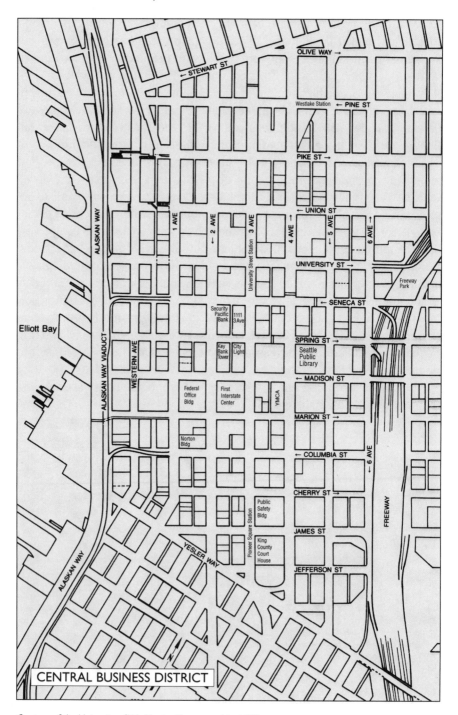

CENTRAL BUSINESS DISTRICT

*Courtesy of the University of Washington Press, copyright 1992.*

backed by a new generation of Seattle capitalists. Among them were financiers C. F. White and C. H. Cobb, railroad builder H. C. Henry, timber and retail magnate C. D. Stimson, lumberman and shipbuilder D. E. Skinner, and E. A. Stuart, a former mule skinner who canned the first Carnation Evaporated Milk on a Kent Valley farm. Over the next two decades, each man's name would grace a major building in the new Metropolitan Tract, thanks to "Major" John Francis Douglas, the company's energetic manager. His greatest achievement was the Olympic Hotel, built in 1924 with the aid of $2,750,000 in community bond sales.

The opportunity for the orderly and planned development of the Metropolitan Tract helped to usher in a new era of downtown construction that lasted until the Depression. This coincided with a fortuitous intersection of several forces: the maturity of resident architects such as Carl Gould and John Graham Sr., the wealth of enlightened investors such as C. D. Stimson, and D. E. Skinner, the zenith of an urban progressive movement led by technocrats such as R. H. Thomson and J. D. Ross, and the availability of modern building technologies and materials.

Foremost among the last was the use of terra cotta to clad structural steel frames. At the end of the nineteenth century, the fear of fire and acceptance of steel frame construction led to the growing use of terra cotta instead of wood, stone, or brick to clad large buildings. This humble semifired ceramic (literally, "cooked earth") was once reserved for sewer pipes and roofing tiles. It was also lightweight, fireproof, and could be cast in virtually any form, color, or texture. Much of the terra cotta used in Seattle was locally mined and fired by the Denny-Renton Clay & Coal Company, based at First and Jackson with its plant on the site of Boeing Field, and by the Northern Clay Company in Auburn (both were taken over by Gladding McBean in 1925).

Frank Lloyd Wright said of the material, "It is in the architect's hand what wax is in the sculptor's hand." Indeed, the first thirty years of the century might be dubbed the "Age of Terra Cotta" in downtown Seattle, embodied in a remarkably harmonious ensemble of sensitive and high-quality buildings. The standard was set by the first master plan for the Metropolitan Tract, prepared in 1907 by the New York partnership of John Mead Howells and I. N. Phelps Stokes and their local representative, Abraham H. Albertson. The influence of the École des Beaux-Arts is readily evident in their surviving masterpiece, the Cobb Building, completed in 1910 on the northwest corner of Fourth Avenue and University Street.

The Howells and Stokes plan was only partially executed, beginning with the White Building in 1908. It featured ornamental terra-cotta Indian heads that were probably modeled by Victor Schneider and reportedly inspired by the photography of Edward S. Curtis, who lived in Seattle when not on one of his pioneering ethnographical expeditions. The Indian head motif was used on other buildings and such ornaments can be found on the Cobb, as well as

This prospectus announces construction of the Cobb Building at Fourth and University as the city's first building designed for the medical and dental professions.

in Rainier Square's concourse and at the Museum of History and Industry.

The White was joined in 1909 by the Henry, and in 1915 by the Stuart. The coordinated facades of what became the White-Henry-Stuart Building fronted Fourth Avenue between Union and University Streets, and later "annexes" filled out the rest of the block by 1923. The Howells and Stokes team also designed the Metropolitan Theater (where the Olympic now stands), the Arena, and the Stimson Building—all long gone.

The rapid progress in the Tract before World War I inspired other developers to shift "uptown" from Second Avenue. Carl Gould succeeded Louis Mendel as Charles Bebb's partner in completing the Fischer Studio Building on Third Avenue and the flatiron Times Square Building between Olive and Stewart in 1915. That same year, Alexander Pantages built his namesake theater at Third and University (below the Cobb, since demolished). In 1916, developer Joseph Gottstein gambled on a new form of entertainment and directed architect B. Marcus Priteca to abandon a planned backstage and loft for his new Coliseum Theater at Fifth and Pine, making it one of the first auditoriums in the United States dedicated expressly to the exhibition of moving pictures.

D. E. Frederick took a gamble of his own when he retained John Graham Sr. to design Frederick & Nelson, the city's largest department store yet, at the "distant" corner of Fifth and Pine Street in 1916. A decade later, the Bon Marché followed Frederick & Nelson's lead and erected its block-sized flagship store, also designed by John Graham Sr., at Fourth and Pine. Large new Rhodes (now owned by the Seattle Art Museum) and Penney's stores were also completed on Second Avenue in the late 1920s, but they could not forestall that street's gradual decline.

The prosperity of the Roaring Twenties fed a second building boom in and around the Metropolitan Tract, while the converging traffic of streetcars, interurban trains, and automobiles turned the "Westlake Mall" triangle formed by Westlake Boulevard, Fourth Avenue, and Stewart Street into the city's busiest intersection. With so many potential patrons, the surrounding area attracted Seattle's grandest theaters. Priteca created his masterwork, the Orpheum, at the corner of Stewart and Westlake in 1927 and aided Rapp and Rapp in

designing the Paramount at Ninth and Pine, Henry Bittman designed the whimsical Music Box on Fourth, and Sherwood Ford gave the Mayflower Theater (later the Seventh Avenue Music Hall) an incongruously Moorish flair.

Not to be outdone, Robert C. Reamer replicated the inner sanctum of the Forbidden City in the 5th Avenue Theater, contained within his design for the Skinner Building, the Tract's most ambitious office block yet in 1926. Reamer also designed the dignified 1411 Fourth Avenue Building for C. D. Stimson, which helped to expand the Tract's design influence beyond its legal boundaries. By then, Art Deco had dethroned Beaux Arts and cities measured their vigor by the height of their skyscrapers.

Art Deco was not a single style but a pluralism of design motifs inspired by the 1925 "Exposition des Arts Décoratifs" in Paris. It superseded the organic formalism of Art Nouveau and merged with the functionally "honest" architecture advocated by Louis Sullivan and Frank Lloyd Wright prior to the triumph of bare-boned Bauhaus and International Modernism. Architects abandoned the "revival" (i.e., imitation) of Gothic, Classical, and Renaissance designs and treatments advocated by the École des Beaux-Arts and found in Deco a stylish way to ornament and accent the ziggurat-like setbacks of ever taller buildings. The results were often vaguely Mayan, Egyptian, and, on the West Coast, Oriental.

The new fashion yielded several handsome buildings, including Henry Bittman's octagon-crowned United Shopping Tower (now the Olympic Tower) at Third and Pine and Sherwood Ford's muscular Washington Athletic Club at Sixth and Union. John Graham Sr. was also an enthusiastic exponent of Deco, as reflected in his designs for the Exchange Building (see Lower Downtown in the Pioneer Square section) and the Bon Marché, but the form achieved its highest expression in Seattle with completion of the Northern Life (now Seattle) Tower at Third and University in 1929. Designed by Abraham H. Albertson, with Joseph Wilson and Paul D. Richardson, the 27-story building's massing, colors, and textures consciously mimic Seattle's nearby mountains in many aspects, ranging from a cavernous lobby to a craggy, three-spired crown.

Unfortunately, as the Northern Life Tower rose, the stock market plummeted. Downtown development went into a deep coma that lasted three decades. The area began to stir in 1954 when the new University Properties Co. (now Unico) took over development of the Metropolitan Tract. Organized by Roger L. Stevens, an energetic real estate developer and theatrical producer based in Detroit, and locally managed by James M. Ryan, Unico retained NBBJ as its resident architects.

NBBJ developed a new master plan "2009" (the year the Unico lease was to expire; it has since been extended) and targeted the decrepit Post-Intelligencer Building for replacement. Unico also decided to undo the University of Washington (UW) regents' error in selling part of the tract to the federal government and worked out an elaborate deal whereby Unico built a new post office in return for a larger footprint for what became the Washington Building on the southwest corner of Fourth and University.

Along with the Norton and Logan Buildings and the new downtown library, the Washington Building marked the arrival of the International style in Seattle in 1959. It also announced Minoru Yamasaki's architectural debut as an associate of NBBJ. After completing his triumphant U.S. Science Pavilion (now the Pacific Science Center) for the Century 21 World's Fair, Yamasaki returned to the Metrolitan Tract to create the graceful IBM Plaza in 1964.

By then, Interstate 5 had been completed in a deep and ugly trench that severed downtown from First Hill on the east and destroyed thousands of inner-city residences. This route had been controversial from the early 1950s, when the state originally proposed a turnpike with tolls and rejected city pleas for inclusion of rights-of-way for rail transit. The state also rebuffed architects Paul Thiry and Victor Steinbrueck's suggestions for a "lid" over the freeway to reunify the city center. (Their cause was later taken up by civic reformer James Ellis, who successfully championed designs for bridging I-5 with Freeway Park and, later, the Convention Center.)

Battle lines were also being drawn over Westlake Mall, which had declined rapidly despite the 1962 opening of the southern terminus of the Monorail. Architects such as Fred Bassetti proposed closing cross streets to create a lively urban commons. Merchants, led by the Central Association, replied that sealing off Westlake

The former Washington Building opened in 1959 as the first new structure in the Metropolitan Tract in decades. It is flanked by the older 1411 Fourth Avenue Building *(foreground)* and the Cobb Building.

Mall would only drive more shoppers to suburban malls. Against the backdrop of these tensions, Minoru Yamasaki's next design precipitated one of Seattle's most divisive urban design debates.

In 1974, Unico announced that it would level the White-Henry-Stuart Building and its Fifth Avenue annexes. The planned replacement was nothing if not audacious: Yamasaki proposed to balance a 28-story office tower on a tapering pedestal above a block-wide shopping plaza. The concept divided both the architectural profession and the community. When the design was unveiled, citizens were still debating the aesthetics of the huge Seafirst Building (now the 1001 Fourth Avenue Building), completed in 1968 and immediately tagged as "the box the Space Needle came in." Many were also mourning the loss of the beloved Stimson Building, replaced by the lackluster Financial Center in 1973.

In May of that same year, historic preservation had been institutionalized as an official City Landmarks Preservation Board with the power to protect a designated structure over an owner's objections. Recently passed environmental laws also gave protesters, led again by Allied Arts and Victor

The flared base for the new Rainier Tower looms over the last wall of the White-Henry-Stuart Annex in this 1977 view south on Fifth Avenue. Minoru Yamasaki's daring design triggered a bitter preservation fight that ultimately led to the listing of several Metropolitan Tract Buildings on the National Register. *(Frank Shaw)*

Steinbrueck, a powerful new weapon by mandating impact statements for government projects, which included the proposed "Commerce Tower" by dint of the UW regents' authority over the Metropolitan Tract.

Despite these instruments, preservationists and critics failed to topple Yamasaki's tower, which was completed in 1979 above what is now called Rainier Square, but they scored some moral victories by persuading the regents to allow the listing of the Skinner and Cobb Buildings on the National Register of Historic Places. Both the UW and Unico strenuously objected to city landmark designation, however, and the courts ruled in 1980 that the Metropolitan Tract was off limits as a state-controlled site. The urban design debate also led to development of Rainier Square as a more pedestrian-friendly shopping plaza and underground arcade. (The upper level of Rainier Square's shopping atrium now houses the Seattle Architectural Foundation and a permanent exhibit celebrating the first century of the Seattle Chapter of the American Institute of Architects.)

The next great downtown debate climaxed in the late 1980s. A dramatic boom in high-rise construction, spurred by Reaganomics and developers' fear of impending tighter land use laws, coincided with the digging of the Downtown Transit Tunnel, and so disrupted the downtown that some joked that Seattle had adopted Beirut as its latest sister city. Amid this turmoil, City Council rejected a final citizen bid to preserve Westlake Mall as open space. By 1989, Peter Steinbrueck had inherited his late father's lance and shield, and he and another future City Council member Margaret Pageler won voter approval of a "Citizens Alternative Plan" (CAP) to cap downtown building heights. The next year, newly elected mayor Norm Rice closed Pine Street to traffic through "Westlake Park" (but voters recently approved reopening the

From left to right, the towers of the Seafirst Fifth Avenue Center, Gateway Center, and Seafirst Columbia Center loom over the Dutch gables of the Rainier Club at Fourth and Marion. *(Paul Dorpat)*

street to aid Nordstrom's redevelopment of the abandoned Frederick & Nelson department store).

Neither the CAP initiative nor landmark designation could save one of downtown's most beloved theaters, the Music Hall. Property owners pled economic hardship to win city permission to demolish the movie palace in 1992, and it seemed that the venerable Eagles Temple and Paramount Theaters might soon meet the same fate. Fortunately, new laws and incentives were enacted in time (see Historic Downtown Theaters later in this section).

Thanks to such reforms and the eternal vigilance of citizen preservationists, one can still catch fleeting reflections of the past amid the glass canyons of downtown Seattle.

## Retail Core Walking Tour

Given the size of the Central Business District (CBD), this tour focuses first on the main retail district. Outlying buildings of interest are then noted.

### ▌ North on Fourth Avenue from University Street

**The Cobb Building** was completed in 1910 and is the only surviving structure executed under the original Howells and Stokes master plan. Abraham Albertson assisted in planning what was advertised as the first building on the West Coast designed expressly for the medical and dental sciences. Among the Cobb's innovative features was a built-in vacuum cleaning system.

Walking north takes you to **Puget Sound Plaza** (the former **Washington Building**), completed in 1959 on the site of the 1902 Post-Intelligencer Building. Its spare geometry and gleaming marble face preview Minoru Yamasaki's emerging style and confidence as an architect.

The Cobb Building *(left)* faces the coordinated facades of the White, Henry, and Stuart Buildings, ca. 1915.

The block opposite is filled by **Rainier Square** and Yamasaki's inverted spire, completed in 1979 after a bitter battle that failed to preserve the original **White-Henry-Stuart** complex. The Square's interior pedestrian corridor leads east under Fifth and Sixth Avenues to terminate at the One and Two Union Square Buildings. The route features several historical displays treating downtown, the Metropolitan Tract, and the Boeing Company and contains one of the White Building's original Indian head ornaments. The upper level of the building's atrium houses the offices of the **Seattle Architectural Foundation** and a permanent exhibit of the city's first century of architectural achievement and development.

### ■ North on Fourth from Union Street

R. C. Reamer designed the handsome Art Deco sandstone facade of the **1411 Fourth Avenue Building**, which opened in 1929 as one of the city's premier business addresses. Reamer also designed the smaller **Great Northern**

**Building** that opened the same year on the northeast corner of Fourth and Union. This building's rather forlorn northern neighbor was designed by Thompson and Thompson and built for J. M. Anderson in 1910.

Returning to the west side of Fourth, the terra-cotta-clad **1417 Fourth Avenue (Holland-Equitable) Building** dates from 1920 and was completed by Arthur Wheatley. The west side of the block terminates with the green marble base of the **Joshua Green Building**, designed for the banking and "Mosquito Fleet" magnate by the ubiquitous John Graham Sr. in 1913. It faces the **Fourth and Pike Building** (formerly the Ligget), designed by George Willis Lawton and Herman A. Moldenhour and completed in 1927.

### ■ North on Fourth to Pine Street

The western side of Fourth Avenue between Pike and Pine has been taken over by new buildings such as Century Square, dubbed the "Remington Shaver

Building" for its barrel roofs. We'll visit Westlake Park on the opposite side of Fourth a little later in this tour.

The block between Fourth and Third Avenues and Pine and Stewart Streets has been filled by the **Bon Marché** since 1929, when the first four floors of John Graham Sr.'s design were completed. Not long after the new store opened, a biplane ran out of fuel and the pilot made an emergency landing on the Bon's block-long roof, which spurred county plans to develop Boeing Field. The original cornice was removed and final stories added in the 1950s, and the building underwent a sensitive interior remodel in the late 1980s.

### ■ Heading East on Olive
Walking east across Fourth brings you to the **Mayflower Hotel** (originally The Bergonian; Stuart & Wheatley, 1926), which resisted absorption into the grand plans for Westlake Center and was refurbished in the late 1980s. It faces north onto the **Times Square Building**, which fills the wedge created by diverging Stewart and Olive Streets.

This elegant flatiron was designed by Bebb and Gould for "Colonel" Alden Blethen, energetic and imperious publisher of the *Seattle Times*, and completed in 1916. The *Times* relocated its headquarters to a more restrained Deco redoubt (designed by R. C. Reamer; see the discussion of the Cascade community in North of Downtown) on Fairview Avenue in 1930, and Times Square was remodeled by Bumgardner Architects for retail and office tenants in 1983, but the relief above its Olive Street entry still celebrates the craft of newspaper journalism and publishing.

Proceeding east on Olive leads you to the pedestrian triangle at Fifth and its statue of **John H. McGraw**, sculpted by Richard Brooks in 1909. McGraw served as King County sheriff during the anti-Chinese riots of 1886 (see the International District) and was elected the state's second governor in 1892. He was also an early investor in the *Seattle Post-Intelligencer*, which may explain why his back is turned to the *Times'* old home.

Crossing Fifth brings you to the **Medical and Dental Building**, designed by John Creutzer with A. H. Albertson in 1925. The northeast corner of Olive and Sixth is occupied by the **Seattle Trust Building** (Stoddard & Son, 1925).

### ■ Side Trip North on Sixth Avenue to Stewart
The nearest of the **Westin Hotel's** two "corncob" towers took the place of the **Orpheum** in 1969. The theater and its superior acoustics were widely praised as B. Marcus Priteca's finest achievements when the Orpheum opened in 1927 (see the later discussion of Historic Theaters). The pedestrian triangle formed by Sixth, Stewart, and Westlake was once filled with commuters waiting for streetcars and interurban trains. Now head east on Stewart to Seventh.

Between Sixth and Seventh Avenues, Stewart Street is fronted by two fine examples of downtown development in the mid-1920s, the **Lloyd Building** and the **Vance Hotel**, both designed by Victor Vorhees, who is best known for his bungalow designs. Turn south on Seventh Avenue and head back to Olive.

The **Tower Building** rising from the northwest corner of Seventh Avenue was designed by Earle W. Morrison and completed in 1931. The northeast corner of Seventh and Olive marks the gravesite of another movie-vaudeville palace, the **Music Hall**, designed by Sherwood Ford in 1928 and demolished in 1992 despite a long, acrimonious preservation campaign (see Historic Downtown Theaters). This led to new land use laws and financial incentives to protect remaining historic theaters. Now head west on Olive to Sixth

Avenue. Nordstrom recently announced that it will build its corporate headquarters on this site.

## ■ Heading South on Sixth to Pine Street

Most of the west side of Sixth between Stewart and Pine is occupied by the former **Frederick & Nelson** department store, now being rehabilitated as **Nordstrom's** retail flagship. The original five-story department store was designed by John Graham Sr. and completed in 1918. Graham's son, John Jr., won the commission to add another five stories in 1950. He removed his father's "Neo-Renaissance" cornice and marquees, but did not tamper with its terra-cotta veneer or other ornamental details. John Graham Jr. also preserved the pattern of the original building's fen-

The Paramount Theater was recently rehabilitated with the aid of new incentives prompted by the demolition of other historic movie palaces. It is seen here from Convention Center station of the Downtown Transit Tunnel. *(Paul Dorpat)*

estration to create a sparer, more "modern" facade. Although this father-and-son design succession offends some purists, the store exterior received Seattle Landmark designation in 1996. The block east of the store will be occupied by a new parking-retail-theater complex by 1998.

You may proceed west on Pine to Westlake Center or take the following excursion three blocks east.

## ■ Side Trip East on Pine to the Paramount

James E. Blackwell was responsible for the traditional terra-cotta treatment of the **Sixth and Pine Building** (formerly the Shafer Building, 1924) on the southwest corner of its namesake intersection. It is abutted on the south by Henry Bittman's older **Decatur Building**, built by Louisa Denny Frye in 1922.

The 1929-vintage **Roosevelt Hotel** at Seventh and Pine was recently refurbished. The tower's economical Art Deco ornamentation and penthouse setback are further products of John Graham Sr.'s prolific pen.

The two-story **Pande-Cameron Building** on the southwest corner of Ninth and Pine dates from 1928 and is a fine example of the many elegant terra-cotta retail buildings designed by Henry Bittman. Its neighbor on the east is one of the beneficiaries of Seattle's historic theater reforms.

**The Paramount**, the largest and grandest of Seattle's surviving movie palaces, was designed by the Chicago firm of Rapp & Rapp with B. Marcus Priteca and completed in 1928. Its lobby and auditorium were refurbished in 1994 under the supervision of NBBJ (see Historic Theaters).

The nearby **Camlin Hotel** on the south side of Ninth was designed by Carl J. Linde and opened in 1926. It is to be renovated as part of a new development, but its delightfully retro "Cloud Room" restaurant and lounge may not survive. It faces the **Convention Center Station of the Downtown Transit Tunnel,** which runs beneath Seattle to the International District. Downtown's original "intermodal transit center" can be found a block north at Stewart. The present-day **Greyhound Bus Station** was built in 1927 by Stone & Webster's Pacific Northwest Traction Company as the Seattle terminus for its interurban trains and motor coaches (rail service ended 12 years later).

Ninth Avenue marks the limit of the downtown's eastward expansion during the 1920s but for a lone sentinel, the **Olive Tower** (E. W. Morrison), built at Olive and Boren in 1928. We now head back west on Pine Street to Westlake Center.

### ■ West on Pine to Westlake Center

The former **"Westlake Mall"** has been an urban design battleground since the late 1950s, when Fred Bassetti and other architects first proposed banishing automobiles from the tangled intersection of Westlake, Fifth, Fourth, Pine, and Pike and converting the triangle into a civic plaza. Horrified downtown retailers accepted the closing of only one block of Westlake between Pike and Pine, which became the southern terminus of the **Monorail** in 1962.

Political trench warfare sputtered into the mid-1980s. Shortly before his death in 1984, architect-activist Victor Steinbrueck tried to break the stalemate by blessing Mayor Charles Royer's plan for a park on the south side of Pine and a new **Westlake Center** retail arcade and office tower on the north. After the site was cleared in 1987, Victor's son Peter led a last-ditch campaign to preserve the entire site as open space. Although this failed, it triggered the successful CAP initiative to limit downtown building heights in 1989.

Westlake Center was developed by the Rouse Company and has proved successful in re-energizing the down-

town's retail core since 1989. The project's completion was briefly delayed while engineers changed plans so that the Monorail could round the office tower's corner to reach the third-story terminal above Fifth Avenue. The Center and other nearby retailers also feature underground entries to the **Westlake Station of the Downtown Transit Tunnel**. This impressive cavern was designed by Brent Carlson and features a "terra-cotta park" designed by Jack Mackie and some of Seattle's finest public art.

While **Westlake Park** has succeeded as a popular gathering place, it also has had to overcome serious design and construction problems. To maximize the sense of openness and unite an awkward space, landscape architect Robert Hanna established a common paving pattern (based on a native basket design) for the Center's plaza, Pine Street, and the formal Westlake Park, which is dominated by Bob Maki's "Westlake Star Axis/Seven Hills" ensemble of sculptures, square arch, and fountain. Initial reviews were mixed, although skateboarders especially enjoyed the final product—and were promptly banned from the park.

A more daunting problem arose when buses and trucks quickly dislodged Pine Street's granite paving stones. After a round of expensive repairs, newly installed mayor Norm Rice closed the street to traffic in 1990. It remained so until 1997, when, following a public vote, the street was reopened to limited traffic as a precondition for Nordstrom's investment in the abandoned Frederick & Nelson building. If you think this is the last chapter in the saga of Westlake Mall, you don't know Seattle.

Most of the hypotenuse of Westlake Park is defined by the former **Nordstrom** store, whose 1973 remodel united three older buildings. The upper stories of the largest of these, the **Ranke** (Louis Svarz, 1926) are still visible at the corner of Fifth and Pike. The rest of the Westlake wedge is fronted by the **Seaboard Building** (formerly the Northern Bank & Trust; William Doty Van Siclen), which in 1909 was one of the first large "uptown" buildings erected outside of the Metropolitan Tract. Now head east on Pike to Fifth Avenue.

## ■ South on Fifth from Pike

The **Banana Republic** store on the northeast corner of Fifth and Pike occupies the terra-cotta shell of the former **Coliseum Theater,** designed by B. Marcus Priteca. It opened in 1916 as one of the nation's first auditoriums dedicated to the exhibition of moving pictures (see Historic Theaters). The theater's original domed marquee (gone since the 1950s) is echoed by the rotunda entry of the new City Centre building that fills most of the east side of Fifth between Pike and Union.

The northeast corner of Fifth and Union is occupied by one of Seattle's first International-style structures, the **Logan Building**, built in 1959 and designed by Mandeville and Berge. The entire east side of Fifth Avenue between Union and University is fronted by the **Skinner Building**. Its warm Wilkeson sandstone (quarried near Mount Rainier) was a favorite material

of architect Robert C. Reamer. Completed in 1926, the Skinner's dignified Renaissance exterior conceals the oriental fantasia of the **5th Avenue Theater**. Gustav Liljestrom was chiefly responsible for the lavish interior, inspired by several imperial chambers within Beijing's Forbidden City. The theater was listed on the National Register in 1978 and carefully restored at a cost of $2.6 million under the supervision of Richard McCann, a colleague of the late B. Marcus Priteca. The refurbished theater reopened in July 1980 and is now operated by a nonprofit association devoted to staging musical road shows.

Minoru Yamasaki's "cyber-gothic" **IBM Building** has stood on the southeast corner of Fifth and University since 1964. Its sunken plaza features a fountain by James Fitzgerald, whose work also graces the courtyard of the nearby Plymouth Congregational Church.

## ■ West on University Street

The majestic **Four Seasons Olympic Hotel** rises from the block between Fifth and Fourth Avenues and University and Union Streets. Financed in large part by a community bond drive, the Olympic was designed by George Post & Company with Bebb and Gould.

The Wilkeson sandstone facade of R. C. Reamer's Skinner Building still graces the east side of Fifth Avenue between University and Union Streets. The distant City Centre was a product of the development boom of the mid-1980s.

The Four Seasons Olympic Hotel dominates Fourth Avenue in this photo taken soon after its completion in 1928. While it remains Seattle's premier hotel, most of its neighbors in this view have perished. *(Old Seattle Paper Works)*

Seattle's premier hotel was built in stages between 1924 and 1929 around the older Metropolitan Theater (Howells & Stokes, 1910). After Helen Hayes took her final curtain call on December 4, 1954, the Metropolitan was demolished to create a "motor entrance" on University Street. The street itself was dubbed "Victory Square" during World War II and hosted numerous war bond rallies and patriotic ceremonies.

The hotel was managed by Seattle-based Western (later Westin) Hotels for many decades. The Four Seasons took over the property in 1980, a year after the Olympic was listed on the National Register, and launched a $55 million, three-year remodel coordinated by NBBJ, Frank Nicholson, and John North. The southwest corner of Fourth and University is occupied by the rather forlorn plaza of the **Financial Center**, where the **Stimson Building** stood from 1924 until 1970. The new tower's

skybridge to the Olympic sparked a civic debate, over the protection of view corridors and street-level activity, that continues to the present day. Better to cast your eyes northwest to gaze upon the Cobb's Beaux-Arts facade and recall the past glories of Denny's Knoll.

## OTHER CENTRAL DOWNTOWN BUILDINGS

Because other properties of historic or architectural interest are scattered through the downtown, the following are less walking tours than inventories of each major avenue from Stewart on the north to Columbia on the south. We will skip First Avenue, which has been treated in other sections.

### ■ Second Avenue
As noted earlier, Second Avenue became the spine of Seattle's "second downtown" as business and retail activi-

This view of "lower downtown" was taken from the Smith Tower soon after its 1914 opening. The large office block on the left is the Central Building at Third and Madison. The gabled original wing of the Rainier Club is located near the center, at Fourth and Marion, below the dome of the First United Methodist Church. The downtown's original Carnegie Library stands two blocks north on Fourth. The spired structure to its east is the early Sisters of Providence Hospital, where the Federal Courthouse now stands. *(Lawton Gowey)*

ty expanded north from Pioneer Square. The street became the main route for "Golden Potlatch" parades, Seattle's first annual summer festivals, in 1911.

Second Avenue was the original home of the **Bon Marché** and **Frederick & Nelson**, and **Penney's** and **Rhodes** department stores later anchored its north end. The former was demolished in 1988 for the Newmark Tower at Pike Street, but the stately sandstone **Rhodes** (Thomas, Grainger & Thomas, 1927) at Second and Union survives as an annex to the new **Downtown Seattle Art Museum** (Robert Venturi, 1991).

Another vestige of Second's past retail prominence is the Venetian Renaissance facade of the J.S. Graham Department Store, now the refurbished **A.E. Doyle Building** (Doyle & Merriam, 1919; Ibsen Nelson, 1973), at Second and Pine. The **Second and Pine Building** (originally the **Haight Building**) on the southeast corner is

another handsome terra-cotta structure designed by S. Jennings and completed in 1908 for offices; it was remodeled for apartments in 1991 by Johnson Architects and Planning. The northwest corner of Second and Pike is occupied by the **Eitel Building** (W. D. Van Siclen, 1906), which has seen far better days.

The **Brooklyn Building** (unknown, 1890) on the southeast corner of University once housed a burlesque theater and pool hall. It was remodeled in the late 1980s as part of the development of the adjacent Washington Mutual Tower.

A third department store, **Baillargeon's**, has stood on the northeast corner of Second and Spring since 1907, although a succession of banks has occupied it in recent decades. Designed by Saunders and Lawton, and remodeled by Doyle and Merriam, this building's eastern face now features a trompe l'oeil mural painted in 1981 by Richard Haas. Second Avenue's other notable buildings are discussed in the

108

Lower Downtown tour included with the section on Pioneer Square.

## ■ Third Avenue

Until 1911, Third Avenue terminated at Denny Hill, which rose sharply north of Pine Street. Its belated development as a commercial street was eclipsed by the Metropolitan Tract, but it nevertheless attracted some significant buildings early in the twentieth century.

The west side of Third between Pine and Pike is lined with three superb examples of early downtown architecture. The youngest is Henry Bittman's Art Deco masterpiece, the **Olympic (United Shopping) Tower** (1929) at Pine. A little to the south rises the oldest, the eccentric **Fischer Studio Building**, begun by Charles Bebb in partnership with Louis Mendel and finished in 1915 with Carl Gould. The building was designed for musicians, complete with an ornate recital hall on its top floors, and is now divided into condominiums. The south end of the block is filled by the former **Republic Building**, now **Melbourne House**, designed by Lawton and Moldenhour and completed in 1927.

Despite these once-fashionable building addresses, Third Avenue never fulfilled its potential as a major retail address. Except for the Bon Marché, major stores either remained on Second Avenue or skipped over it to settle on Fourth and Fifth Avenues. The old "dime stores" were not so fussy. The most prominent of these was the **F.W. Woolworth** store at Third and Pike. Although it reflects standardized design by Harold B. Hamhill's New York office, the former Woolworth's (currently a Ross clothing outlet) is cherished today for its warm terra-cotta facade and 1939-Moderne styling.

It faces the older home of another former five-and-dime, the **Kress Variety Store** (E. J. Hoffman, 1923), on the southwest corner of Third and Pike. The

Henry Bittman's Art Deco tower graces the corner of Third and Pine. *(Paul Dorpat)*

nearby **Mann Building** is another example of Henry Bittman's fine terracotta detailing. Built in 1926, it long contained the Embassy Theater and is slated for rehabilitation.

Woolworth's shares its block with the **Joseph Vance Building** at Union, designed by Victor Vorhees and completed in 1929. Several pieces of the building's terra-cotta facade fell in 1995, prompting a complete restoration of the exterior. Between 1903 and 1959, the east side of Third between Union and University was dominated by an imposing Neoclassical post office. Its first neighbor on the south was the turreted Gothic pile of the original Plymouth Congregational Church. This was succeeded in 1913 by the Pantages (later Palomar) Theater, and then by a parking garage in 1964.

The manmade mountain of the

The terra-cotta facades of the Woolworth's and Kress variety stores still frame the intersection of Third and Pike, but their original tenants departed long ago.

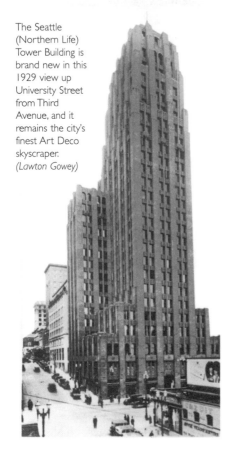

The Seattle (Northern Life) Tower Building is brand new in this 1929 view up University Street from Third Avenue, and it remains the city's finest Art Deco skyscraper. *(Lawton Gowey)*

**Seattle Tower** rises from the southeast corner of Third and University. Originally named the **Northern Life Tower** and completed in 1929, this building is, in the opinion of most critics, the city's finest Art Deco skyscraper. Its massing and brickwork (which gradually lightens as it ascends) were designed by Abraham Albertson with Joseph Wilson and Paul Richardson to evoke an alpine spire thrusting up from the earth. Similarly, its moody, richly ornamented lobby engulfs the visitor like the subterranean hall of a fantastical mountain king.

The Seattle Tower's southern neighbor is the older and more utilitarian **Telephone Building**, designed by Bebb & Gould and completed in 1920. Now owned by USWest, it still serves as a major telecommunications center. The former **Earl Hotel**, now the **Seattle Hotel**, on the south side of Seneca dates from 1929 and was designed by V. W. Vorhees. The remaining significant structures on Third are discussed in the Lower Downtown tour.

## ■ Fourth Avenue

We have already treated Fourth Avenue in detail north of Seneca. The little terra-cotta building on the southwest corner of Seneca was designed for a bank branch by Henry James in 1922 and currently houses a **Starbuck's** coffee house. It faces an empty lot that is slated for a new hotel.

The "new" Main Branch of the **Seattle Public Library** was designed by Leonard Bindon and John L. Wright with Decker, Christiansen & Kitchin. Completed in 1960, the building's Fifth Avenue plaza features George Tsutakawa's *Fountain of Wisdom*, his first public commission. The library is one of the city's better expressions of the International style, but it is now hopelessly obsolete. Some old-timers still yearn for the original Carnegie Library erected on the site back in 1906.

The former **Seafirst Building** standing opposite the library on Fourth Avenue was the city's first modern high-rise office building. Designed by NBBJ, the 50-story "black monolith" opened to less than enthusiastic reviews in 1969 (see downtown history), but rumors of the sale of its signature sculpture, Henry Moore's *Vertebrae*, triggered an instantaneous preservation movement in the late 1980s and a quick retreat by the building's owners.

The southwest corner of Fourth and Madison has housed the downtown **YMCA** since 1909 in a building designed by James Stephen. A new, taller wing was designed by Albertson, Wilson and Richardson and completed on the northwest corner of Fourth and Marion in 1931. It stands kitty-corner from a recreational center for a different social stratum, the **Rainier Club.**

Founded in 1888 by the city's more rambunctious business and professional leaders, the Rainier Club rented a number of venues before purchasing a lot on the southeast corner of Marion in 1902 for construction of a permanent home. It retained Spokane-based architect Kirtland Cutter, well known in Seattle for C. D. Stimson's First Hill mansion (see First Hill). He abandoned his original Tudor-style design for a more fanciful, Dutch-gabled facade reportedly inspired by England's Aston Hall. The building was completed in 1904 and was overflowing by 1928, when the Club retained Carl Gould to design a new wing. Gould extended Cutter's original facade but added the Georgian portal that now serves as the main entry, along with his own Art Deco grilles, lamps, and ornaments for the lobby and new club rooms. The expanded Club opened in 1929 and recently underwent an extensive interior remodel that preserved the spirit of Cutter and Gould.

George Tsutakawa's first public fountain still gushes and burbles on the Fifth Avenue plaza of the Seattle Public Library. *(Paul Dorpat)*

Kirtland Cutter's design for the Rainier Club was inspired by a Jacobean manor. Pictured here soon after completion in 1904, the Club seems to be set in a rural estate rather than the heart of a growing city.

## ■ Fifth Avenue

The **YWCA** Building at Fifth and Seneca was designed by Édouard Frère Champney during his brief partnership with Carl Gould and opened in 1913. As the supervising architect for the 1909 Alaska-Yukon-Pacific Exposition on the UW campus (see Northeast Seattle section), Champney had a romantic flair, but his plans for this building's clock tower and roof garden were not executed.

The sloping lawn between Seneca and Madison is guarded by the austere visage of the **Federal Courthouse**, designed by Louis A. Simon with Gilbert Stanley Underwood and completed in 1940. Its courtrooms have echoed to many historic trials, and the lawn was a frequent battleground during antiwar demonstrations of the 1960s and early 1970s. Plans for a new courthouse are now under discussion, and the building's future is cloudy. This site was previously occupied by the first **Sisters of Providence Hospital** in Seattle, designed in 1882 by Mother Joseph with Donald MacKay. Providence

Hospital relocated to Eighteenth Avenue (see Central Area) in 1910.

The **First United Methodist Church** has stood at the southwest corner of Marion since 1907. The nave was designed by James Schack and Daniel Huntington as a large central rotunda, and it houses numerous public lectures in addition to church services.

The high-rise lingams east and south of the church testify to Seattle's downtown boom in the 1980s. In 1984, the seventy-six-story Seafirst Columbia Center captured the title of "tallest building west of the Mississippi" once claimed by the Smith Tower. The shorter but more phallic Keybank Gateway Tower is slated to become the new Seattle City Hall by A.D. 2000.

## ■ Sixth Avenue

Rising from the northeast corner of Fifth and Union, Sherwood Ford's eagle-encrusted Art Deco tower for the **Washington Athletic Club** has exuded vigor and confidence since 1930. It stands its ground with dignity against the brash youth of Unico's One and Two

Children frolic in the fountains and cascades of Freeway Park, built in 1974 in an effort to heal the deep gash created by I-5 and reconnect downtown with First Hill. (*Frank O. Shaw*)

Union Square buildings, which will be lucky to age as gracefully. Two Union's construction in 1989 entailed demolition of another of Henry Bittman's terra-cotta low-rises, the **Hubbel Building** (1922).

The eastern side of Fifth between University and Seneca marks the edge of **Freeway Park**, whose development was spearheaded by urban visionary James Ellis 20 years after architects Paul Thiry and Victor Steinbrueck first proposed "lidding" the planned downtown freeway to preserve downtown's connection with First Hill. This delightful urban oasis was designed by Lawrence Halprin with Angela Danadjieva and features waterfalls and plazas for summer concerts. The first phase was completed in 1976, and the healing of the Freeway's gash was extended north with construction of the Washington State Trade and Convention Center in the late 1980s.

The **Women's University Club** building on the southwest corner of Spring was designed by Abraham H. Albertson with Édouard Frère

Champney (see earlier discussion of YWCA) and completed in 1922. The site was previously occupied by **St. Francis Hall**, which housed the city's first Jesuit school in 1891 and planted the seed for Seattle University.

### ■ Seventh Avenue

In addition to the previously mentioned **Tower Building**, **Roosevelt Hotel**, and **Eagles Building**, two other notable buildings survive on Seventh. Henderson Ryan's distinctive Mediterranean-style **Waldorf Hotel** (now low-income apartments) has stood on the northeast corner of Pike since 1907, but it is now doomed by expansion plans for the nearby **Washington State Trade and Convention Center.** The **Eagles Building** at Seventh and Union was designed by Henry Bittman for the Fraternal Order of Eagles in 1925. The building was owned by the Convention Center until 1996, when it was sold to ACT for restoration as **Kreielsheimer Place** (see the following section on Historic Downtown Theaters).

The home "Aerie" of the Fraternal Order of Eagles has been preserved and adapted as Kreielsheimer Place and the new home of ACT Theater. It abuts the Washington State Trade and Convention Center, which spans I-5 at Union Street. *(Paul Dorpat)*

The ubiquity of public timepieces such as this one, located near Fourth and Pine, led some to call Seattle the "City of Clocks." *(Paul Dorpat)*

## ■ Street Clocks, Then and Now

Architectural historian Lawrence Kreisman notes that Seattle was once known as "the city of clocks," because of the downtown's ubiquitous public timepieces. At the turn of the nineteenth century, most of these street clocks were supplied by Mayer & Company to jewelers, who used them, ironically, to advertise watches. Vintage downtown street clocks can be found standing (and occasionally operating) at 1427 Fourth, near Pike; 409 Pike, near Fourth; 1529 Fourth, near Pine; 1206 First, near Seneca; and 720 Second, near Columbia. Two new street clocks were erected in 1990 as part of the street-level improvements in connection with the Downtown Transit Tunnel: Heather Ramsay's *Pendulum Clock* on Third Avenue near University, and Bill Whipple's *Question Mark Clock* on Pine near Fifth.

## ■ Historic Downtown Theaters

Credit long months of gray skies and relentless rain for nourishing a thriving theatrical culture in Seattle. Entertainment centers such as the Frye and Squire's Opera Houses were among the city's first large buildings, and the amusement of thousands of transient gold prospectors helped to establish the fortunes of vaudeville impresarios such as Alexander Pantages, John Considine, and John Cort. Their architects, notably Seattle's B. Marcus Priteca, created fantasies of stone and terra cotta that were as transfixing as anything on stage or screen.

Today, Seattle's census of Equity theaters is second only to that of New York City, but there was a time when it seemed the curtain would never rise again downtown. The sequence of decline was familiar: first the movies drove out vaudeville and burlesque between the world wars, then suburban expansion scattered audiences to the malls and multiplexes.

Two dozen operating theaters managed to survive until downtown construction rebounded in the late 1950s. The first to go was the **Metropolitan Theater**, designed by Howells & Stokes and completed in 1911. It was later engulfed by the Olympic Hotel and finally consumed to create the University Street entry. Next came the **Palomar** (formerly the **Pantages**), designed by Priteca in 1913 and demolished for a garage in 1964. Then Priteca's acclaimed **Orpheum** was leveled in 1968 and replaced by the first of the Westin Hotel's two cylindrical towers, followed a few years later by the silencing of Henry Bittman's whimsically Baroque **Music Box.**

Robert Reamer's **5th Avenue Theater** in the Skinner Building (1926; see the earlier discussion of the Metropolitan Tract in this District's History) might have met the same fate but for the bitter fight over the new Rainier Tower in the mid-1970s. Its owners, Unico, accepted a National Register listing (but not Seattle Landmark designation) and invested millions in a careful restoration of the Forbidden City–inspired lobby and auditorium. The 5th Avenue is now operated

The demolition of the Orpheum in 1968 cast a long shadow over downtown's historic theaters, but new regulations and incentives should assure a brighter future for surviving theaters. *(Frank O. Shaw)*

by a nonprofit association specializing in musicals, which often fill its 2,130 seats.

Such philanthropy was not available to the Clise family, who owned the **Music Hall** at Seventh Avenue and Olive. Although it was originally named the **Mayflower**, Sherwood Ford designed the huge theater as an architectural "Night in the Gardens of Spain," complete with gigantic sandstone urns and Moorish arches. It opened in 1929 and hosted Seattle Symphony concerts under Sir Thomas Beecham's baton, as well as films and revues. Despite a succession of theatrical tenants, the Music Hall steadily declined into the 1980s, when its owners applied to remove Seattle Landmark designation so the site could be redeveloped.

Appeals and lawsuits stalled demolition until late 1991, when Allied Arts launched a new campaign to protect other endangered properties. Mayor Rice convened a "Theater Advisory Group" (TAG), which recognized that historic theaters were "worth more dead than alive" due to rising property values. TAG recommended a revolving fund to

purchase landmark theaters' "transfer-
able development rights" for resale to
developers seeking to enlarge planned
buildings on other downtown sites. In
cases in which owners of landmarks
plead economic hardship, TAG called
for a ban on "speculative" demolition
unless credible redevelopment plans
were in place. City Council enacted
these reforms in 1993 and gave remaining historic theaters a new lease on life.

The first theater to apply the new
rules was the **Paramount**, at Ninth and
Pine. Priteca advised the Chicago firm
of Rapp & Rapp in the Paramount's
design, and it opened in 1928 with
3,000 seats and the largest Wurlitzer
organ on the West Coast. After decades
of decline, the theater was purchased
by former Microsoft executive Ida Cole
in 1993 and remodeled under the
supervision of NBBJ. The Paramount
reopened as a venue for major road
shows and productions in 1995. In
addition, Cole plans to remodel the
adjacent apartment tower for offices
and studios.

NBBJ also supervised conversion of
the **Coliseum Theater** at Fifth and Pike
into a flagship store for Banana
Republic in 1995. Designed by B.
Marcus Priteca for real estate developer
John Gottstein, the Coliseum started out
to be a conventional vaudeville house
in 1914. The advent of motion pictures
changed this scheme, and a planned
backstage and curtain loft were abandoned. The theater opened in 1916 as
the first true movie palace in Seattle
and, arguably, in the nation. The
Coliseum suffered some heavy-handed
modernization in the 1950s and lost its
unique domed marquee. NBBJ undertook a much more sympathetic exterior
restoration, and the interior store is contained within a freestanding shell that
preserves the possibility for restoring
the auditorium at a future date.

While city landmark reforms did not
apply to the Coliseum (it had already

This view north along Fifth Avenue from the late
1920s frames the Coliseum Theater's former
marquee in the center. The nearer buildings have
been replaced by City Centre. Farther north
stands the original five-story Frederick & Nelson
Department Store and the taller Medical-Dental
Building. The street ends at the Orpheum
Theater, since replaced by the Westin Hotel.
*(Rev. Dennis Anderson)*

sold its development rights), they
played a key role in saving the **Eagles
Building** at Eighth and Union. This
building housed Aerie No. 1 of the
Fraternal Order of Eagles, a "working-
men's club" dedicated to mutual benefit
and social reform.

The Eagles counted architect Henry
Bittman among their members, and his
finely detailed Second Italian
Renaissance Revival design incorporated a large ballroom-auditorium, a banquet hall, dining and club rooms, fifty-
plus apartments, a vault for members'
possessions, and a bowling alley.
Completed in 1925, the building served
as headquarters for the Eagles' long
campaign for national old-age pensions.
After President Franklin Roosevelt

signed the act creating Social Security in 1936, he awarded the pen to the Eagles in gratitude for their efforts.

The Eagles Building declined until the late 1960s, when its auditorium enjoyed a brief renaissance as Seattle's leading rock and roll venue. The slide resumed, and the State Trade and Convention Center acquired the property in the mid-1980s. Landmark designation prevented outright demolition, but years of neglect nearly accomplished the same result.

Shortly after the city's new historic theater laws took effect, **A Contemporary Theater**, or "ACT," negotiated with the Convention Center to take over the Eagles Building for its new home. The sale of development rights helped to fund a $35 million exterior restoration and internal conversion, creating two separate theaters and 40 units of low-income housing, all designed by Callison Architecture. The Eagles Building reopened in 1996 as **Kreielsheimer Place** (after a major benefactor) and is one of Seattle's best examples of adaptive reuse of a landmark structure.

The **Moore Theater** at Second and Virginia is the oldest survivor of Seattle's theatrical golden age. It was built by James Moore as part of his new hotel and completed in 1907 (see the Denny Regrade in the following section). Thanks to Edwin Houghton's superior acoustical design, there isn't a bad seat among the 1,400 in the hall. Although the auditorium's uppermost balcony has been closed due to newer seismic standards, the theater remains an active venue for concerts and smaller productions. The theater's owners have not as yet sought city aid for restoration, but it's available if and when they need it.

## BELLTOWN, DENNY REGRADE, AND SEATTLE CENTER

### Orientation

The area stretching north of Stewart Street to Mercer Street between Eighth Avenue and Elliott Bay is usually dubbed the Denny Regrade, acknowledging the area's forcible flattening by city engineers early in the twentieth century. It incorporates the older Belltown district west of Second Avenue and Seattle Center, roughly bounded by Broad Street, Mercer Way, Denny Way, Fifth Avenue, and First Avenue North.

### Belltown and Denny Regrade History

Reginald Heber Thomson became Seattle's city engineer in 1892. He designed the town's first modern sewers and established a water system that remains the region's largest a century later. But roads and boulevards were Thomson's first love, especially if they were straight and level. Thus, Seattle's topography presented the Scots-Irish engineer with a daunting challenge, and no irregularity of nature affronted him more than Arthur Denny's damn hill.

Denny Hill rose steeply north of Pine Street between Second and Fifth Avenues, then descended gradually to the north across William Bell's claim. It

R. H. Thompson became Seattle's city engineer in 1882. His enduring monument (or lack thereof) is the absence of Denny Hill. *(E. S. Curtis; Rainier Club)*

was defined on the west by a precipitous bluff that dropped from Second Avenue to the edge of Elliott Bay. This confined "Belltown" to First and Western Avenues and largely isolated it from the downtown precincts to the south. (Bell left Seattle in 1855 and actually had little to do with his namesake land claim.)

Denny Hill stuck in R. H. Thomson's craw because he believed it blocked the city's manifest destiny of northward expansion. Having seen the power of hydraulic mining in California, he knew that the hill could easily be sluiced into the bay, but he was frustrated by Arthur Denny's stubborn ambition to lure the territorial legislature to his own "Capitol Hill" (not to be confused with the present-day hill northeast of downtown).

Finally persuaded in 1889 that the seat of the new state government was firmly planted in Olympia, Denny began to erect an enormous hotel, which he named for himself. The Panic of 1893 halted work before the interior was complete, leaving the turreted Victorian shell of the Denny Hotel to hover over Seattle's landscape for a decade like an architectural Mrs. Haversham, abandoned at the altar of Denny's great expectations.

James A. Moore, a flamboyant developer in his own right, bought and completed the 100-room pile as the Washington Hotel. He personally handed the first guest keys to President Teddy Roosevelt and his entourage on May 23, 1903. Moore built his own tram to transport guests to the top of Denny Hill and started building his own namesake theater and hotel on its western slope.

Thomson started nibbling at Denny Hill's flanks while trying to wear down Moore's resolve. Economics finally convinced Moore to abandon the high ground in 1906, and he erected a modern New Washington Hotel (now the Josephinum) at Second and Stewart. Thomson wasted no time tearing into Denny Hill, but it took five years to vanquish his foe west of Fifth Avenue (the rest of the eastern slope was regraded in 1929 and 1930). When property owners balked at selling, engineers carved around their lots, sometimes leaving houses stranded a hundred feet in the air atop "spite mounds." These manmade buttes fell by 1911, giving Seattle vast new tabula rasa upon which to sketch its urban visions.

The first and most famous of these was drawn by Virgil Bogue, a protégé of the Olmsted brothers (who had been retained to plan Seattle's park system

This nineteent-century drawing and 1903 view of the Washington (Denny) Hotel's lobby give a sense of its Victorian opulence—and Seattle's loss when it was regraded out of existence two years later. *(Paul Dorpat; Asahel Curtis)*

Thomson's engineers were already nibbling at Denny Hill's western flank in this 1905 view from Second and Pine Street. *(A. Curtis, University of Washington Library Special Collections. Neg. 8137)*

"Spite mounds" rise like man-made buttes amid the Denny Regrade, giving some sense of Denny Hill's original height. (*A. Curtis, Washington State Historical Society. Neg. 18733*)

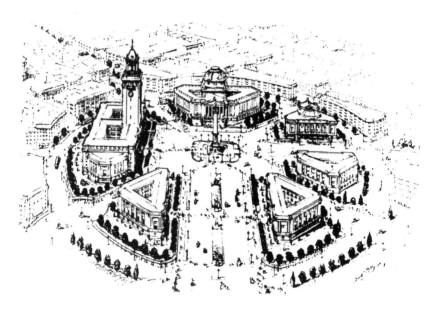

Virgil Bogue's audacious Civic Center would have radiated out from the intersection of Fourth and Blanchard Street, but voters rejected the plan in 1912.

in 1903). Bogue was hired by the new Municipal Plans Commission in 1910, and he delivered a comprehensive schema the following year. Reading like a manifesto of the City Beautiful movement, the Bogue plan proposed to remake Seattle in the image of the "Civic Idea...a consciousness demanding the recognition of organic unity and intelligent system."

These words were made flesh in his design for a new Civic Center, an ensemble of Beaux-Arts government buildings, not unlike San Francisco's City

Hall complex, radiating outward from the intersection of Fourth and Blanchard. The plan basically relocated downtown Seattle to the new Regrade, which horrified property owners south of Pine Street and precipitated a bitter battle between reformers, led by Thomson, and the "landlord trust." Divided, confused, and wary of the potential bill for Bogue's dreams—which included a rapid transit tunnel from downtown to Kirkland on the far shore of Lake Washington and purchase of Mercer Island for a city park—voters rejected the plan in 1912 by nearly two to one.

*Courtesy of the University of Washington Press, copyright 1992.*

Modern condo towers are now springing up in the Denny Regrade, finally fulfilling R. H. Thomson's vision — 75 years late. *(Paul Dorpat)*

Thomson's blank slate remained mostly blank for the next half-century, thanks to two key factors. First, the automobile, which was barely mentioned in Bogue's plan, facilitated the city's rapid expansion into outlying areas and obviated the Regrade's original raison d'être to serve horse-drawn vehicles stalled by Seattle's steep hills. Second, skyscrapers such as the new Smith Tower, which City Beautiful planners despised, allowed owners to concentrate business development (and raise property values) within the existing downtown.

Hotels, apartments, warehouses, and car dealerships slowly filled the Regrade's vacant lots with functional but largely undistinguished structures. The cheap land attracted marginal businesses to service the downtown. Labor unions raised meeting halls and a Central Labor Temple at First and Broad, and film distributors dotted the area with ornate "jewel box" auditoriums in which to preview new releases for theater owners. The older strip of Belltown west of Second Avenue fell into disrepair and disrepute as an upland adjunct of the harbor and berth for visiting sailors.

The Regrade's modest success as a working class neighborhood fell far short of Thomson and Bogue's lofty ambitions, but this did not dissuade succeeding generations of planners and developers from fantasizing "better" futures for the area. The next major step was taken in the mid-1970s when the city approved new zoning to encourage construction of a high-rise residential district. Reality again disappointed the planners, and young artists, musicians, and entrepreneurs took advantage of the area's low rents to establish a thriving mini-SoHo colony of studios, galleries, cafes, and clubs.

In the early 1980s, developer Martin Selig launched a one-man boom of new office construction in the area. The condo craze and superheated real estate market of the Reagan years promoted more construction — and nearly bankrupted a few developers when the tax reform of 1986 popped their financial bubbles. A new round of high-rise construction began in the early 1990s, and many fear that gentrification will soon drive out the Regrade and Belltown's surviving bohemian element.

Blame it all on R. H. Thomson. As Judge Thomas Burke lamented 80 years ago, "It would have been much better to have saved Denny Hill" by tunneling under it "while preserving the natural beauty that means so much to any city."

## Exploring Belltown and the Regrade

The terms "Belltown" and "Denny Regrade" are now used interchangably, although by tradition the former designates the area west of Second Avenue. The district is home to a new wave of fine restaurants (chiefly along First and Second Avenues), galleries, music clubs, and hip bars and taverns. One caution: the area around Third and Bell seems to have become a permanent outdoor drug market, especially after dark.

Surviving structures of historical or architectural interest are scattered randomly from Denny Way on the North to Stewart Street on the South, and from Sixth Avenue on the east to Western Avenue. Among the more important are described in the following paragraphs.

The **Securities Building** at Third and Stewart was designed by John Graham Sr. and completed in 1913 (a wing was later added on the east). It features a handsome L-shaped lobby opening on Third and Stewart.

The **Josephinum** at Second and Stewart began life in 1908 as James Moore's New Washington Hotel. It was designed by the St. Louis firm of Eames & Young, and now serves as a Catholic residence for the elderly.

The New Washington Hotel (now the Josephinum) and neighboring Moore Theater and Hotel, shown here ca. 1910, still dominate Second Avenue between Stewart and Virginia Streets. *(Webster & Stevens, Photographers; Loomis Miller)*

B. Marcus Priteca's Natatorium at Second and Lenora lost its domed foyer in the 1950s when it was remodeled to host revival meetings. *(Lawton Gowey)*

**The Moore Theater and Hotel**, 1932 Second, was begun as an annex to James Moore's "old" Washington Hotel atop Denny Hill. Designed by Edwin Houghton, the theater is still in active use and highly esteemed for its superior acoustics.

**Bethel Temple**, 2033 Second, occupies the former **Crystal Swimming Pool**, an ornate natatorium designed by B. Marcus Priteca in 1915. Its large, domed marquee was removed in the 1950s, and the pool was planked over for religious services.

The **Austin A. Bell Building**, 2326 First, which bears the name of William Bell's son, opened in 1889. Its fanciful Neo-Gothic front was designed by Elmer Fisher and survived a later fire. A new structure is now being built behind and north of the facade, which will be restored.

**Fire Station No. 2**, at Fourth and Bell, dates from 1920 and is an example of D. R. Huntington's work as city architect. Nearby apartment and commercial buildings, including the popular Two Bells Tavern, typify the modest but practical styles of construction that began to fill the Regrade in the early 1920s.

**Group Health Cooperative Administration and Conference Center**, Sixth and Wall, was originally built in 1948 to house the offices and presses of the *Seattle Post-Intelligencer*. The building was designed by the New York firm of Lockwood-Greene with NBBJ. The entry rotunda was formerly crowned with a large globe circled by revolving neon letters announcing, "It's in the *P-I*." This artifact was relocated in the late 1980s to the *P-I*'s new headquarters on Elliott and can be seen from the waterfront. Group Health Cooperative, which was founded in 1946 and is the nation's largest consumer-governed health care system, occupied the building in late 1987.

**Tilikum Place**, Denny and Cedar, features a dramatic, full-figure statue of Chief Sealth, "firm friend of the Whites," by James. A. Wehn in 1912. James Rupp's guide, *Art in Seattle's Public Places*, says that Wehn cast his Pioneer Square bust of Sealth from the orginal mold for this statue, but destroyed the model to protest the city's plan to use an inferior foundry; he later reconciled with the city and sculpted a new figure. The triangle and fountain were rehabili-

The former Belltown Hotel *(foreground)* burned down years ago, but the Austin Bell Building's Victorian facade survived and is now being renovated. *(Lawton Gowey)*

The *Seattle Post-Intelligencer's* trademark globe glowed with neon at Sixth and Wall from 1948 to 1988, when the newspaper moved its offices to Elliott Avenue. Its former building, sans globe, now houses the administrative offices of Group Health Cooperative.

tated in 1975 under the supervision of Jones & Jones architects. In the early 1990s, cleaners scraped away decades of paint to discover that the statue had originally been covered in gold leaf, which has now been restored.

The **KOMO Broadcasting Studio building**, Fourth and Denny, was designed and erected by the Austin Company in 1948. It is regarded as Seattle's finest example of Streamline Moderne, and the lobby is graced by a delightful mural celebrating the miracle of radio.

### SEATTLE CENTER HISTORY

While the new Denny Regrade languished in the 1920s, a Civic Center of sorts began to take shape on its northern fringe.

The site of the present-day Seattle Center was dubbed "Potlatch Meadows" by early settlers in the mistaken belief that the natives held their tribal festivals on the land. More likely, they cleared the area in order to snare low-flying ducks as they commuted between Lake Union and Elliott Bay.

Seattle.
When the Klondike
was struck - 1896
(J. Andrews
Photo

David and Louisa Denny used to grow sweetbriar roses and pasture cattle on their land, variously dubbed "the swale" or "the prairie" and now the site of Seattle Center.

The area's first white residents, David and Louisa Denny, simply called it "the prairie," and little grew there other than Louisa's sweetbriar roses and forage for cattle, horses, and mules until 1928. That year, the city opened a new Civic Auditorium (now the Opera House), funded with a bequest from the estate of Pioneer Square saloonkeeper James Osborne. An ice arena and a 35,000-seat athletic field were added soon after. The army built a large armory (now the Center House) in 1939, and the Seattle public schools completed Memorial Stadium for high school football games in 1948.

When planning got under way in the late 1950s for the "Century 21 Exposition," as the Seattle World's Fair was known officially, the Civic Center offered a natural location for the event. Millions in public and private funds were raised under the leadership of Eddie Carlson, Joseph Gandy, and Ewen Dingwall to expand the site and build both temporary pavilions and permanent facilities.

Paul Thiry served as supervising architect for the Fair, and Lawrence Halprin directed the original landscaping. The old Civic Auditorium was remodeled and sheathed in brick to create the Opera House, and the playhouse was built in hopes of attracting a permanent drama company. The armory was drafted into K.P. duty as the "Food Circus." The state built the Coliseum (Key Arena) to house its "World of Tomorrow" exhibit, and the federal government financed construction of what is now the Pacific Science Center. Sweden's Alweg Systems subsidized a double-tracked Monorail line from the fair to Westlake Mall, while local investors underwrote erection of Seattle's new civic totem, the Space Needle. The Fair opened April 21, 1962, and closed 10 million visitors later on October 21.

It even turned a modest profit.

The World's Fair helped to transform Seattle from a rather provincial backwater into a genuinely cosmopolitan port

When they were completed for the 1962 Seattle World's Fair, the Space Needle and the Monorail became instant urban totems.

city, and it created a lasting legacy of important civic buildings for the arts, professional sports, and major community events such as the annual Bumbershoot arts festival over Labor Day weekend. It accomplished Bogue's vision in a way he would never have predicted — by giving Seattle a true "center" combining carnival rides and high culture.

## EXPLORING SEATTLE CENTER

The Center grounds offer a pleasant afternoon's stroll, and usually bustle at night with concerts, ballet or opera in the Opera House; plays at the Bagley

Wright Theater, Intiman Playhouse, and new Seattle Children's Theater; Supersonics basketball in the Key Arena, Totems hockey in the Mercer Arena; and programs at the Pacific Science Center and other facilities. The "Fun Forest" amusement area also attracts large crowds day and night during summer months. Paul Allen's "Music Experience Project," celebrating Seattle-born rock guitarist Jimi Hendrix and other local stars, should also prove to be a major draw upon completion of Frank Gehry's design just east of the Monorail terminal in 1998. Be warned that multiple events can quickly fill nearby parking lots and garages. If you're based downtown, avoid the crush by taking the Monorail from Westlake Center.

The major structures created for the 1962 World's Fair are described in the following paragraphs.

**The Space Needle.** The Fair's signature structure is now Seattle's unofficial symbol. It began as a doodle on a cocktail napkin drawn by Fair chairman Eddie Carlson while visiting Stuttgart's giant broadcast tower in 1959. Architect John Graham Jr., who had designed the world's first revolving restaurant for a Honolulu hotel, took charge of translating Carlson's fantasy into a real structure. Victor Steinbrueck came up with the graceful tripod, and John Ridley created the two-story "flying saucer" crown for the spinning restaurant and observation deck.

Fair organizers asked King County commissioners to fund the $4 million needed for construction, but they declined. It's probably just as well; given how the county-owned Kingdome turned out, Seattle might have ended up with a "Space Mushroom." A private consortium of investors rallied to back the project (which remains privately owned), and contractor Howard S. Wright's workers erected the 602-foot tower in an astonishing eight months. The structure is anchored to the earth by nearly 6,000 tons of concrete, laid in history's largest continuous pour in April 1961, and the tower incorporates more than 3,000 tons of steel. Deliberately designed to flex, the Needle's top-house can sway several feet in high winds, and it has withstood one major earthquake so far without damage.

**Monorail.** A pair of Fifties-Moderne trains covers the 1.3-mile distance between Seattle Center and Westlake Center in a little less than two minutes. Now operated by Seattle Center, the Monorail was privately financed for the Fair and designed by Sweden's Alweg Systems, and it is one of the world's few rapid transit systems that actually makes a profit.

**Pacific Science Center.** This elegant cathedral to science was designed by Minoru Yamasaki with NBBJ for the U.S. pavilion at the Fair. Now operated by a nonprofit foundation, the Center

houses an Imax theater, a "lasarium," and numerous exhibits and hands-on demonstrations for kids.

**Key Arena.** Paul Thiry's masterpiece started out as the Washington State Pavilion and was designed for conversion into a sports "coliseum" after the fair. The structure's innovative tentlike roof had one small flaw: it leaked, which resulted in the first and only NBA basketball game ever called on account of rain. The building was completely remodeled in 1993 to create the new Key Arena, but Thiry's original vision remained intact—even if his roof didn't.

**International Fountain.** Japanese designers Kazuyuki Matushita and Hideki Shimizu created this musical lawn sprinkler whose numerous jets are synchronized by computer with a sound system.

**Opera House.** Sir Thomas Beecham may have had the drafty, accoustically inert Civic Auditorium in mind when he warned Seattle in 1941 that the city

Minoru Yamasaki's graceful arches still soar above the courtyard of the Pacific Science Center, originally built for the World's Fair.

Paul Thiry's Coliseum was recently remodeled as "Key Arena" and given a new roof that, it is hoped, will not lead to future "rainouts" of Sonics basketball games.

was headed for the "cultural dustbin." The original structure survived Sir Thomas's brief tenure as conductor of the Seattle Symphony and was transformed by the firm of Chiarelli and Priteca into a modern Opera House for the Fair. It is now the permanent home for the Seattle Opera and the Pacific Northwest Ballet (whose new Phelps Center was recently completed next door). The symphony will move downtown and occupy the new Benaroya Symphony Hall in 1998.

**Intiman Playhouse.** The playhouse was occupied by the Seattle Repertory Theater from 1963 until 1982, when this group relocated to the Bagley Wright Theater farther west on the Center grounds. Intiman Theater later remodeled the Playhouse for its own, smaller productions.

Courtesy of the University of Washington Press, copyright 1992.

# 2

# East of Downtown

## FIRST HILL

### Orientation

City planners define First Hill as the area bounded by Pine Street on the north, Dearborn on the South, Fourteenth Avenue on the east, and Interstate 5 on the west. Most Seattle residents think of First Hill in more restricted terms, as the western slope of the ridge cresting along Boren Avenue between Jackson and Pike Streets. The area now embraces "Pill Hill," refering to the major hospitals and medical centers clustered near the intersection of Madison and Boren.

### History

First Hill was literally the first ridge encountered by Seattle's founders when they settled on the eastern shore of Elliott Bay in spring 1852. Rising steeply to a crest nearly 350 feet above the bay, the ridge was quickly logged to supply Henry Yesler's mill at the foot of Skid Road (Yesler Way), but settled more slowly.

Hostile natives descended First Hill to attack the village of Seattle on January 26, 1856, but they were repulsed by cannon fire from the USS *Decatur,* anchored in Elliott Bay. After peace was restored, a system of crude

Opposite: Depression-era economies allowed the architects of St. Joseph Church to produce a less costly but more daring design. *(Paul Dorpat)*

aqueducts (hollow logs elevated on stilts) was built to transport water from the top of Spring Street to the growing town below.

Although platted by Arthur Denny in the mid-1860s, the crest and eastern slope of First Hill remained little more than a scrubby clear-cut until 1883, when Colonel Granville Haller built "Castlemount," a luxurious estate on the block bounded by James, Cherry, Broadway, and Minor. Many of the town's most prominent "first families" followed his example, including the Carkeeks, Fryes, Dennys, and Burkes, and began building grand new homes to escape

Native warriors swooped down First Hill to attack the village of Seattle on January 26, 1856. (MOHAI)

By the 1890s, many of Seattle's "first families" had relocated to First Hill. *(A.Curtis, Museum of History and Industry)*

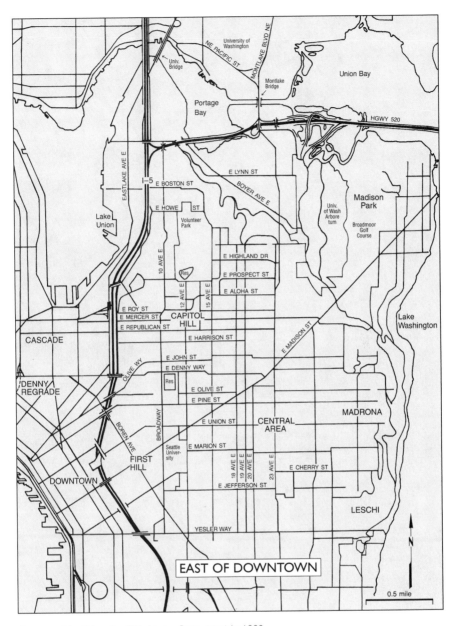

*Courtesy of the University of Washington Press, copyright 1992.*

the noise and smell of the business district. As such, First Hill ranks as Seattle's original residential suburb.

The southern extremity of First Hill was originally named Yesler Hill, but it earned the epithet "Profanity Hill" from loggers who had to scale its steep western grade on the way to fell trees. Lawyers maintained this tradition as they ascended James or Jefferson Street to file lawsuits at the old County Courthouse, located where Harborview now stands.

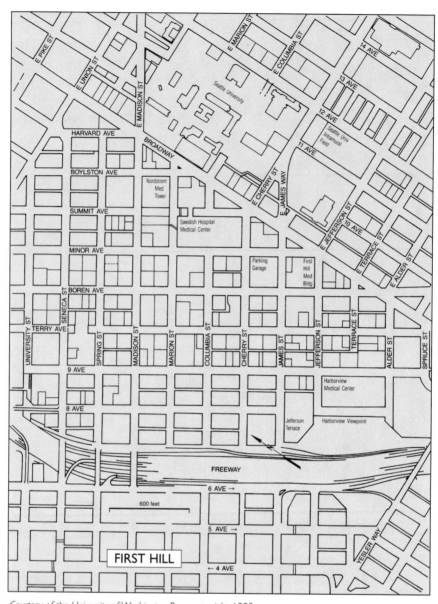

Thanks to regrades and streetcar lines, ordinary families began to invade First Hill's patrician precincts by the end of the nineteenth century. One newspaper lamented, "Society on First Hill had barely got started when up jumped the city." Some wealthy families fled to more remote compounds on Capitol Hill, the Lake Washington shore, the Highlands, and Broadmoor, but others stood their ground and helped to create a lively and economically diverse community housing poor immigrants, rich dowagers, and many in between.

Mrs. Emily Carkeek hosted costume parties and the first meetings of the Seattle Historical Society in her First Hill mansion. *(Museum of History and Industry)*

Apartments and hospitals soon took the place of many of the mansions and estates, and the construction of Interstate 5 in the mid-1960s severed the area from the business district below. This rift was partially healed by Freeway Park in 1974. The neighborhood was rediscovered in the 1980s by condo developers, and its resident hospitals have expanded manyfold. Despite this, First Hill retains a fine collection of stately mansions, apartment blocks, churches, and other historic structures.

## Points of Interest

We move up First Hill's western slope from the downtown. With the exception of Harborview Hospital, Trinity Episcopal Church, and Yesler Terrace, most of the following structures are clustered within a few blocks north or south of Madison. For a self-guided walking tour, park near the intersection of Madison and Boren and stroll the nearby blocks.

**Trinity Episcopal Church,** 609 Eighth. The original church suffered a catastrophic fire in 1901, a decade after construction. John Graham Sr. was retained to rebuild and expand the church on a traditional English model, and it has changed little since reopening in 1903.

**Harborview Hospital,** 325 Ninth. Although significantly expanded since the original tower's completion in 1931, Harborview still displays the powerful Moderne lines and masses established by Harlan Thomas with his son Donald and partner Clyde Grainger. Thomas was

Trinity Episcopal Church is dwarfed by downtown high-rises in this modern view.
(Paul Dorpat)

chair of the University of Washington's (UW) architectural school during this period, by the way. Harborview is owned by King County and managed by UW as a teaching hospital. Its emergency trauma and burn centers are regarded as national leaders.

**Yesler Terrace,** Eighth at Yesler. Although not recommended as a tourist destination, Seattle's first public housing project deserves mention as a significant architectural and social landmark. Its development was advocated by Jesse Epstein, a leading reformer in the 1930s and Seattle Housing Authority director in the 1940s, to replace decaying tene-

ments on the edge of Seattle's Japan Town. Design was coordinated by J. Lister Holmes and involved several leading architects. The efficient townhouses and terraced landscaping (designed by Butler Sturtevant) established a progressive paradigm upon completion in 1943, but later generations were compelled to rethink the wisdom of merely replacing old ghettos with new ones.

**Fourth Church of Christ Scientist,** Eighth and Seneca. Designed by George Foote Dunham and completed in 1922, this handsome terra-cotta sanctuary was recently purchased by Historic

Seattle for conversion into a concert hall for chamber music ensembles.

**St. James Cathedral,** Ninth Avenue at Marion Street. The design of First Hill's most prominent historic landmark is credited to Heins & LaFarge of New York, which dispatched W. Marbury Somervell and Joseph S. Cote to supervise construction and thereby established them in Seattle. Dedicated by Bishop O'Dea as the new center of Catholicism in the Northwest on December 22, 1907, the cathedral originally featured a large central dome in addition to its twin spires. Miraculously, no one was injured when this dome collapsed under the weight of a record snowfall shortly past 3:00 P.M. on February 2, 1916. The cathedral suffered some equally unfortunate remodeling in the 1950s, but much of its original

grandeur was recently restored (including a small cupola over a new central altar) by a team of Bumgardner Architects led by Don Brubeck.

**Frye Art Museum,** 704 Cherry. Originally designed by Paul Thiry and completed in 1952, this private art museum was established by the descendents of pioneers Charles and Emma Frye to exhibit their collection of European figurative and landscape paintings. The museum was recently remodeled and expanded. Thiry's design for his own 1946 office can be found nearby at 800 Columbia Street.

**Summit School,** 1415 Summit. James Stephen served as the Seattle School District's lead architect from 1899 until 1908, and this 1905 structure is one of his finest creations. It still func-

A sensitive remodel revived St. James Cathedral's former glory in 1996. *(Paul Dorpat)*

tions as a school, although with a curriculum its builders would be hard-pressed to understand.

**The Hotel Sorrento,** Madison at Terry. This elegant, Mediterranean-style hostelry was designed by Harlan Thomas. Unofficially dubbed the "Honeymoon Hotel," the Sorrento boasted the city's first rooftop restaurant, and its cheerful, wood-panelled lobby is a popular spot for brunch and receptions.

**The University Club,** northeast corner of Boren and Madison. Originally built as Martin Van Buren Stacy's second Seattle residence in 1889, this mansion has housed the University (Men's) Club since 1901. Its former garden was also the original home of the Seattle Tennis Club, which relocated to the west shore of Lake Washington in 1919.

**Historical Display, Swedish Medical Center,** southeast corner of Boren and Madison. A new wing of the Swedish Medical Center now occupies the former estate of pioneer contractor and stonemason Morgan Carkeek. The home was completed in 1885, and

Carkeek's wife, Emily, presided over Seattle society for many decades by sponsoring such diverse activities as costume balls and the founding of the Seattle Historical Society. The Carkeek mansion was demolished in 1939 for a gasoline "superstation," which in turn fell for expansion of the medical center. The history of the property and First Hill is retold by an attractive display in the new building's lobby.

**"Pill Hill."** A rich history of service and innovation led to First Hill's prominence in the medical arts, although few original structures survive to testify to its roots. The tradition began with Mother Joseph and Mother Praxedes, who established the Sisters of Providence's first Seattle hospital at Fifth and Jefferson. This later moved due north to Fifth and Madison, where the Federal Courthouse now stands, and then leapfrogged First Hill to relocate at Seventeenth and Cherry in 1911.

Meanwhile, Episcopalians founded the short-lived Grace Hospital at Summit and Union (where Summit School now

Harlan Thomas's elegant Hotel Sorrento has graced First Hill since 1908. *(Lawton Gowey)*

The former Stacey Mansion at Madison and Boren has long housed the University Club. *(Loomis Miller)*

stands) with the idea of challenging Catholics' virtual monopoly on health care. Dr. T. T. Minor, a popular physician and early mayor, also lived on First Hill until his death in 1889, and Minor Avenue honors his memory.

Dr. Nils Johanson tried to establish a hospital at Belmont and Olive but was rebuffed by neighbors in 1908. Two years later, Dr. E. M. Rininger built his 40-bed Summit Hospital at Summit and Olive. A month before the hospital was to open, Rininger's auto collided with an interurban streetcar and he died in Seattle's first fatal car wreck. Dr. Johanson and his Scandinavian-American backers quickly raised $91,000 to buy Summit and renamed it Swedish Hospital; they didn't even have to change the monograms on the linen.

Drs. James Tate Mason and John Blackford established one of the city's first group practices in 1917. They opened their new clinic and hospital three years later on Terry north of Madison and christened it "Virginia Mason" after Tate's daughter.

Another long-time First Hill institution, Cabrini Hospital, recently closed. It was established in 1915 by Mother Cabrini in the former Perry Hotel (demolished in 1996), then only six years old. The Fred Hutchinson Cancer Research Center was founded on First Hill in 1974, but it has since moved most of its work to a new campus near Lake Union. This leaves Swedish and Virginia Mason to rule the Pill Hill roost, while Harborview dominates old "Profanity Hill."

**Stimson-Green Mansion,** 1204 Minor. Spokane-based architect Kirtland Cutter designed this English half-timbered mansion for timber magnate C. D. Stimson in 1901. Its numerous rooms showcase a potpourri of styles ranging from Arts and Crafts to baronial Gothic to Moorish smoking den. When the Stimsons relocated to the Highlands, just north of Seattle, in 1914, banker Joshua Green moved his family in. Patsy Collins, C. D.'s granddaughter, now rents the home for special events through a nonprofit foundation. The nearby man-

The Stimson-Green Mansion is brand-new in this 1901 view. *(Patsy Collins)*

The recently rehabilitated Garrand Building was the original home of Seattle University and Immaculate Conception parish. *(Paul Dorpat)*

sion at 1117 Minor was designed by Henry Dozier and completed in 1907 for developer and "Tidelands King" Henry H. Dearborn.

**The Gainsborough,** 1017 Minor. The textured brickwork and terra-cotta ornamentation of this handsome apartment tower, erected in 1930, represent one of Earle W. Morrison's last Seattle commissions. Other examples of his work include 1223 Spring apartments, and the Olive Tower on the edge of downtown. Bertram D. Stuart designed the nearby Marlborough tower in 1926.

**Catholic Archbishop's Residence,** 1104 Spring Street. This audacious mansion was designed for W. D. Hofius by A. Walter Spalding in 1902. Its Gothic porch may have caught the eye of Bishop Edward John O'Dea, for the diocese bought the home for his residence in 1920 and it has served his successors ever since.

**Piedmont Apartments,** 1215 Seneca. This curious apartment-hotel block, with its Palladian windows and Baroque ornamentation, was designed by Daniel Huntington and Arch Torbitt and later housed the Salvation Army's **Evangeline Young Women's Home.**

**Sunset Club,** 1021 University. Joseph S. Cote made creative use of the Georgian Revival Style in creating this 1916 private clubhouse.

**Firehouse No. 25,** Harvard and Union. A Somervell and Cote collaboration, this large brick fire station was completed in 1908. In recent decades it has housed counterculture radio studios and professional offices.

**First Baptist Church,** Harvard at Spring. Completed in 1912, this Perpendicular Gothic Revival church was designed by Ulysses Grant Fay with Russell & Babcock.

**Seattle University,** Broadway and Madison. The modern campus serves some 10,000 students and marks a transitional zone between First Hill and the Central Area on the east. Seattle University grew out of the city's first Jesuit boys' school, established in 1891 by Fathers Victor Garrand and Adrian Sweere, S.J., at Sixth and Seneca. Development of the present campus began in 1894 with completion of the original Church and School of the Immaculate Conception, now named for Father Garrand, who designed it in collaboration with John Parkinson. The building was rehabilitated a century later by Duarte-Bryant architects.

The Neo-Gothic Administration Building, completed in 1941, was designed by John Maloney, who went on to create numerous Catholic churches and school buildings. Also of note, Seattle Unversity's newly remodeled Fine Arts Building on Madison Street incorporates one of the original powerhouses for the Madison Street Cable Railway. Seattle University's new St. Ignatius Chapel was designed by Steven Holl.

# CENTRAL AREA

## Orientation

This sprawling residential district is roughly bounded by Twelfth and Rainier Avenues on the west, Thirtieth Avenue on the east, Madison Street on the north, and I-90 on the south. It lacks a single business or cultural center but is organized around several crisscrossing major arterials, including Madison, Cherry, and Union Streets, Twenty-third East, and Martin Luther King Jr. Way.

The Central Area contains several pockets of high crime, which should make the visitor cautious, particularly after dark.

## History

For many Seattleites, the Central Area is virtually synonomous with Seattle's black community and, alas, with urban poverty. In both respects, this view is stereotypical and ignores the district's rich tapestry of racial, economic, and social diversity.

The ridge to the east of First Hill (cresting along Nineteenth Avenue East) was dubbed "Second Hill" or "Renton Hill," after Captain William Renton, who logged the area to supply his Port Blakely Mill Company. Residential development of the area did not begin until the late 1890s. The area was soon dominated by working-class families who migrated to Seattle to toil in its booming railroad, shipbuilding, fishing, and coal mining industries. In this respect, the area might be thought of as Seattle's first multiethnic, working-class neighborhood.

Seattle's black community also settled here — by choice at first, and then by necessity. William Grose (sometimes spelled "Gross") planted the seeds in 1890. Grose was a freeman and sailor who had settled in Seattle in 1860 and made his living as a cook. He was one of a dozen or so blacks in Seattle at the time; the first, Manuel Lopes, arrived in 1852 (some say 1858) and set up a barber shop in Pioneer Square.

Grose opened his own restaurant, Our House, near Yesler's Wharf in 1876, and he was popular with citizens of all races. Marine engineer Robert Moran credited Grose for lending him the capital he needed to found what became Seattle's largest shipyard. Grose saved enough money by 1882 to pay Henry Yesler $1,000 in gold for 12 acres near the intersection of East Madison and Martin Luther King Jr. Way, an area now dubbed "Madison Valley."

Following the Great Fire of 1889, Grose subdivided his "ranch" and sold lots to other relatively prosperous African-Americans. Meanwhile, poorer families and transient workers tended to locate along Jackson and Yesler, above Pioneer Square. By 1900 this area and Madison Valley had become the informal centers of

William Grose was Seattle's leading African-American businessman in the late 1800s.
*(Esther H. Mumford)*

Seattle's black community, which accounted for 400 residents out of the city's total of more than 80,000. The spiritual glue that linked them was provided by pioneering churches such as Mt. Zion Baptist and African Methodist Episcopal.

Although black workers encountered hostility from many early labor unions and were manipulated by unscrupulous employers, there was enough work, albeit largely unskilled, to attract nearly 2,500 new black residents by 1915. Many whites responded to this influx with formal covenants and cold shoulders that prevented blacks (along with Jews, Japanese, Chinese, and Filipinos) from buying or renting homes in newer neighborhoods such as Capitol Hill and the "suburbs" north of the Ship Canal.

Thus, when some 15,000 blacks migrated to Seattle to work in its shipyards and airplane factories during World War II, there was only one community open to them. This translated into a pattern of de facto residential and school segregation that persists to the present day. Reform came slowly: Seattle voters rejected an open housing law in 1964; the first black member of the city council, the late Sam Smith, was not elected until 1967; riots and racial violence wracked the Central Area during the late 1960s; and serious efforts to desegregate schools did not commence until the 1970s.

As of this writing (1997), blacks constitute only 10 percent of Seattle's population, yet the city is led by a black mayor, Norm Rice; King County government is headed by a black County Executive, Ron Sims; and Seattle schools are managed by a black Superintendent, John Stanford. That's more than tokenism, although there is much work to be done both within and beyond the Central Area to alleviate the legacy of decades of social and economic injustice.

The Central Area was also an early center for Seattle's Jewish community. The first synagogue, Ohaveth Sholum, was founded in 1889 at Eighth Avenue and Seneca on First Hill. The second, Bikur Holim, was established to the southeast at Thirteenth and Washington Street in 1891 and relocated to Seventeenth and Yesler in 1914. Seattle's largest synagogue, Temple De Hirsch, was established in 1899 and built a permanent home in 1907 at Fifteenth Avenue and Pike Street.

Though relatively small, Seattle's Jewish community provided the growing town with important leaders such as banker and street railway financier Jacob Furth, mayor Bailey Gatzert, educator Nathan Eckstein, and social reformer Jesse Epstein. Beginning in 1903, the city also attracted a large number of Sephardim, including the first members of the influential Alhadeff family, and it now boasts the fourth largest Sephardic community in the United States. Antisemitism bloomed rather late in Seattle and was largely dispelled by the 1960s, thus preventing a forced concentration of Jews into any single neighborhood.

## Points of Interest

The Central Area is still dotted with many Victorian-era homes testifying to its early settlement, but more modern and modest residences predominate. The following list focuses on major public and institutional structures found along major arterials.

**Temple De Hirsch,** 1511 East Pike. The original temple, built in 1907, was succeeded in 1960 by a new building designed by Detlie & Peck with B. Marcus Priteca. The earlier building was demolished in 1992, but several of its columns have been preserved in a garden setting.

**Langston Hughes Cultural Arts Center,** Seventeenth at Yesler Way. This Byzantine-inspired synagogue was designed by B. Marcus Priteca in 1912 as the second home for Seattle's first Jewish congregation, Bikur Holim. It was converted into a community center in the late 1970s.

**Church of the Immaculate Conception,** Eighteenth Avenue at East Marion. Designed by the Aberdeen, Washington, firm of Clark & McInnes with ample input from Father Adrian

Sweere, S.J., this grand sanctuary opened in 1904 as the new center of Seattle's first Jesuit parish (it was taken over by the diocese in 1929).

**Providence Medical Center,** Seventeenth at East Cherry. This is the third and largest Seattle hospital built by the Sisters of Providence. It was designed by Somervell & Cote and opened in 1911.

**Firehouse No. 23,** Eighteenth Avenue at East Columbia. Designed by the firm of Evertt & Baker in 1909, this handsome brick structure was adapted by Ted Bower in 1970 to house the Central Area Motivation Project and a community center.

**Horace Mann School,** Twenty-fourth at East Cherry. The former Walla Walla Elementary School was designed by Charles Saunders and George W.

The former Bikur Holim synagogue now houses the Langston Hughes Cultural Center. *(Paul Dorpat)*

The spire of Providence Hospital has towered over the Central Area since 1911. *(John Cooper)*

Lawton in 1901. Renamed in honor of the father of American public education, the Georgian Colonial Revival school was surplused in the 1970s but is still used for community programs.

**Douglass-Truth Branch Library,** Twenty-third at East Yesler. The former Henry Yesler Memorial Library was one of several library commissions designed by W. Marbury Somervell with a new partner, Harlan Thomas. The building opened in 1914 and blends Renaissance Revival with a touch of the Mediterranean and a dash of California style. Rededicated in 1975 to honor Frederick Douglass and Sojourner Truth, the library contains a special collection of African-American literature.

This small Carnegie Library at Twenty-Third Avenue and East Yesler now bears the names of Frederick Douglass and Sojourner Truth. *(Paul Dorpat)*

145

Lightning bolts add a dramatic touch to Fire Station No. 6. *(Paul Dorpat)*

**Firehouse No. 6,** Twenty-third at East Yesler. Architect B. Dudley Stuart adorned this 1931 cast concrete structure with a dramatic lightning-bolt grille.

**James Garfield High School,** Twenty-third at East Alder. Floyd A. Naramore served as chief architect for the Seattle Public School District from 1919 until 1931 and designed some two dozen elementary, secondary, and special education buildings. He preferred a Georgian style but also experimented with other approaches; Garfield represents his sole use of a Jacobean motif. Opened in 1923 and expanded in 1929, Garfield is also significant as Seattle's first "magnet school" in early efforts to promote voluntary desegregation.

**Martin Luther King Jr. Park,** 2200 Martin Luther King Jr. Way. This African-inspired monument was designed by Robert Kelly and dedicated in November 1991 on the 30th anniversary of the great civil rights leader's sole visit to Seattle.

## CAPITOL HILL

### Orientation

This diverse residential district occupies a crude triangle bounded by Interstate 5 on the west, Madison Street on the southeast, and Boyer Avenue on the northeast. Its primary north-south arterials are Broadway Avenue East and Fifteenth Avenue East.

## History

Much of Capitol Hill was first platted by Arthur Denny prior to 1861, but development was slow to follow. The city purchased 140 acres from John Colman in 1876, which were later divided between "City Park" and Lake View Cemetery, and new streetcar lines began to spur residential construction after 1891. The park was renamed Volunteer Park in 1901 to honor veterans of the Spanish-American War, and a large reservoir was built.

Construction of the Broadway High School followed in 1902, by which time the flamboyant James A. Moore (see Downtown Seattle) had begun developing the ridge running south from Volunteer Park to Howell Street. He planned an upscale neighborhood to succeed First Hill as the choice of Seattle's founding families and nouveau riche and dubbed it "Capitol Hill," after a similar area in Denver. (This has led to confusion with downtown's former Denny Hill, which Arthur Denny had briefly touted as "Capitol Hill" in hope of attracting the state capital to Seattle; see Downtown Seattle.)

The Olmsted brothers made Volunteer Park the jewel in the crown of their 1903 parks plan. Scrubby second-growth trees and bushes were uprooted and replaced by more elegant plantings, fountains, pools, broad promenades, and a recreational pavilion. The large brick-sheathed "standpipe" was erected in 1907, followed by construction of the miniature Crystal Palace botanical conservatory in 1912 and the first home of the Seattle Art Museum in 1932.

The stretch of Fourteenth Avenue directly south of Volunteer Park was nicknamed "Millionaires' Row," and it is still graced by scores of substantial homes, as is the Harvard-Belmont Historic District on Capitol Hill's northwest

James Moore developed "Millionaires' Row" immediately south of Volunteer Park. *(Webster & Stevens; Old Seattle Paper Works)*

## The Olmsted Legacy

John C. Olmsted and Frederick Law Olmsted Jr. were invited by the city of Seattle to design the young city's park system in 1902. The Olmsted Brothers had inherited the mantle of their father, Frederick Law Sr., as the leading apostles of the "City Beautiful" movement, which saw parks, boulevards, and other public amenities as instruments for elevating the spirtual as well as physical level of urban civilization amid the

Frink Park and Lake Washington Boulevard were completed in 1909 and remain part of the Olmsted brothers' enduring legacy in Seattle. *(Seattle Municipal Archives)*

chaos and squalor of the early industrial age.

The Olmsteds accepted the city's commission on condition that officials pledge to set aside 5 percent of the city's existing area, or about 2,000 acres, for parks and play fields. By this time Seattle already owned about 500 acres, including the large tracts that would become Volunteer and Woodland Parks, the Arboretum, and the Jefferson Golf Course. Visionary park superintendent E. O. Schwagerl had written the city's first park plan in 1894, and Mayor George Cotterill blazed more than 20 miles of trails to serve the city's 10,000 bicyclists—out of a population of 50,000.

John C. Olmsted arrived in Seattle in the winter of 1902–03 to survey the landscape and returned to Brookline, Massachusetts, to begin developing a plan with his stepbrother. This scheme was updated and expanded after a series of annexations tripled Seattle's land area in 1907. Even before this was complete in 1908, work had begun on key elements such as Lake Washington Boulevard, Green Lake, and Ravenna Park.

The Olmsteds were natural allies of Seattle's progressives and suggested colleague Virgil Bogue to write the city's first Comprehensive Plan. Although voters rejected this in 1912 (see Denny Regrade), they approved a $4 million bond issue to implement the Olmsteds' park plan.

The Olmsteds, particularly John, worked on Seattle park designs for another 30-plus years. They also laid out the grounds for the Alaska-Yukon-Pacific Exposition and future Quadrangle on the University of Washington campus, Fort Lawton, and Capitol Hill's Millionaire Row.

While financial constraints prevented full development of their park and boulevard plan, the legacy of Olmsteds' work in Seattle is regarded as the nation's most complete expression of their dreams for a "City Beautiful." The brothers would no doubt be pleased to know that Seattle now contains more than 5,000 acres of parks, equaling 9 percent of its total area, and nearly 23 miles of scenic boulevards.

slope. Architect-builders such as Frederick Anhalt also accommodated less affluent renters in gracious apartment buildings and courts, and convenient streetcar service to both the downtown and the University District attracted residents of all incomes and backgrounds.

The area thrived until the post–World War II exodus to the suburbs, and construction of I-5 severed it from Lake Union and the downtown in the early 1960s. The area rebounded in the 1970s as a new generation of "young urban professionals" rediscovered Capitol Hill's charm and convenience and began restoring its housing stock. It also became the neighborhood of choice for many members of Seattle's large gay and lesbian community, who help to fuel a lively street scene along Broadway and Fifteenth Avenue East.

## Points of Interest

Given the size of Capitol Hill, I have highlighted a few districts and points of interest. This is a great area to explore by car, bike, or on foot. We start with Lake View Cemetery and Volunteer Park and generally head south, visiting first the east side of Fifteenth Avenue and then the west.

**Lake View Cemetery,** 1554 Fifteenth Avenue East. For some of the honored pioneers buried here, Lake View was their fourth resting place, having been forced out of earlier graveyards by the city's relentless expansion. Chief Seattle's daughter "Princess" Angeline lies here, along with David "Doc" Maynard and his second wife; capitalists Henry Yesler and Dexter Horton; Washinton's first governor, Elisha P. Ferry; most of the early Denny and Boren clans; and Civil War veterans of the Grand Army of the Republic.

**Volunteer Park,** between East Prospect and East Galer Streets and Federal Avenue East and Fifteenth Avenue East. You may enter Volunteer Park via Galer on the northeast corner, or Prospect on the south side. This park was originally purchased in 1876 but left wild until construction of the reservoir in 1901. Edward Otto Schwagerl, a pioneering landscape architect who also served as superintendent of parks,

Chief Seattle's daughter Angeline now resides in Lake View Cemetery, not far from the graves of the Denny family and other white settlers who displaced her people. *(Paul Dorpat)*

laid out plans for the area, but his designs were superseded in 1903 by those of the Olmsted brothers. The park's name honors veterans of the Spanish-American War, a colonial adventure that had a major impact on Seattle's economy and forged early and enduring links to the Philippines.

The Olmsteds' plan for a more formal system of garden paths and recreational areas was largely complete when the reservoir's standpipe tower opened in 1907 and offered hardy stair climbers a sweeping view of the city (and now an Olmsted exhibit). A botanical conservatory was added on the park's north end in 1912, and a memorial (sculpted by H. A. McNeil) was erected near the reservoir to honor Judge Thomas Burke, who died in 1925.

John Olmsted tolerated these intrusions on his design, but he strenuously

Carl Gould's stunning design for the original Seattle Art Museum in Volunteer Park now houses an extensive collection of Asian art. *(Old Seattle Paper Works)*

"Wireless" stock dealer George Parker got to live in his magnificent Capitol Hill mansion for only a year before being sent to federal prison in 1910. *(Paul Dorpat)*

opposed the city's decision to allow Dr. Richard Fuller to locate his Art Institute of Seattle (later Seattle Art Museum) on the grounds. Olmsted was ignored, which virtually ended his work in Seattle. Carl Gould designed a spare but striking Moderne gallery (the Depression scotched plans for a more elaborate building), which opened in 1933. The building was rededicated in 1994, as the Seattle Asian Art Museum, to display an extensive collection of Orientalia begun by Dr. Fuller and his mother.

**Millionaires' Row.** The blocks immediately south of Volunteer Park were developed by James Moore to house Seattle's latest generation of entrepreneurs. During the early 1900s they built grand monuments to their new wealth, and none was grander than the Neo-Classical Revival mansion that Frederick Sexton designed for George H. Parker at **1409 East Prospect,** just outside the southern entrance to Volunteer Park. Parker earned his millions unknowingly peddling what proved to be worthless stock in a company that claimed to represent "wireless" inventor Guglielmo Marconi in the United States. The fraud was exposed in 1910, just a year after Parker moved into his new home. He relocated involuntarily to the federal prison on McNeil Island, but was later pardoned. A few decades later the "Parker Mansion" was occupied by an exiled Russian count who led a pseudo-scientific cult, the Light Bearers, and offered believers spiritual communication with the cosmos. Most recently, it was owned by a former television anchorwoman—thus maintaining its "wireless" connection.

**Stevens Neighborhood.** This well-preserved residential area stretches east of Volunteer Park from Fifteenth Avenue East to Twenty-third Avenue. Its pleasantly eclectic mix of architectural styles showcases Tudor Revivals, Queen Annes, bungalows, classic boxes, and English cottages built early in the 1900s

for Seattle's emerging middle class. The neighborhood is anchored by Isaac Stevens Elementary School (named for the Territory's first governor), 1242 Eighteenth Avenue East, a frame Colonial Revival structure designed by James Stephen. Opened in 1906, the school is a designated landmark and is currently undergoing renovation.

**St. Joseph's Catholic Church,** 732 Eighteenth Avenue East. The present home of Seattle's second (and sole surviving) Jesuit parish turned out far differently in 1930 than originally planned. Thanks to the Depression, Jesuits abandoned plans for a traditional but more expensive Gothic design and let A. H. Albertson, Joseph Wilson, and Paul Richardson experiment with structural concrete for a daringly modern and unadorned expression of early Romanesque masses and motifs.

**Academy of the Holy Names,** 728 Twenty-first Avenue East. Evicted from north Beacon Hill by the city's massive regrade, the Sisters of the Holy Names relocated their academy for young girls to this imposing Beaux-Arts edifice in 1908. It was designed by the team of C. Alfred Breitung and Theobald Buchinger, who created several important Catholic buildings early in the century.

**St. Mark's Episcopal Cathedral,** 1245 Tenth Avenue East. Shifting to the west side of Volunteer Park, we find another artifact of the economies imposed by the Depression on Seattle's church builders. St. Mark's impressive Neo-Byzantine bulk was designed by the San Francisco firm of Bakewell and Brown and left bare out of financial necessity. Édouard F. Champney (see University of Washington in Northeast Seattle) served as supervising architect, but he died a year before the cathedral opened in 1930.

**Harvard-Belmont Historic District.** St. Mark's stands just beyond the northern limit of Seattle's only residential his-

Samuel Hill's mansion (Hornblower & Marshall, 1909) stands on East Highland Drive, near St. Mark's Episcopal Cathedral. *(Paul Dorpat)*

toric district. Named for its two primary streets, Harvard and Belmont, the district is bounded by East Roy on the south, St. Mark's on the north, Broadway East on the east, and I-5 on the west. It contains scores of handsome homes dating from the early nineteenth century and reflecting a variegated but harmonious tapestry of architectural styles. While the district's homes were originally built for wealthy families such as that of railroad magnate Horace C. Henry, they now serve a more economically diverse population. The area's tree-lined streets offer a delightful afternoon's stroll.

The district's southeast edge is anchored by Arthur Loveless's charming **Studio Building,** at 711 Broadway East. Completed in 1933, the building's brickwork, larger dormers, and delightful courtyard mimic the architecture of England's Cotswold villages. It faces the former home of the **Women's Century Club,** designed by Pierce A. Horrocks in 1925. The Club now houses one of Seattle's first independent movie theaters, the Harvard Exit. The Studio Building shares its block on Roy with a miniature version of George Washington's Mount Vernon home, designed for the **Rainier Chapter of**

**the Daughters of the American Revolution** by Daniel Huntington in 1925 and now rented for receptions and private parties.

The next block to the west is filled by the home of the **Cornish School (now College) for the Allied Arts,** founded by Nellie Cornish in 1914. The present Mediterranean-influenced building was designed by A. H. Albertson with Paul Richardson and Gerald C. Field and opened in 1921. Over the years, the Cornish faculty has included dancer Martha Graham, painter Mark Tobey, and musical renegade John Cage.

**The Apartment Buildings of Frederick W. Anhalt.** Capitol Hill is dotted with charming apartment courts created by self-taught architect and contractor Frederick William Anhalt during the 1920s and 1930s. Inspired by the village architecture of England and Normandy, Anhalt built cozy apartments within miniature châteaus and manor houses, complete with turrets, leaded-glass windows, individual fireplaces and chimneys, elaborate masonry and terra-cotta flourishes, and landscaped courtyards. Several of his creations may be found in or near the Harvard-

Belmont Historic District at 710 Belmont Place, 730 and 750 Belmont Avenue East, and 1005 and 1014 East Roy Street.

**Broadway East.** This bustling thoroughfare was widened in 1931 to accommodate the traffic generated by its surrounding neighborhood and streetcar commuters. Many of the avenue's original storefronts survive, and a recent spate of construction has added several new "urban markets." Broadway's sidewalks are usually jammed with a parade of humanity of all sizes, shapes, colors, incomes, genders, and orientations.

Nellie Cornish (top) moved her "School of the Allied Arts" to Capitol Hill in 1914. *(Cornish)*

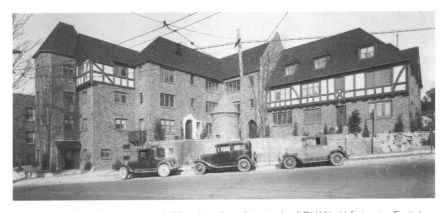

Frederick Anhalt's quaint apartment buildings have brought a touch of Old World fantasy to Capitol Hill since 1920.

Only the central hall of the former Broadway High School survives today and is used for a performance hall.

**Broadway Performance Hall,** Broadway at Pine. This imposing stone hall is all that survives of the original Broadway High School (later Edison Technical School), completed in 1903 and designed by William E. Boone with James M. Corner. The school's original north and south wings were demolished for the new Seattle Central Community College campus, but the central structure was preserved and adapted for use as an auditorium. Its neighbors include several handsome fraternal halls dating from the early 1900s, one of which now serves as the Egyptian Theater.

**Plymouth Congregational Columns,** Pine Street above I-5. These four columns were salvaged from the original 1912 Plymouth Congregational Church, designed by John Graham Sr. They were relocated to the present site when the new church was built in the early 1960s.

# CENTRAL LAKE SHORE FROM LESCHI TO MONTLAKE

## Orientation

The slopes above Lake Washington from the foot of Yesler Way to the Montlake Bridge contain several of Seattle's most charming and best preserved neighborhoods. These include Leschi, Madrona, Denny Blaine, Madison Park, and Montlake. From downtown Seattle, head due east on Yesler to Thirty-first Avenue and wind down through Frink Park to Lake Washington Boulevard. Then turn north (left) along the shoreline and through the Arboretum to Montlake. As an alternative route from downtown, follow Madison Street to Madison Park, where McGilvra Boulevard East links to Lake Washington Boulevard.

## History

When the first whites arrived in Seattle, Lake Washington's western slopes and beaches were already home to Nisqually Indians, led by Chief Leschi. He refused to sign the 1855 Point Elliott Treaty, which confined most of Puget Sound's tribes to inadequate reservations, and led the native rebellion of January 1856. Despite strong protests from many whites, including Bing Crosby's great-grandfather, Leschi was hanged on February 19, 1858, on trumped-up murder charges stemming from an unrelated ambush.

The hills above the lake shore were extensively logged to feed Henry Yesler's mill, and a few hardy homesteaders established farms, but there was little development before 1888. On September 27 of that year, J. M. Thompson completed his Lake Washington Cable Railway, with cars running east on Yesler Way from Pioneer Square to the lake and returning on Jackson Street.

The real goal of Thompson and his backers (including Henry Yesler) was to attract home buyers. To this end, they established an amusement park and small menagerie at Leschi, where small cross-lake steamers offered transportation to the virtual wilderness on the eastern shore and Mercer Island, then called "East Seattle." Thompson repeated this formula with the Madison Street Cable Railway in 1889, which terminated at Madison Park, another amusement area, built by developer and judge John J. McGilvra. Seattle's first professional baseball team played its inaugural game at Madison Park in 1890, and ferries offered transportation for fans from Kirkland across the lake.

The next major phase of development followed construction of Lake Washington Boulevard in 1909. The route was designed by the famed Olmsted brothers, John and Frederick Law Jr., as part of Seattle's first comprehensive parks plan (see "The Olmsted Legacy" on page 148). Completion

The Lake Washington Cable Railway began operating from Pioneer Square to Leschi Park in 1888.
(Lawton Gowey)

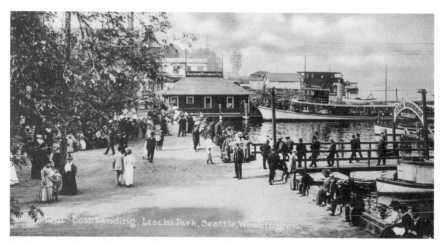

Pavilions, cross-lake ferries, and a small zoo once attracted cable car riders to Leschi Park and spurred the area's development in the 1890s. *(Oregon Historical Society)*

of the Lake Washington Ship Canal in 1917 lowered the lake by nine feet and allowed the addition of bathing beaches and facilities between the boulevard and the shoreline. These improvements spurred residential expansion and creation of new neighborhoods such as Madrona on the slope between Leschi and Madison Park.

To the north, Montlake was first slated for development by Thomas Mercer, who named "Union Bay" and "Lake Union" in 1854 in farsighted anticipation of a canal linking Lake Washington with Salmon Bay. This would wait 63 years, but a shallow ditch was dug by Judge Thomas Burke in 1885 to allow passage for logs between Union Bay and Portage Bay. The University of Washington campus relocated to the north side of Portage Bay a decade later and hosted the 1909 Alaska-Yukon-Pacific Exposition. That same year, developers Corner and Hagen dubbed their new subdivision "Montlake," and the opening of Montlake Bridge in 1925 secured the neighborhood's popularity with professors and professionals.

The development of Broadmoor Country Club in 1923–1927 created one of the city's first "gated communities," laid out by Vernon Macan between Madison Street and the marshy southern shore of Union Bay. The University of Washington Arboretum was landscaped in the early 1930s largely with labor of Civilian Conservation Corps workers and funds from the Works Progress Administration. The Museum of History and Industry opened near the Arboretum's northern portal in 1950, and the Seattle Parks Department later established the Foster Island nature trail.

The government played a less positive role in the 1960s and 1970s when highway planners aimed the Evergreen Point (Albert D. Rosellini) Floating Bridge at the heart of Montlake and proposed to route the R. H. Thomson Expressway through the Arboretum and Central Area. Environmental activists such as Margaret Tunks and Roger Leed and Montlake resident Maynard

Arsove failed to sink the bridge plan, but they succeeded in erasing R. H. Thomson from the books (while greatly reducing plans for I-90's expansion; see Southeast Seattle section).

## Points of Interest

The following is a motor tour that begins at Frink Park above Leschi and follows Lake Washington Boulevard north to Madison Park, heads southwest along Madison, and then traverses the Arboretum to Montlake. Feel free to veer inland to cruise the area's pleasant neighborhood streets, but be prepared to get lost among numerous dead ends.

**Frink Park.** The road that winds through this wooded ravine from Thirty-first to Leschi leads under a low bridge which is one of the few surviving artifacts from the Lake Washington Cable Railway. The park is one of several strung by the Olmsteds like pearls along the Boulevard from Seward Park to the Arboretum.

**Leschi Park.** The menagerie, pavilions, and ferry terminal are long gone, but restaurants and marinas still provide a pleasant diversion at the foot of Yesler Way.

**Madrona Park.** The bathhouse was built in 1919 and remodeled in 1970 to house the Madrona Dance Studio.

**Denny Blaine Park.** This little lakeshore park is framed by residences ranging from humble cottages to imposing mansions. Several were designed by Ellsworth P. Storey between 1903 and the mid-1920s, including the chaletlike "Storey Houses" at 260 Dorffel Drive East.

**McGilvra Boulevard East and Thirty-ninth Avenue East.** At this point, we take a right off Lake

Some of Ellsworth Storey's finest residential designs can be found near Denny-Blaine Park. *(Paul Dorpat)*

Vaudeville impresario Alexander Pantages' grand mansion still stands near Madison Park. *(Paul Dorpat)*

Washington Boulevard, which veers inland toward the Arboretum. Head north on Thirty-ninth Avenue/McGilvra Boulevard East to Madison, and turn right toward the lake.

**Madison Park.** The bathing beach lies adjacent to a cozy little business district, which was served by streetcars until 1940. Pioneer Hall, just south of the park, was built by Judge McGilvra and donated to Seattle in 1910. A walk north along Forty-third Avenue East will lead you past the charming Lake Court Apartments, designed in 1936 by Paul Thiry.

**Madison Street.** Ascending Madison will take you through the Washington Park neighborhood. A typical Colonial Revival mansion, the Samuel Hyde House was designed by Bebb and Mendel and built in 1908 near the corner of Thirty-seventh East. The Walker-Ames House, at 808 Thirty-sixth East, a Bebb and Gould design from slightly later, and it now serves as the official residence for the president of the University of Washington. The great vaudeville impresario Alexander Pantages once lived at 1117 Thirty-sixth East in an eclectic California Mission Revival mansion designed by Clayton Wilson and Arthur Loveless. The gated

neighborhood of Broadmoor lies across Madison, but access is limited to residents and authorized guests.

**The Arboretum.** A right turn at the intersection of Madison and Lake Washington Boulevard takes you into the Arboretum. This 62-acre tract was originally deeded to the City of Seattle by the Puget Mill Co. in 1900 and named Washington Park. The Olmsted plan replaced an existing bicycle path with the Boulevard in 1909, and wealthy neighbors raced horses on the grassy mall now dubbed Azalea Way.

The park remained largely undeveloped until the early 1930s, when the University of Washington leased it from the city for establishment of a formal arboretum. Two notable amenities lie just inside the park's Madison Street entrance: the Japanese Garden and a stone caretaker's cottage designed by Arthur Loveless and Lester Fey in 1927.

At the opposite end of the park, note the abandoned freeway ramps curving off of Highway 520. These modern temples to the automobile date from 1962 and were intended to link the Evergreen Point Floating Bridge with the R. H. Thomson Expressway. They give a hint of the environmental

The Washington Park Arboretum contains a Japanese Tea Garden near its Madison Street entrance. *(Frank Shaw)*

The Montlake Bridge is seen here from the east soon after completion in 1925. *(Old Seattle Paper Works)*

damage this project would have caused had voters not canceled it in 1970.

**Museum of History and Industry,** 2700 Twenty-fourth Avenue East. "MOHAI" lies a few blocks northwest of the northern entrance of the Arboretum, and is enisled between the traffic of Highway 520 and the Montlake Cut. Housed in a handsome Miesian structure designed by Paul Thiry in 1950, MOHAI contains a variety of exhibits and artifacts representing the region's history. Nature lovers will also enjoy a stroll on the trail leading from the museum through the Foster Island wetland.

**Seattle Yacht Club,** 1807 East Hamlin. A left turn on East Hamlin off Montlake East will bring you to this Colonial Revival structure. Designed in 1919 by John Graham Sr., it has been modified and expanded several times, but its original mock lighthouse survives.

**The Montlake Bridge.** Blaine & Associates did the heavy lifting for this bascule bridge, which opened for the first time in 1925, but Carl Gould supplied the Neo-Gothic control towers to echo his plan for the University of Washington on the north side of the Montlake Cut.

# 3

# North of Downtown

## CASCADE, SOUTH LAKE UNION, AND EASTLAKE

### Orientation

The Cascade neighborhood is a large mixed-use area extending north of Denny Way to the southern shore of Lake Union, and it contains several significant structures as well as Seattle's chief maritime historical centers. Eastlake Avenue leads to the University District and borders the city's largest houseboat colonies. Westlake passes through a more industrialized area on the way to Fremont.

### History

Lake Union was named by Thomas Mercer in 1854 in expectation that a canal would ultimately link it with Lake Washington, Salmon Bay, and Puget Sound. Sixty-three years would pass before his vision became reality.

The area between Denny Way and the south shore of Lake Union was platted in the 1860s by David Denny, who was the first of many planners to envision intensive development of the district. Although Denny built a successful lumber mill on the lake, most of his dreams were unrealized. Meanwhile, shipbuilders and other maritime businesses rose along the shore

Opposite: James Stephen's monumental Queen Anne High School now houses condominiums. (Paul Dorpat)

This crude log canal at Montlake marked the first attempt to link Lake Washington with the waters to the west. *(University of Washington Library Special Collections. Neg. UW4290)*

and a comfortable working-class neighborhood gradually took form, which was dubbed "Cascade" despite the fact that nearby Capitol Hill obstructed any view of that mountain range.

In 1890, L. H. Griffith won a "build-off" with competing streetcar companies by completing a line of track that traversed the district diagonally from Fourth and Pike to the west shore of Lake Union in just five days. This route established Westlake Avenue and later crossed the the murky stream draining Lake Union at Fremont to serve north-end communities such as Ballard. A year later, David Denny's Rainier Power and Railway Company built a line along Eastlake that also crossed the future Ship Canal at Latona, superseding

Nothing ever came of Virgil Bogue's 1911 proposal for a "Grand Central Station" at the south end of Lake Union, but this hasn't prevented planners from dreaming up new futures for the Cascade neighborhood.

Eddie Hubbard *(left)* and William E. Boeing have just landed on Lake Union with the very first bag of international U.S. Air Mail ever delivered. *(Boeing)*

a private ferry, to serve the University District. His grand development plans were dashed by the Panic of 1893, which bankrupted his company.

The Cascade area was targeted for dramatic renewal by Virgil Bogue's 1911 "Plan of Seattle." He proposed a Grand Central Station and large ferry terminal for the south end of the lake, along with a major apartment district, but voters rejected the scheme. Thanks to such "benign neglect," the Cascade area attracted large numbers of immigrants from Scandinavia, Greece, and the Balkans. Poorer families moored ramshackle houseboats along Westlake and Eastlake amid shipyards, mills, and canneries.

History was made on—and over—Lake Union in 1916 when lumber magnate William E. Boeing established the Aero Club in a converted boat house at the foot of Roanoke Street. He and his partner, Navy Lieutenant Conrad Westervelt, built their first aircraft here, a spindly floatplane christened "the B & W," which lifted off from Lake Union for the first time in June 1916 with Herb Munter at the controls. (This plane and a twin were later sold to New Zealand and were the first aircraft to operate among its islands.)

A month later Boeing incorporated the Pacific Aero Products Company, which would later bear his name (see Georgetown in Southwest Seattle). On March 3, 1919, Boeing and copilot Eddie Hubbard landed on Lake Union in a CL-4S floatplane bearing 60 letters from Vancouver, British Columbia, and completed history's very first international airmail delivery. By then, Boeing had shifted his production to the "Red Barn" on the Duwamish River, but Lake Union remains a busy floatplane terminal to this day.

This spectacular aerial view shows the downtown, Lake Union, and north Seattle as they appeared in the mid-1920s.

The opening of the Ship Canal and Chittenden Locks in 1917 had enhanced Lake Union's industrial potential, and planners' dreams for lakeshore parks and neighborhoods were shelved. New factories, auto dealerships, and similar businesses intruded on Cascade's residential areas. Completion of I-5 turned Mercer Street into a major access road and effectively cut off the south shore of Lake Union from the city. It also blockaded Eastlake from Capitol Hill.

Over the years many of Westlake's houseboats were displaced by industrial and maritime uses, but the colonies on the east shore and Portage Bay survived despite official disapproval and landlubbers' disdain. The chief appeal of "floating homes" was their low cost, but some residents also valued the bohemian life-style they represented. Thus was set the stage for some sharp conflicts with city planners and private developers in the late 1960s and 1970s. Former Communist Party member and journalist Terry Pettus led the successful campaign to secure protection for floating homes, but were he alive today he would probably wince at the recent Yuppification of some of the city's once humble houseboat colonies.

In the past decade the Cascade area has attracted new development, including the campus of the Fred Hutchinson Cancer Research Center. The district remains an irresistible tabula rasa in the eyes of some urban visionar-

164

ies who can't seem to see the existing neighborhood. A major citizen effort, sparked by *Seattle Times* columnist John Hinterberger, proposed razing much of the area to create a vast "Seattle Commons" park, flanked by upscale condominiums and high-tech business centers. Reprising their skepticism toward the Bogue plan, voters rejected this scheme twice in 1996, and the homes and businesses of Cascade will likely be left in peace for another decade or two.

## POINTS OF INTEREST

**Denny Park,** Dexter Avenue and Denny Way. Although it was the third tract of parkland donated to the city, this gift of Arthur Denny became the first dedicated city park in 1884. The modernistic administration center of the Seattle Department of Parks was built in 1948 and designed by the team of Young, Richardson, Carleton and Detlie.

**Norway Hall,** Boren Street and Denny Way. This fanciful center for the Norwegian community was designed by a native son, Sonke Englehart Sonnichsen, and opened in 1915.

**The Seattle Times,** Fairview Avenue North at John. Robert C. Reamer designed this restrained Art Deco edifice for the *Seattle Times* when it moved from Times Square in 1930.

**Center for Wooden Boats and NW Seaport.** Two major maritime historical centers are based adjacent to the Naval Reserve pier at the foot of Terry Avenue North. The Center for Wooden Boats was founded to preserve both wooden vessels and the art of their construction. The older NW Seaport works to save and restore significant ships, including the three-masted coastal schooner *Wawona,* launched in 1897 and the first

The Center for Wooden Boats and Northwest Seaport moorage for the schooner *Wawona* share the south end of Lake Union. *(Paul Dorpat)*

vessel to be designated a National Landmark, the lightship *Relief* (1904), and early tugboat *Arthur Foss* (1889).

A third institution, the Puget Sound Maritime Museum, hopes to establish permanent exhibits in the Naval Reserve Center in the near future. Several major restaurants and retailers have recently occupied the nearby piers and lakefront along Fairview

St. Spiridon's Russian Orthodox Cathedral has been a Cascade neighborhood landmark since 1938. *(Paul Dorpat)*

A biotechnology laboratory now occupies the former Lake Union Steam Plant. *(Paul Dorpat)*

North. The *Virginia V,* launched in 1922 and the last Mosquito Fleet steamer still operating on Puget Sound, often calls at this complex.

**Immanuel Lutheran Church,** Yale Avenue North at Thomas. The early religious center for Cascade's large Scandinavian population was designed by Watson Vernon and completed in 1912.

**St. Spiridon Russian Orthodox Cathedral,** Yale Avenue North at Harrison. Considering its golden onion domes and lofty nave, we might dub this 1938 design by Ivan Pavlov "St. Basil's of Seattle."

**City Light Steam Plant (now Zymogenetics),** Eastlake East at Fairview East. Daniel Huntington designed this handsome generator building in 1911. Water piped down Capitol Hill from Volunteer Park powered its first turbines, followed by steam boilers. The building was adapted by a biotechnology company in the early 1990s, which replaced its six decaying smokestacks with smaller facsimiles.

**Fairview Avenue East Houseboats.** Seattle's largest houseboat colony hugs the eastern shore of Lake Union along Fairview Avenue East

Floating homes have shared Lake Union with float planes since 1916, when the first Boeing-built aircraft took off from its waters. *(Paul Dorpat)*

from Terry Pettus Park at East Newton Street to East Roanoke, where, alas, nothing remains of William Boeing's original Aero Club hangar.

# QUEEN ANNE HILL AND MAGNOLIA

## Orientation

Seattle's tallest hill lies immediately northwest of downtown, and its summit can be reached via a steep ascent up Queen Anne Avenue North from Mercer Street. Magnolia's hill lies farther northwest, beyond the "Interbay" gulch between Smith Cove and Salmon Bay. From downtown, Magnolia is best accessed via Fifteenth Avenue West and the Magnolia Bridge at West Garfield Street. To visit Fishermen's Terminal on Salmon Bay or Discovery Park on Magnolia's northwest tip, take the West Emerson ramp off Fifteenth West and follow the signs.

## History

Towering 456 feet above Elliott Bay's average high tide, Queen Anne is the tallest of Seattle's original "Seven Hills." The others are neighboring Magnolia, First Hill, Capitol Hill, Beacon Hill, West Seattle's central ridge, and the late, lamented Denny Hill, long since sluiced into the bay (some also count the Central Area's Second, or Renton, Hill, but that makes eight and spoils the Roman allusion).

On January 24, 1853, David Denny filed a claim on land including the southeastern slope of Queen Anne Hill and Lake Union. He and Louisa Boren, who had trekked at his side along the Oregon Trail from Cherry Grove, Illinois, were married that same day by Justice of the Peace Doc Maynard. Dr. Henry Smith, John Ross, Edmund Carr, and Thomas Mercer arrived that summer and filed claims for the rest of the Hill and its adjacent Smith Cove and Salmon Bay shorelines. George Kinnear later bought a large parcel on the Hill's western slope.

Actual development of these properties proceeded slowly until the 1880s, when the first transcontinental rail service (via Tacoma) spurred a dramatic rise in Seattle's population and wealth. The Hill's San Francisco-like setting and sweeping views were a natural magnet for the city's nouveau riche, and the area took its name from the numerous new homes built in the then-popular Queen Anne style.

The Hill's main north-south thoroughfare was dubbed "Temperance Street" after the abstemious politics of its middle-class residents. Getting up its slope remained a daunting challenge for man and beast, sober or otherwise, until 1890 when the Front Street Cable Railway established a line from downtown to the crest. A decade later, the cable cars were replaced with electric streetcars, but they still required a boost in ascending renamed Queen Anne Avenue's steep southern grade.

The solution was a pair of weighted counterbalance cars running in tunnels beneath the tracks. An ascending streetcar hooked itself to a cable linked to a counterbalance poised at the top of the hill and then used its descending mass to help haul it up the hill. Similarly, a descending streetcar pulled the underground counterbalance back up to the crest. This system operated until 1940, when Seattle's transit system converted to electric and diesel buses, and many old-timers still refer to Queen Anne Avenue's south approach as "the Counterbalance."

John Olmsted was very taken with Queen Anne Hill's scenic potentials, but existing development did not allow the broad boulevards he favored. In 1910, the Parks Board approved a less ambitious route ringing the crown of the hill, but few improvements were actually made beyond street tree plantings along Bigelow Avenue North and W. R. B. Wilcox's spectacular retaining walls on Seventh and Eighth Avenues. Completion of Highway 99 (Aurora

Streetcars prepare to tackle Queen Anne Avenue's steep grade. The ascent and descent were assisted by weighted cars running in tunnels beneath the tracks, which gave the street its informal name, "The Counterbalance." (*Lawton Gowey*)

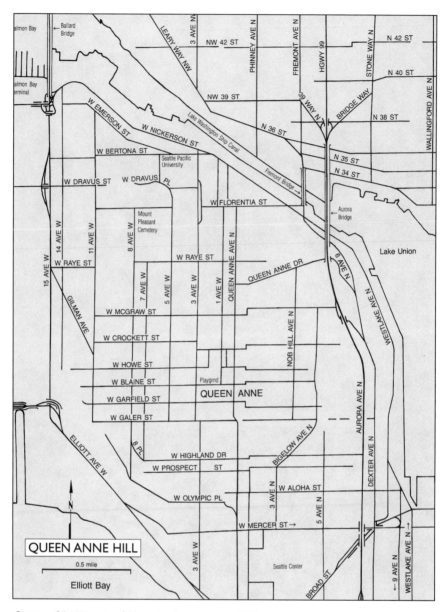

*Courtesy of the University of Washington Press, copyright 1992.*

Avenue North) created panoramic vistas for motorists driving along the Hill's lower-eastern flank, but these views are fast disappearing behind a wall of condominiums and apartment buildings.

Development of Magnolia lagged behind Queen Anne by several decades, although both mounds were annexed to Seattle in 1891. The first spurt followed completion of the Great Northern Railway in 1893, which entered Seattle from the north and originally terminated at Smith Cove, where J. J. Hill built giant piers to service his transpacific steamships. The Port

The Olmsted brothers designed the original grounds for Fort Lawton on Magnolia.

of Seattle later took over this location to develop the longest pier on the West Coast, which the Navy commandeered during World War II.

In 1895, the City of Seattle ceded a military reservation covering much of Magnolia's northwest quadrant to the Department of War, which named it Camp Lewis. As America prepared to enter World War I, the Olmsteds laid out plans for present-day Fort Lawton. The base was used to house Axis prisoners of war during World War II and was slated as a nest for antiballistic missiles during the Cold War. In 1970, the Pentagon surplused most of the fort and returned the land to the City of Seattle for "pacification" as Discovery Park. Salish tribes pressed a treaty claim on the area with lawsuits and angry demonstrations (Jane Fonda was there), but this was settled in 1977 with establishment of the tribal-managed Daybreak Star Arts Center in the park.

The southern and western fringes of Magnolia Bluff are lined with many imposing homes dating from the 1920s and 1930s, and the rest of the hill is given over to pleasant middle-class neighborhoods.

## Points of Interest on Queen Anne Hill

Queen Anne's tree-lined streets offer a pleasant drive and many stunning vistas of the city. It's easy to get lost, but if you travel in any direction long enough, you'll run out of hill and regain your bearings. From downtown, just head north up First Avenue past Seattle Center to Roy Street, jog left (west), and turn right on Queen Anne Avenue North, which bisects the hill from north to south. Note that streets and avenues west of Queen Anne Avenue are labeled "West" while avenues on the east side bear the suffix "North"; streets are left without such directional additions.

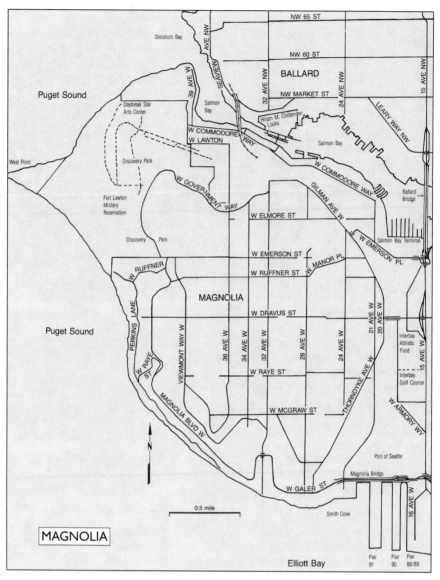

*Courtesy of the University of Washington Press, copyright 1992.*

### ▦ Mini-Tour of Highland Drive and Southeastern Queen Anne Hill

Proceed up Queen Anne Avenue North and turn right at Highland Drive. The large half-timbered French Gothic **"Chappel House"** at 21 Highland dates from 1906. It was designed by San Francisco architect Edgar Matthews for W. M. Chappel, a descendant of French immigrants, who struck it rich in the Alaska goldfields and founded the Rainier Heat & Power Company (see the International District).

The lower road at the fork leads into **Bigelow Avenue North,** a "street" owned by the Parks Department. This pleasant residential drive skirts the eastern slope of Queen Anne Hill and is a segment of a formal **Queen Anne Boulevard** that was only partially realized (see Eighth Avenue in the following mini-tour). We will instead take the upper road.

**The Riddle House** at 153 Highland is named for its original owner, Charles Riddle, not for any puzzles it may contain. Designed by E. W. Houghton and built in 1893, this "shingle-style" mansion is one of the neighborhood's oldest standing structures.

Turn left up Second Avenue North and head two blocks north to the former **Queen Anne High School,** between Lee and Galer Streets. Designed by James Stephen and opened in 1909, this massive Beaux-Arts edifice was surplused by the school district in 1981 and converted into condomiumiums by Historic Seattle with the aid of Bumgardner Architects. A jog west on Lee Street will take you past **Observatory Park.** The first and smaller of the two standpipe towers was built in 1901 to hold water pumped all the way from Capitol Hill's Broadway reservoir.

Return to Queen Anne Avenue via Garfield Street and turn left. The intersection of **Galer and Queen Anne Avenue North** is a classic streetcar business district. Between 1901 and 1940, streetcar motormen paused here briefly to connect or disconnect their cars from cables running to the subterranean **counterbalance** system that helped them master Queen Anne Avenue's precipitous grade.

### ▦ Mini-Tour of Southwestern Queen Anne Hill

If continuing the preceding tour on Queen Anne Avenue North turn right at West Galer Street or head up from downtown and take a left on West Galer. This street honors (phonetically at least) Jacob Gaylor, who built a prominent house on the Hill in 1884.

The former **West Queen Anne Public School** fills the south side of West Galer between Fifth and Sixth Avenues West. The original two-story

The original standpipe on top of Queen Anne Hill has been joined by a forest of broadcast and microwave towers. *(Paul Dorpat)*

The former Kinnear Mansion exemplified the architectural style that gave Queen Anne Hill its name.

school was designed by Skillings and Corner and opened in 1895. In the late 1970s the building was rescued from demolition by Historic Seattle and converted into condominiums, which established the successful formula for later saving Queen Anne High School (mentioned earlier).

To view one of Seattle's more interesting homes, turn right at Sixth West, then left on West Blaine Street, and right on Eighth West. The Romanesque Revival **Shorrock House** at 1432 Eighth West was designed in 1904 by John Graham Sr. for British emigré Ernest Gladstone Shorrock and restored after a 1930 fire.

The ornamented balustrade and light standards along **Eighth Avenue West** give a hint of what the Olmsteds had hoped to achieve on the Hill. The elaborate retaining wall and public stairways were designed by W. R. B. Wilcox in

1913. The most dramatic view of these features can be found below **Marshall Viewpoint** at the intersection of Seventh West and West Highland.

Heading east on West Highland leads you past several impressive mansions, including Bebb & Mendel's **Kerry House** (1906) at 421 and **Stimson House** (1910) at 415. The most distinctive design is found at 222 West Highland: the **Black House.** Designed by Andrew Willatsen for J. C. Black in 1914, this Prairie-style home reflects the influence of Frank Lloyd Wright on his former student.

The nearby Tudor-style **Victoria Apartments,** 100 West Highland, were designed by John Graham Sr. in 1911. **Kerry Park** fills much of the south side of West Highland. Donated by former millhand-turned-millionaire Alfred Sperry Kerry (whose home survives at 421 West Highland), the park protects one of Seattle's most spectacular vistas from the encroachment of banal condo towers such as its eastern neighbor. The park's central sculpture, *Changing Form*, was created by Doris Chase and installed in 1971.

We now turn right (south) on Queen Anne North and right again onto West Prospect. The large Victorian home at **108 West Prospect** was built in 1892 by former Mayor John Franklin Miller, who also donated "Franklin Place" one block west. Turn left (south) at First Avenue West, then right (west) on West Kinnear Place.

The **Ankenny House** stands below West Kinnear at 912 Second West. When Rollin Valentine Ankenny purchased this property in the late 1880s, it was overshadowed by a giant cedar dating from the time of Marco Polo. The tree was revered by natives and had been used as a landmark by early white trappers and explorers. Unswayed by neighbors' protests and a native curse, Ankenny felled the "Powwow Tree" in 1891, but it took him 20 troubled years to finally finish his new home.

Proceed along West Kinnear and take the lower road at the fork. The large

W. R. B. Wilcox's dramatic retaining wall and stairs below Marshall Viewpoint reflect the Olmsteds' unrealized vision for a Queen Anne Boulevard. *(Frank Shaw)*

Queen Anne-style home at **520 West Kinnear Place,** built for Rachel Mable in 1890, typifies the early architecture that gave the Hill its name. The Prairie-style home at **515 West Kinnear Place** was designed by Andrew Willatsen in 1915, along with houses at **320 and 218 West Kinnear Street**.

A left on Seventh West and again on West Olympic Place leads you past the **Chelsea Apartments,** at 620, designed by Harlan Thomas with engineer Charles Collins as a residential hotel. The Chelsea's Mediterranean flourishes, deep bay windows and original roof garden made it one of the city's finest addresses and established Thomas's reputation when it opened in 1907. A Mrs. Enegern established an early Montessori School in the building in 1913.

The Chelsea faces **Kinnear Park,** which was donated to the city in 1889 by early developer George Kinnear. Head east on West Olympic to Second West and you will encounter the **Delamar Apartments,** designed by Daniel Huntington and the last surviving building constructed by George Kinnear. Turn right at Second West, then left on West Roy to return to Queen Anne Avenue.

### ■ Northwest Queen Anne Hill

If you head back up the Hill, the following points of interest can be found in its northwestern neighborhoods.

**Mt. Pleasant Cemetery,** West Raye Street at Fifth Avenue West. We shift now to the north end of Queen Anne, beginning with this historic cemetery. The original 10-acre site was purchased by the International Order of Odd Fellows in 1879 for its members. The cemetery gradually expanded to 40 acres with areas purchased by or reserved for Free Methodists, the Chaveth Sholem (the city's first Jewish cemetery), Temple De Hirsch, the Chong Wa Benevolent Society, and, most recently, Muslims.

Among the honored dead are pioneer Methodist ministers David Blaine and Daniel Bagley, historian Clarence Bagley, Asa Mercer of "Maidens" fame, early governor John McGraw, and proletarian members of the Industrial Workers of the World ("Wobblies") and Woodsmen of the World.

**Seventh Church of Christ Scientist,** 2555 Eighth Avenue West. This fantastic, vaguely Byzantine sanctuary was created in 1926 by Harlan Thomas in partnership with his son Donald and Clyde Grainger. A straight shot down Eighth will lead you to the area of the southwestern Queen Anne mini-tour described earlier.

## POINTS OF INTEREST IN MAGNOLIA AND SALMON BAY

### ■ Fishermen's Terminal

West Emerson Place. From downtown, take Fifteenth Avenue North to the foot of the Ballard Bridge and follow the signs to loop over the highway and head west on Emerson. The terminal was established by the Port of Seattle in 1913 to house fishermen whose traditional Salmon Bay moorages were imperiled by construction of the Lake Washington Ship Canal. It was expanded in 1946 and completely rebuilt in 1988. The dramatic memorial to the more than 460 Seattle fishermen lost at sea since 1900 was sculpted by Ron Petty and dedicated in 1988.

### ■ Fort Lawton and Discovery Park

West Government Way at Thirty-sixth Avenue West. Take Fifteenth West from downtown and follow the Fishermen's Terminal signs to West Emerson Place, which intersects with Gilman Place West. Turn right and head west; the arterial ultimately turns into West Government Way and enters the park. Originally named Camp Lewis in 1895,

Vessels crowd Fishermen's Terminal in this 1920s view looking toward Ballard. *(Port of Seattle)*

Fort Lawton was developed in 1916 according to plans drawn by the Olmsted brothers. Many of the original officers' quarters and barracks survive, but they have deteriorated since the early 1970s when most of the base was decommissioned and returned to the City of Seattle. This 534-acre tract was named Discovery Park in honor of the vessel that carried Captain George Vancouver into Puget Sound. Discovery is Seattle's largest park, and most of the grounds have been intentionally left largely unimproved to provide habitat for bald eagles, raccoons, and other wildlife. It also houses the Day Break Star Arts Center, designed by Lawney Reyes and operated by United Indians of All Tribes since 1977 in settlement of native treaty claims to the original Fort Lawton site.

### ■ Magnolia
West Galer Steet and Magnolia Boulevard West. From downtown, take Fifteenth Avenue West to the Magnolia Bridge, which puts you at West Galer Street and leads to Magnolia Boulevard East. This route, partially laid out by the Olmsteds, offers stunning views of Smith Cove and Elliott Bay, and the adjoining neighborhoods feature many handsome homes dating from the 1920s and 1930s. You may follow the Boulevard around to the southern edge of Discovery Park at West Emerson Street.

# 4

# Northwest Seattle

## BALLARD

### Orientation

Like some other Seattle areas, Ballard is a "city within a city," but with a decidedly Scandinavian accent. It is best reached from downtown via Highway 99/Aurora Avenue or Elliott/Fifteenth Avenue West and the Ballard Bridge. Northwest Market Street is the main thoroughfare and connects with historic Ballard Avenue and the Chittenden Locks, where it becomes Seaview Avenue Northwest and continues to Golden Gardens. One caveat: the slowness and peculiar parallel parking techniques of Ballard drivers are the butt of many Seattle jokes, which are all true.

### History

In 1852, Ira Wilcox Utter filed the first homestead claim in the future Ballard. Although miles north of Seattle, he was not alone. The area had long been populated by a Duwamish community called the Xacho-absh, or "Lake People." They maintained villages on the shores of the Shilshole and Salmon Bays long after other natives relocated across the Sound under the terms of the 1855 Point Elliott Treaty.

The area was logged and settled at a fair pace. Seattle's growth spurt during the 1880s prompted Judge Thomas Burke to purchase 720 acres north of Salmon Bay, which he platted as the "Farmdale Homestead." He and his rail-

Opposite: Ron Petty's *Animal Storm* pylon at Wallingford Center celebrates the neighborhood's biodiversity. *(Paul Dorpat)*

179

road partner, Daniel H. Gilman, knew that the Great Northern Railroad planned to enter Seattle from the north, and the two men joined with John Leary and others to form the West Coast Improvement Company in 1888. They laid a spur along Salmon Bay for their Seattle, Lake Shore and Eastern Railroad (which crossed the canal at Fremont) and named their new district "Gilman Park."

At about the same time, William Rankin Ballard, master of the Puget Sound stern-wheeler *Zephyr,* lost a coin toss with a business partner and took ownership of 160 acres of supposedly worthless timberland adjoining Farmdale in payment of a business debt. He then met Midwestern lumber magnate Charles Douglas Stimson and persuaded him to buy a defunct sawmill on Salmon Bay. Ballard later joined forces with Leary, Burke, and Gilman, and his "losing bet" yielded a cool $1,000 per acre.

Captain Ballard managed Gilman Park and lent his name to the new city when it incorporated in 1890. A census that year enumerated 1,636 residents living between Salmon Bay and the future Northeast Sixty-fifth Street. The area grew rapidly as railroad and streetcar service expanded in the 1890s. Developers pushed the rails out to Golden Gardens and built an amusement park to attract home buyers, while another line served Loyal Heights on the

A streetcar rounds the corner of Twentieth Avenue Northwest and Ballard Avenue in this 1909 scene. *(Lawton Gowey)*

Ballard's mills made it the "Shingle Capital of the World" in the early 1900s. *(Lawton Gowey)*

bluff above. Private ferries also offered passage from Ballard to nearby towns on Puget Sound.

Ballard built itself a handsome city hall in 1899 and decreed a perfect balance between vice and virtue by limiting saloon licenses to the number of the city's churches. In 1901, Fred Sander began building an interurban street railway north toward Everett and laid 12 miles of track by 1907. (Sander's line was bought by Stone & Webster the following year, and the line was rerouted through Fremont to Seattle.)

Meanwhile, 6,000 miles to the east, tensions between Scandinavian states and fears of Bismark's Germany combined with famine and unrest in Norway to spark a mass migration to the United States. Jobs in Puget Sound mills and fisheries attracted thousands to cross the continent to the Northwest's "second frontier," and many settled in the new town of Ballard. Although Scandinavians never constituted more than a third of Ballard's population, they imprinted their strong ethnic identity on the entire community, and the preference of some for snuff and chewing tobacco soon earned it the nickname "Snoose Junction."

In the early 1900s, Ballard declared itself the "Shingle Capital of the World" (producing 333 billion shingles in 1898 alone) and eagerly awaited the construction of the long-debated Ship Canal (see "Seattle's Big Ditch" on pages 182-183), but its municipal services could not keep up with growth. Chronic deficiencies in the water supply, including the discovery of a dead horse in the town's sole reservoir, persuaded most Ballardites that it was time to join Seattle.

The vote to annex passed by 996 to 874 on November 6, 1906, and the City of Ballard ceased to exist on January 1, 1907. Like West Seattle, which also joined Seattle that year, Ballard was never fully absorbed, and it has maintained its unique cultural and civic character in the 90 years since annexation.

## Seattle's Big Ditch

In 1854, Thomas Mercer named Lake Union and Union Bay in full confidence that a canal would soon link Lake Washington and Salmon Bay via these waters. In fact, this northern route had a lot of competition, and the stakes could not have been higher for Seattle's early developers.

In 1867 the Navy expressed its desire for a base in or near Seattle. Clearly, a freshwater moorage would be best to reduce the corrosion of ship hulls, but this required access to Puget Sound. Nature provided a linkage of sorts between salt and fresh water via the Black River slough, which flowed from Lake Washington's southern tip into the meandering Duwamish. This route was too shallow for most boats, and it was ruled out by the amount of dredging required to make it navigable.

The northern route attracted more interest, but it also entailed a lot of digging. A natural dam at Montlake separated Lake Washington from Portage Bay and Lake Union, while only a murky stream flowed between the latter and Salmon Bay at Fremont. John Pike tried to dig a narrow canal at Montlake in 1860, and Judge Burke completed a passage for logs in 1883. Assuming a deeper and wider cut at Montlake, schemes were floated to bypass Salmon Bay and reach Elliott Bay via alternate canals from south Lake Union to Smith Cove.

Former territorial governor Eugene Semple had another idea: dig a canal from south Lake Washington through Beacon Hill, and use the fill to cover the Duwamish mudflats and create a giant "Harbor Island" for future piers and industry. He won state approval in 1895 and started digging in 1900, but railroad interests feared dilution of their control of Seattle's central harbor, and capitalists such as Thomas Burke and the Great Northern's J. J. Hill had gambled on the northern canal. Semple's political and financial backing soon dried up. (Auto traffic now "flows" through his canal, and the battle over Harbor Island was resolved when voters created the Port of Seattle in 1911.)

Exasperated with the delays, developer James Moore offered to front the money to dig the government's canal in 1906. The Army Corps of Engineers assigned Major Hiram M. Chittenden to supervise the effort, but Moore quickly exhausted his funds with little progress. Chittenden surveyed the project and recommended a large lock between Salmon and Shilshole Bays and a deep cut at Montlake. Congress finally approved the plan in 1910, but complaints by Ballard mill owners (who would lose their accustomed log pond on Salmon Bay) postponed the start of construction until November 1911.

The work proceeded slowly and involved many daunting engineering challenges. Lake Union stood 8 feet above the high-tide level of Puget Sound, and Lake Washington was almost as high again. Once open, the canal would lower the latter lake by 9 feet, cut off its Black River drainage, strand many water-dependent businesses on the lake shore, and interfere with major salmon migrations. Chittenden super-

Dredges toil at the future site of the Chittenden Locks in this view from about 1914. *(U.S. Army Corps of Engineers)*

Admiral Peary's Arctic flagship *Roosevelt* opens the Chittenden Locks on July 4, 1917. *(U.S. Army Corps of Engineers)*

vised the engineering solutions, while Bebb and Gould designed the buildings for the government locks. Carl English later planted a delightful garden on the grounds, and a public fish ladder was installed to give migrating salmon passage over the weir at the mouth of Salmon Bay.

Seattle's dream of a canal became reality on July 4, 1917, when the USS *Roosevelt,* which had carried Admiral Peary's North Pole expedition to the Arctic eight years earlier, led a marine parade through the new lock. Ironically, the Navy had by then already established its Puget Sound base at Bremerton, and the beams of new warships soon outgrew the dimensions of the largest of the two locks.

Bascule bridges were completed across the canal at Ballard, Fremont, the University District, and Montlake during the next decade. Work on the Lake Washington Ship Canal was not declared complete until 1934—80 years after Thomas Mercer first predicted such a project. In 1956, the Corps of Engineers rededicated the government locks as Hiram M. Chittenden Locks, to honor the man who had finally cut Seattle's equivalent of the Gordian knot.

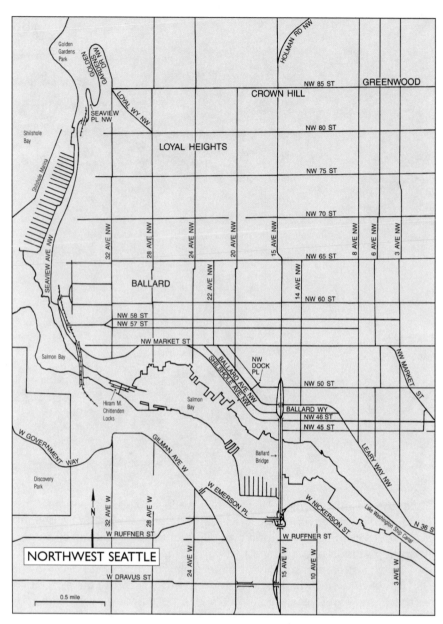

*Courtesy of the University of Washington Press, copyright 1992.*

## POINTS OF INTEREST

**Carnegie Free Public Library,** 2026 Market. Funded with Andrew Carnegie's gift of $15,000, the Ballard library was designed by Henderson Ryan and opened in 1905. It was superseded by a new facility in the 1960s and now houses a collection of antique dealers.

**Fire Station No. 18,** Market at Russell Avenue Northwest. Designed by Bebb and Gould in 1911, its unusual Dutch gable gives the structure Mission-style flair. The building now houses a music club.

**Market Street Business District.** Most of the buildings lining Market date from 1913 to the early 1930s, when retail activity shifted away from the older Ballard Avenue. Market Street is dominated by the **Ballard Building,** designed by William R. Grant and erected in 1927 by the Fraternal Order of Eagles at Twenty-second Northwest. The district resembles a small midwestern town, and one could quickly forget that it is actually situated within a far larger city. Bergen Park honors Seattle's first sister-city and was dedicated by King Olav V of Norway in 1975.

**Ballard Avenue Historic District.** No less a personage than King Carl XVI Gustav of Sweden read the official proclamation establishing the Ballard Avenue Historic District on April 11, 1976. He also dedicated the park and bell tower on the site of the original **Ballard City Hall** at Twenty-second

Northwest and Ballard Avenue. Most of the buildings on the Avenue were built between 1890 and 1915, and they offer an opportunity to stroll a century into the past.

Notable structures include **Vik Apartments** (1926) at 5425 Ballard, featuring a Mission-style facade; the **Jones Building** (1901) at 5405 Twenty-second Northwest, home of Ballard's original post office and the Sunset Hotel; the **G.S. Sanborn Building** (1901) at 5323 Ballard Avenue, the district's sole example of Richardsonian Romanesque; the former **Scandinavian-American Bank** (1902) and the **Ballard Savings & Loan** (1914) at Northwest Vernon Place, whose pediment extols "Thrift"; the corbie-gabled **C.D. Stimson Co. office,** designed by Kirtland Cutter in 1913 at 2116 Northwest Vernon Place;

Ballard City Hall is long gone, but its bell resides in a new tower on its original site. *(Nordic Heritage Museum)*

The main lock disgorges a flotilla of fishing and pleasure boats into Salmon Bay. *(U.S. Army Corps of Engineers)*

and the imposing **Cors & Wegener Building** (1893) at Twentieth Northwest. The Historic District ends a block south at Northwest Dock Place.

**Hiram M. Chittenden Locks,** 3015 Northwest Fifty-fourth Street (Market Avenue becomes Fifty-fourth and then Seaview Avenue as it progresses westward). Completed in 1917, the former government locks are now named for the engineer who guided their construction. Bebb and Gould designed the buildings, with their curious hut-like roofs, and Carl English planted the botanical garden which now bears his name. You may cross the lock gates and weir blocking the mouth of Salmon Bay and view salmon struggling up the fish ladder on the Magnolia side of the waterway. The grounds contain a visitor center and small museum.

**Shilshole Marina and Golden Gardens,** Seaview Avenue Northwest. The statue of Leif Eriksson was dedicated in 1962, and the Port of Seattle completed the long-stalled **Shilshole Marina** a year later.

In the 1890s a streetcar line carried sunbathers (and potential home buyers) to **Golden Gardens,** a private park established by Olive and Harry Treat. The city purchased the site in 1922; a half-century later it was proposed as the home for the city aquarium, but this ended up downtown after a bitter battle.

**Nordic Heritage Museum,** 3014 Northwest Sixty-seventh Street. Housed in the former Webster Elementary School (unknown, 1907), this delightful museum features exhibits and walk-through dioramas tracing the Scandinavian immigration and its impact on Ballard and the Pacific Northwest.

186

# FREMONT

## Orientation

Fremont, arguably Seattle's liveliest neighborhood, bills itself as "the Center of the Universe." From downtown it is served by its own bascule bridge linking Westlake and Dexter Avenues with Fremont Avenue, Thirty-sixth Avenue North, and Leary Way (leading to Ballard).

## History

Fremont is named for the Nebraska hometown of two of the area's founders, L. H. Griffith and and E. Blewett, who joined with dentist-entepreneur Dr. E. C. Kilbourne to plat the area in 1888. Its original industry consisted of lumber and shingle mills and an iron foundry, clustered on the north Lake Union shore.

In 1888 developers hired Chinese labor to widen the stream leading to Salmon Bay, but rail transportation is what established the area's early economic fortunes. First to arrive was a spur of the Seattle, Lake Shore and Eastern Railroad, which crossed the future canal from Seattle in 1888 and then followed the north shore of Lake Union to Lake Washington (now the Burke-Gilman Trail).

Griffith and Kilbourne were eager street rail entrepreneurs, but Guy Phinney built the first line in 1890 to carry visitors up the hill from Fremont to his private Woodland Park. Griffith's Front Street line arrived a year later and pushed on to Green Lake. In 1891 the residents of Fremont and its northern neighbors annexed themselves to Seattle. Most of the buildings in Fremont's business district date from 1900 to 1915.

In 1910, Stone & Webster's Seattle-Everett Traction Company (later Pacific Northwest Traction) inaugurated fast interurban service between the two cities via Fremont. Finally, Northern Pacific built its own trestle into Fremont in 1914. That same year, a coffer dam broke during construction of the Ship Canal and washed away several low-level wagon crossings.

In 1916 the Canal's "Fremont Cut" brought more prosperity, as well as a new bascule bridge, even before the locks were finished. On the other hand, completion of the high-level George Washington Bridge for Aurora Avenue in 1932 threw a shadow across Fremont, and the end of interurban rail service in 1939 sent it into eclipse.

Benign neglect and low rents made Fremont an attractive neighborhood for students, bohemians, and artists in the 1960s, and they helped to launch a mini-renaissance in the following decades. Locals boasted that Fremont was "the community that recycles itself" and declared it an "Artists' Republic" in the 1990s. Fremont's annual Summer Solstice street fair and parade express this playful exuberance and should not be missed.

The last of Seattle's tall ships had to escape Lake Union before engineers completed the span of the Aurora Bridge in 1932. *(Greg Lang)*

Harmless pranksters can't resist decorating Richard Beyer's "People Waiting for the Interurban," which is probably the city's most popular work of public art. *(Paul Dorpat)*

The former Fremont carbarn witnessed the end of Seattle's streetcars in 1941 and now houses Redhook Brewery's Trolleyman Pub. *(Lawton Gowey)*

## POINTS OF INTEREST

**Fremont Bridge and Ship Canal.** The bridge dates from 1916 and was the first completed over the new Ship Canal, whose Fremont Cut is bordered by a pleasant tree-lined walkway.

*People Waiting for the Interurban,* Fremont North at North Thirty-fourth. Perhaps Seattle's most popular public artwork, sculptor Richard Beyer's 1978 monument to the Interurban actually sits perpendicular to the line's route up Fremont Avenue. Other notable "monuments" in Fremont include a giant bronze figure of V. I. Lenin salvaged from Eastern Europe, a monstrous Volkswagen-eating troll lurking under the Aurora Bridge at North Thirty-sixth Street, and a sleek rocket ship rescued from a defunct military surplus store in the Denny Regrade.

**Redhook Trolleyman Pub,** Phinney Avenue North at North Thirty-fourth Street. Built in 1905 by Stone &

Webster's Seattle Electric Company, this brick "carbarn" remained in continuous service until the early morning of April 13, 1941, when Seattle's last operating streetcar screeched to a halt at its doors. The building was adapted in 1988 by architect Skip Satterwhite to house the Redhook Brewery and, later, its Trolleyman Pub.

**Fremont Branch Library,** 731 North Thirty-fifth Street. This Carnegie library was designed by Daniel Huntington in a California Mission style and opened in 1921.

**B.F. Day Elementary School,** 3921 Linden Avenue North. The simple elegance of John Parkinson's design for this 1891 school, entered via a dramatic central Roman arch, earned him appointment as the Seattle Public School District's first resident architect. It is the District's oldest operating building and the last surviving example of Parkinson's three-year tenure.

# WALLINGFORD

## Orientation

This comfortable residential neighborhood is framed between Highway 99 and Interstate 5, and Green Lake and Lake Union. It is bisected from east to west by North Forty-fifth Street, which is lined by a busy retail district centered at the intersection with Wallingford Avenue North. It is easily reached from downtown via I-5 or Highway 99/Aurora Avenue, although rush-hour traffic on Forty-fifth can be horrendous.

## History

The neighborhood takes its name from developer John Wallingford, who platted the area in the 1880s, and it now embraces James Moore's Latona community; both neighborhoods were annexed by Seattle in 1891 along with Fremont and Green Lake. The area was served by David Denny's north-end streetcar line, which crossed the neck of Portage Bay at Latona, and a later east-west line on North Forty-fifth helped spur residential development in the 1900s. A trestle bridge at the foot of Stoneway was removed during construction of the Ship Canal.

### POINTS OF INTEREST

**Wallingford Center,** Forty-fifth Avenue North at North Wallingford. Designed by James Stephen and opened in 1904, the former Interlake School was converted by Bruce Lorig & Associates into a retail center with apartments on its second story in the early 1980s. Ron Petty's 1985 bronze and aluminum pylon, *Animal Storm,* celebrates the neighborhood's wildlife in relief.

**Home of the Good Shepherd.** This stately former home for "wayward girls" was designed by Breitung & Buchinger and completed in 1907 amid a large estate and orchard. The Sisters moved on in 1956, and the neighborhood defeated a plan to build a shopping center on the grounds in 1973. The City of Seattle purchased the property three years later for a park and community center, and the building is now managed by Historic Seattle.

**Gas Works Park,** North Northlake Way at Burke Avenue North. Built in 1907 to extract industrial gases from coal and oil, the Lake Union Gas Works fell victim to competition and rising environmental sensitivity in the 1960s. Decades of pollution prevented developers from snapping up its little peninsula, but landscape architect Richard Haag had a different vision. Working with Olson/Walker architects to create a park on the site, he proposed retaining the rusted old cracking towers, pipes, valves, and other machinery as industrial sculptures. The family of the late city council member Myrtle Edwards, who was to be memorialized by the park, were horrified and withdrew the name, but Haag's idea carried the day and in 1978 Gas Works Park became one of Seattle's most popular, as well as distinctive, public spaces.

The former Home of the Good Shepherd is now a community center and park in the heart of Wallingford. *(Paul Dorpat)*

Architect Richard Haag transformed Gas Works Park's cracking towers into an ensemble of industrial sculptures. *(Frank Shaw)*

# GREEN LAKE AND WOODLAND PARK

## Orientation

Green Lake sits between North Fiftieth and Eightieth Streets. It is bordered on the west by Highway 99/Aurora Avenue North and ringed by Green Lake Way; Interstate 5 passes a few blocks to the east. Aurora bisects Woodland Park, with the Woodland Park Zoo on the west and "Lower Woodland Park" on the east. Zoo entrances are found off Phinney Avenue North on the west, North Fifty-ninth Street on the north, and North Fiftieth Street at Fremont Avenue North on the south.

## History

Green Lake is an artifact of the Ice Age, a large pond left by the retreating glacier that sculpted nearby Phinney Ridge and Seattle's other hills and valleys. The area was populated by bands of Duwamish "Lake People" until the 1855 Point Elliott Treaty relocated them.

The first white settler, "Green Lake John" Erhart Saifried, arrived in 1869. A. L. Parker built a sawmill on the lake and ran a rail line down to Fremont. W. D. Wood, Dr. E. C. Kilbourne, Guy Phinney, and other developers bought up the lake and its surrounding clear-cuts in the 1880s and began promoting home sales on the "suburban" tracts.

To entice buyers, Phinney built a private park and menagerie on his "Woodland Park" estate and established a streetcar line from Fremont to its

Green Lake is surrounded by a suburban village in this 1903 view. (A. Curtis, University of Washington Library Special Collections. Neg. 3152)

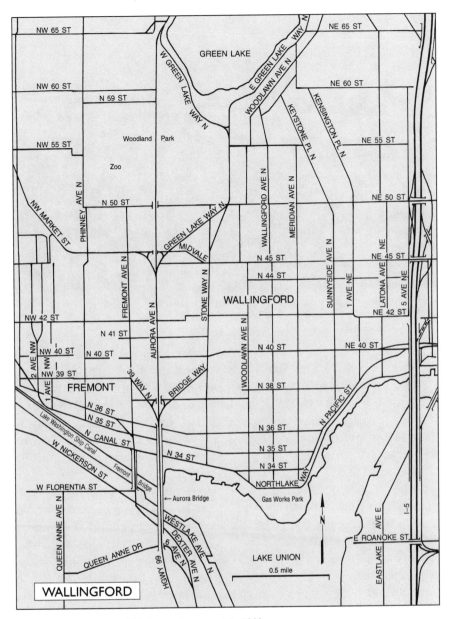

Courtesy of the University of Washington Press, copyright 1992.

entrance off North Fiftieth Street. His widow tried to keep up the property following Phinney's death in 1893, but she finally sold the 200-acre estate to the City of Seattle in late 1899. The $100,000 purchase outraged fiscal conservatives, who thought the park was "too far out" from the city center.

John C. Olmsted disagreed. He recommended an expanded zoo at Woodland Park and acquisition of the rest of Green Lake's shoreline. This was accomplished by 1910, and the city blocked the lake's inflow in order to lower it by 7 feet and create space for lawns and a boulevard. This had the

A small menagerie on Guy Phinney's "Woodland Park" estate was the seed for what is now regarded as one of the nation's 10 best zoos. *(Seattle Municipal Archives)*

unfortunate effect of encouraging algae growth and gave birth to the "swimmer's itch" that still afflicts some bathers despite improved drainage.

The menagerie at Woodland Park was expanded in 1909 with animals transferred from Leschi Park, and Olmsted designed new but less than humane cages and pits for their exhibition. In 1930, the State Highway Commission overruled Seattle's strenuous objections and routed Highway 99/Aurora Avenue through the park, isolating the zoo's 90 acres from the park's lower 130 and Green Lake.

The zoo was improved in fits and starts with WPA projects in the 1930s and parks bonds in the 1960s. After voters killed George Bartholick's bold plan to reunite upper and lower Woodland Parks with a lid over Aurora in 1974, zoo director David Hancocks retained Jones & Jones architects. They devised a radical new plan to house animals in large, open exhibits resembling their native "bioclimatic zones." Thanks to a 1985 countywide bond issue, the aid of the nonprofit Woodland Park Zoo Society, and the leadership of zoo director David Towne, much of this plan has now been implemented, attracting international kudos and one million visitors each year.

### POINTS OF INTEREST

**Green Lake Branch Library,**
7364 East Green Lake Way North. Designed by Somervell & Cote and opened in 1910, this eclectic little Carnegie Library gives the lake a hint of a Mediterranean breeze.

**Twin TeePees Restaurant,**
7201 Aurora Avenue North. This whimsical bit of highway vernacular was erected in 1934 and still serves a great prime rib on Friday nights.

**Woodland Park Zoological Gardens,** North Fiftieth at Fremont

This Mediterranean-style Carnegie Library has faced Green Lake since 1910. *(Paul Dorpat)*

The Twin Teepees Restaurant has served locals and Aurora Avenue motorists since 1934.

North. Donated to the City of Seattle in 1899, the former Phinney Estate included a small menagerie. The Woodland Park Zoo opened in 1904 with additional animals acquired from the private Leschi Park menagerie, and the Olmsted brothers designed new bear pits and cramped cages in 1910. With the exception of the 1909 Ape House (dubbed a "Siminary" because it also housed the first zoo director), none of these early structures survive, and it is just as well. In 1976 director David Hancocks worked with architects from Jones & Jones to develop a radical new plan for presenting animals in spacious exhibits emulating their native habitats, which have since won major awards and set a new standard for zoos around the world.

# 5

# Northeast
# Seattle

## UNIVERSITY OF WASHINGTON CAMPUS

### Orientation

The main entrance to the University of Washington (UW) campus lies at the intersection of Northeast Forty-fifth Street and Seventeenth Avenue Northeast and is best reached from downtown via I-5 (although rush hour traffic is very heavy on Forty-fifth). From Fifteenth Avenue Northeast, on the University's west border, you may enter the main garage at Forty-first Street Northeast and the campus at Fortieth Northeast. A visitors center, located on the corner of Northeast Campus Parkway and University Way Northeast, offers a self-guided tour.

### History

The original Territorial University was founded on Denny Knoll in future downtown Seattle in 1861 (see the Central Business District in the Downtown Seattle section). Its growth and that of the surrounding city compelled a search for an alternate site, which culminated with the Legislature's selection of an undeveloped tract on the north shore of Portage Bay and Union Bay in 1891.

Architect William E. Boone drew up the first plan for the new campus, but actual development was hampered by lack of funds and political wrangling. Frustrated with the delays, Regent David Kellogg stabbed a rotting log with his umbrella and ordered that the University's first building be built

Opposite: The penthouse atop R. C. Reamer's Meany Hotel was the home of the first theater-in-the-round. *(Paul Dorpat)*

there. And so Denny Hall rose on the site and admitted its first students in the fall of 1895.

The next buildings included the first dormitories, Lewis and Clark Halls, and a science building (later named for famed literary scholar and critic Vernon Parrington). A semblance of order was proposed by Professor A.H. Fuller and the Olmsted brothers, who laid out an oval scheme with a "Liberal Arts Quadrangle" in 1904. The plan was put on hold when the campus was selected to host the Alaska-Yukon-Pacific (AYP) Exposition of 1909. John C. Olmsted was retained to design the AYP grounds in order to create permanent infrastructure for the campus. Among these lasting improvements are Rainier Vista and "Frosh Pond."

The AYP's buildings were planned by the San Francisco firm of Howard and Galloway, and they brought their principal designer, Édouard Frère Champney, to Seattle. A veteran of several major expositions, Champney was given free rein in creating an ensemble of suitably operatic and ornate structures (none of which was intended to outlive the fair). Local architects such as John Graham Sr. also contributed buildings and pavilions.

The AYP was a rousing success, but it left few permanent facilities for the University's future use. The Olmsteds returned and crafted a new master plan, which was adopted in 1915 with modifications by Bebb and Gould and John Paul Jones. Actual construction followed over the next decade, but rising costs precipitated a clash between University president Henry Suzzallo and Governor Roland Hartley, who tried to veto construction of the University's new library. Outraged at being overriden by Suzzallo's legislative allies, he stacked the Board of Regents and it fired the president. Voters in turn retired Hartley in 1932, and chastened Regents named the library for Suzzallo after his death a year later.

Another bitter political feud delayed legislative approval of the University's School of Medicine until 1946 (it was opposed by local physicians who did not welcome competition from new doctors), and its "South Campus" became the main focus of campus expansion in the 1950s and 1960s. A clumsy attempt to use the city's urban renewal funds and condemnation authority to this end led to a long battle with neighboring businesses on Portage Bay.

The Legislature approved another spurt of construction as arriving baby-boomers swelled enrollment beyond 30,000, but the turmoil of the 1960s led to the fortresslike architecture of "Red Square," which seemed better suited for defense against barbarian hordes than the education of the young. With more recent construction, notably the new Allen Library and Astrophysics campus, the University seems to have recovered its scholastic equanimity, and today it covers 639 acres and serves 35,000 students.

Children pose during an outing on the the University of Washington's largely undeveloped campus. Its original building, the château-like Denny Hall, welcomed its first students in 1895. *(Carrie Campbell; courtesy Lucy Campbell Coe)*

Édouard Frère Champney and other architects transformed the new campus into a fantasy city for the 1909 Alaska-Yukon-Pacific Exposition, Seattle's first world's fair. *(F. Nowell, University of Washington Library Special Collections. Neg. X2246)*

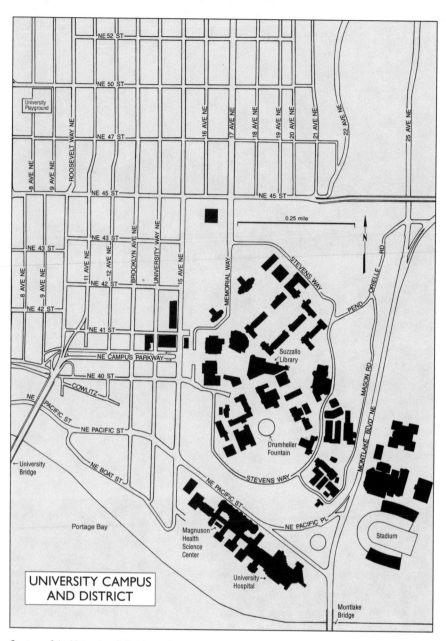

*Courtesy of the University of Washington Press, copyright 1992.*

## Walking Tour

We enter the University campus from Northeast Forty-fifth Street, as the Olmsteds intended. They also designed the Seventeenth Avenue Northeast boulevard, now dubbed "Frat Row," to provide a suitable transition from neighborhood to academe. Note that while visitor parking is available on campus, you may end up at some distance from this gate.

200

Cherry trees bloom in this 1980s view of the "Quad," laid out by the Olmsted brothers and largely realized by Bebb and Gould between 1917 and 1920. *(Frank Shaw)*

The **Thomas Burke Memorial Museum** has occupied its present home, designed by James J. Chiarelli, since 1962. Its diverse collections trace Northwest history from the days of the dinosaur to the region's early human habitation. The museum also includes a charming coffee house. The large killer whale sculpture at the museum entrance was carved by Bill Holm and installed in 1985.

The stone **Observatory** was designed by Charles Saunders and erected in 1895, when clear "suburban" skies offered clear views for its 6-inch refracting telescope. The original instrument is still in use, and the public is allowed to peer through it on selected evenings.

A short side trip east will bring you to Glenn Hughes' **Penthouse Theater,** which relocated from the top of the Meany Hotel (see University District) to

the campus in 1938. In his final commission, Carl Gould designed the circular Moderne building, which was recently shifted from the far side of campus.

Work on the first building on campus, **Denny Hall,** was mostly finished when the first students arrived in November 1885. Designed by Charles Saunders and George W. Lawton, this academic château's belfry contains the University's original 1861 bell.

A stroll southeast down the hill from Denny takes you into **"the Quad,"** originally proposed by the Olmsteds in 1904. Most of its principal buildings were designed by Bebb and Gould and completed between 1917 and 1920. Scanning clockwise from its southwest corner, the Quad is framed by **Savery Hall, Raitt Hall,** the spires of the newer **Art and Music Buildings** (Whitehouse & Price, 1950), **Miller**

**Hall, Smith Hall,** and **Gowen Hall** (Abraham Albertson, 1932). The Quad's venerable cherry trees put on an impressive display in the spring.

Take a moment to admire the numerous grotesques and gargoyles that inhabit the cornices and corbels of these buildings. Alonzo Victor Lewis festooned **Savery Hall** with military and scientific figures befitting the home of the ROTC. **Raitt Hall** was named for Effie Raitt, founder of the University's School of Home Economics, so Gould ornamented it with females figures engaged in mostly domestic (and sexually stereotypical) pursuits. **Miller Hall's** collection is less thematic, but sculptor A. V. Lewis included several recognizable historical and mythological figures for the Univerity's original administration building. Dudley Pratt's menagerie of cartoonish gargoyles (can you find Mickey Mouse?) for **Smith Hall** is the most diverse and delightful on the Quad. In contrast, John Elliott sculpted sober reliefs of famous judges

and barristers for the first law school in **Gowen Hall.**

Exiting the Quad on the west l eads you into **"Red Square,"** which replaced a pleasant lawn with a sea of brick in 1972. **Kane Hall** is notable chiefly for a dramatic mural painted by Pablo O'Higgins in 1945 to celebrate the working-class struggle and defeat of Fascism. It was relocated from the Central Area home of the Shipscalers' union hall to Kane's second floor lobby in 1977.

Red Square's modern fortresses offer a stark contrast to **Suzzallo Library,** Carl Gould's magnificent (and budget-busting) "Cathedral of Books." Allan Clark sculpted its gallery of famous thinkers and used campus athletes as models for the figures of Thought, Inspiration, and Mastery guarding its main entrance. The cavernous undergraduate reading room, which helped to cost president Henry Suzzallo his job, is a must-see. For the sake of economy, the library was completed in 1926 sans

Dudley Pratt created these whimsical figures to ornament Smith Hall on the UW Quad. *(Paul Dorpat)*

the towering spire Gould had planned. Minoru Yamasaki designed the building's complementary east wing in 1962. The 1991 Allen Library was designed by Edward Larrabee Barnes and is a splendid addition to the campus.

Suzzallo frames the Olmsteds' **Rainier Vista** with the Gothic Revival **Administration Building,** designed by Victor N. Jones. In one of his final commissions, Allan Clark decorated the 1949 building with stylized personifications of academic disciplines.

Descending the steps leads you into a second quadrangle, framed by sparer Gothic Revival buildings dating from the late 1920s and 1930s. The central **Frosh Pond** is a survivor of the AYP Exposition of 1909. Lawrence Halprin designed its triumphant **Drumeller Fountain** (named for the regent who financed it) to help mark the University's 100th birthday in 1961.

Rainier Vista's lower lawn is flanked by two stands of trees. The one on the left shelters a large amphitheater, **Sylvan Theater,** which contains four hand-fluted columns salvaged from the University's original downtown building. A trail leads through the arbor on the right side of the lawn into the **Medicinal Herb Garden,** first planted in 1911.

Exiting the Herb Garden path puts you on the campus's west ring road, opposite the Physics/Astronomy

Building, designed by Cesar Pelli and completed in 1996 with a Foucault pendulum. Head north past two artifacts of the AYP. The Beaux-Arts **Architecture Hall** on the west was designed by John Galen Howard (Howard & Galloway) as a museum. It faces the wood-frame **Cunningham Hall,** designed by Saunders & Lawton as the AYP's ostensibly temporary "Women's Building." It now honors photographer and 1907 UW graduate Imogen Cunningham.

Ascending the stairs next to the new **Meany Hall** (the original was condemned after the 1965 earthquake) puts you back on Red Square near the recently expanded **Henry Art Gallery.** The original structure was designed by Bebb and Gould in 1927 to house railroad magnate Horace C. Henry's donated art collection. Lorado Taft's sculpture of *George Washington* was commissioned by the Daughters of the American Revolution and installed for the AYP in 1909.

Head northeast past the recently refurbished **Parrington Hall,** the University's second major building, designed by Timotheus Josenhans and Norris Best Allen and completed in 1904. A left turn onto the main avenue leads you back to this tour's starting point. The University's Visitors Information Center at 4014 University Way Northeast offers a more complete self-guided tour free of charge.

# UNIVERSITY DISTRICT

## Orientation

This lively neighborhood abuts the west and north boundaries of the University of Washington and stretches from Lake Union to Ravenna ravine. From downtown, it is best reached via the Northeast Fiftieth Street ramp off Interstate 5 (avoid Northeast Forty-fifth because it is one of Seattle's busiest arterials). University Way Northeast, called "the Ave" by locals, is the district's main drag.

## History

The University District predates its namesake institution by some 30 years. The area was first settled by Christian and Harriet Brownfield in 1867. This couple was granted one of the territory's first divorces in 1875 "on the grounds of incompatibility of tempers."

The Brownfield homestead was subdivided and passed to new owners, including the parents of "cookbook author" Alice B. Toklas. In 1883, the Lake Washington Improvement Company was incorporated to log and develop the area. It also filed the first "Lakeview" plat and began digging a canal to allow logs to float through the Montlake portage separating Lakes Washington and Union.

The locally owned Seattle, Lake Shore and Eastern Railroad established a line (now the Burke-Gilman Trail) from Fremont along the northern shore of Union and Portage Bays in 1887 and ultimately rounded Lake Washington to reach east side coal mines. E. M. Carr filed a new Kensington plat in anticipation that a ship canal would soon join the lakes, and sold most of the land to developer James Moore in 1890. He began developing the new towns of "Brooklyn" and "Latona."

On February 23, 1891, the Legislature ended three years of debate and voted to relocate the University of Washington campus from downtown Seattle (see the Central Business District, Metropolitan Tract) to "Section 16," a wooded wilderness bordering Union Bay. On May 4 the area's few hundred residents voted to join the City of Seattle, and two months later David Denny's Rainier Power and Rail Company inaugurated streetcar service to the area,

The streetcars and salesmen's coupes have vanished from "The Ave," but the University Book Store still occupies the same location, albeit behind a greatly altered facade. *(Lawton Gowey)*

crossing the future canal via trestle immediately below the present Freeway Bridge. The line then jogged east to "Columbus Avenue" (now University Way) and ran north to present-day Northeast Forty-fifth Street, then little more than a wagon trail, and was later extended to Ravenna ravine, then a private park.

Denny's line went bankrupt during the Panic of 1893, and the arrival of the University's first students in 1895 did little to revive the area. Recovery came slowly, but enough people lived in the area by 1902 to warrant construction of the University Heights (1902) and Latona (1906) elementary schools. At the same time, Charles Cowen had begun developing the neighborhood around Ravenna Boulevard and his namesake park, which were both recommended by the Olmsted parks plan.

The District's success was secured by the spectacular Alaska-Yukon-Pacific Exposition, Seattle's first world's fair, staged on the campus in 1909 (see the University of Washington). Growing University enrollment, expanded streetcar service, and completion of the Lake Washington Ship Canal in 1917 made "the Ave" (Fourteenth Avenue was renamed University Way in 1919) northeast Seattle's primary business district, and this "city within a city" experienced a surge of commercial and apartment construction through the 1920s. The neighborhood also produced Seattle's first (and only, as of 1997) woman mayor, Bertha K. Landes, who was elected to a single two-year term in 1926.

The Depression and World War II were hard on the District, but the G.I. Bill's college loans quickly tripled University enrollment to nearly 15,000 by 1950. That same year, unwelcome commercial competition appeared with the opening of Northgate, one of the nation's first shopping centers, a few miles north. This was followed by the University Village complex east of the District in 1956.

Victor Steinbrueck, then a professor of architecture at UW, suggested that the District fight back by turning the Ave into a pedestrian mall, but this idea was not seriously entertained until the early 1970s. Meanwhile, construction of Interstate 5 between 1958 and 1962 isolated the University Distict from the nearby neighborhoods of Latona and Wallingford and squeezed east-west traffic into Northeast Forty-fifth and Fiftieth Streets, creating near-permanent traffic jams.

University District resident Bertha K. Landes became the first (and only, as of 1997) woman to serve as mayor of Seattle in 1926. *(Museum of History and Industry)*

The mid-1960s established the University District as the unofficial center of Seattle's counterculture. Its veteran corps of beatniks, radicals, and artists had to make room in coffee houses, such as the Eigerwand and the Pamir House, for "fringies," hippies, and student activists of the Baby Boom generation. They protested the war in Vietnam on campus (and on I-5 during the famous "Freeway March" of May 5, 1970) and sampled psychedelic substances peddled by dealers on the Ave, to the horror of local merchants. Business leaders did welcome the appearance of at least one drug during the 1967 "Summer of Love" when the State Legislature finally lifted its 1893 ban on the sale of alcoholic beverages within one mile of the UW campus.

Despite generational and political tensions, attorney and former Planning Commission chair Cal McCune pushed a plan for converting University Way into a pedestrian mall. Thanks in large part to the success of Seattle's first "Street Fair," organized by pacifist and Ave merchant Andy Shiga in May 1970, the idea enjoyed broad community support, but the Ave's mostly absentee landlords rejected the mall in a special tax election in 1972.

The Ave today remains a busy and diverse business district, although its main trade is catering to the needs and whims of the 35,000 students encamped a block away.

## Points of Interest

We start by touring the Ave from its root on Portage Bay to Cowen and Ravenna Parks on the north, with a few jogs east and west on side streets.

**Jensen's Motor Boat Company,** 1417 Northeast Boat Street. One of the last holdouts against UW's relentless expansion, Jensen's is also one of few surviving marine businesses on this stretch of Portage Bay. It was here that Stan Sayre built the Slo-Mo-Shun, a radically new twin-sponson "hydroplane" that revolutionized powerboat racing in 1950.

**Burke-Gilman Trail.** This paved bicycle and jogging path follows the original roadbed of the Seattle, Lake Shore & Eastern Railroad, which was built eastward from Fremont to Union Bay in 1888. Removal of the tracks began in the early 1970s, and work on converting the rest of the route continues to the present day.

**Ye College Inn,** 4000 University Way. This quaint half-timbered lodge was financed by Charles Cowen to house

visitors at the 1909 AYP. It was designed by John Graham Sr. and David J. Myers, who also created several AYP pavilions on the nearby campus.

**Campus Parkway.** This boulevard was created in 1950 with the idea of establishing a more formal entrance to UW, but it now runs into the expanded Henry Art Gallery.

**The Playhouse,** at Forty-first Northeast. This charming brick building was designed by Arthur Loveless for the original Seattle Repertory Theater, founded by Burton and Florence James in 1929. The James' left-wing politics drew the fire of local McCarthyists in the late 1940s, when the building also housed the radical Church of the People, and UW drama department chair Glenn Hughes persuaded the University to take over the facility.

**U.S. Post Office,** 4244 University Way. This utilitarian Moderne building was designed by Gilbert Stanley Underwood in 1937. A later remodel prevents viewing of a WPA mural in its original lobby. The nearby **University Methodist Temple** was designed by John Graham Sr. and completed in 1927.

**University Book Store,** 4326 University Way. Now the city's largest independent bookseller, the University Book Store was established as a campus co-op in 1910 and is still owned by the Associated Students of the University of Washington. It moved to its present location in 1922 and has since expanded many times over.

**Wells Fargo Bank,** University Way at Northeast Forty-fifth. This imposing white Classical Revival building was built in 1913 for the University State Bank. It has served a succession of financial institutions.

**The Wilsonian,** University Way at Northeast Forty-seventh. Built and named by George and Corinne Wilson, this large apartment-hotel was designed by Frank Fowler and built in 1922. One famous tenant was Bertha K. Landes, who became Seattle's first woman mayor in 1926.

**University Heights Elementary School,** University Way at Northeast Fiftieth. Now a community center and the site of Saturday farmers and crafts markets, University Heights was designed by Bebb & Mendel and built in stages between 1902 and 1908.

**Ravenna and Cowen Parks,** University Way at Northeast Ravenna Boulevard. The deep ravine of Ravenna Park was a magnet for nature lovers, and they had to pay owner W. W. Beck a quarter for the privilege of communing with its colossal firs and babbling brook. The Olmsteds coveted the tract and planned Ravenna Boulevard to link it with "University Boulevard" (Seventeenth Northeast) and Green

This gargoyle at Northeast Forty-third Street and Brooklyn Avenue Northeast seems to need the services of a nearby tenant. *(Paul Dorpat)*

Lake. Beck refused to sell, so the Parks Department took the land by eminent domain in 1911. Nearby Cowen Park, in contrast, was donated by Charles Cowen in 1907, less out of altruism than shrewd calculation in spurring development of his nearby holdings.

■ **Side Trip West on Forty-second Street Northeast.**
The **Brooklyn Center** on the southeast corner of Forty-second and Brooklyn Northeast was built in 1891 for the United Methodist Church. **El Monterey Apartments** at 4204 Eleventh Northeast were designed and built by Everett J. Beardsley, who created several fanciful Mediterranean and Spanish Revival apartment blocks around Seattle.

■ **Side Trip West on Northeast Forty-fifth Street.**
The **Neptune Theater** at 1303 Brooklyn Northeast was designed by

Henderson Ryan and billed as one of America's finest neighborhood movie houses when it opened in 1921. (It was rivaled by the Egyptian Theater, which opened on Christmas Day, 1925, on the Ave, but this was converted into a drug store in 1960. The more modest Varsity Theater dates from 1940 and still shows movies.)

The **Edmond Meany Hotel,** 4507 Brooklyn Northeast, was designed by R. C. Reamer and financed through a community bond drive. It opened in 1931 and featured Glenn Hughes' original theater-in-the-round (designed by John Detlie) in its penthouse. The latter name stuck when UW built a free-standing "Penthouse Theater" on campus in 1938. The hotel's own name honors long-time UW history professor and booster Edmond Meany, and it reigned as the District's tallest structure until erection of Safeco's nearby corporate fortress in 1973.

**Showroom,** Northeast Forty-fifth at Roosevelt Northeast. Designed by Schack, Young & Mayers, this early terra-cotta automobile showroom was built in 1926 for a dealership established by UW athletic star Wee Coyle.

**Blue Moon Tavern,** Northeast Forty-fifth near Seventh Northeast. Established in 1934 just outside the one-mile alcohol quarantine around UW, the Blue Moon's eclectic clientele of leftists, literati, and loonies has made it a de facto cultural landmark. At one point in the 1950s, the bellies of at least four award-winning poets—Theodore Roethke, Stanley Kunitz, Carolyn Kizer, and Richard Hugo—might be found pressed up against the bar. The tavern was saved from demolition in 1990 by a populist preservation campaign, and last call has been postponed until 2034.

### ■ Side trip east on Northwest Forty-seventh.

The charming half-timbered **University Presbyterian Church Inn** at Sixteenth Northeast was designed by Ellsworth Storey in 1916 and served as the original home of what is now a much larger congregation.

University Heights Elementary now serves as a community center. *(WSA, Burien)*

One of the nation's first shopping centers, Northgate occupied a suburban wilderness when it opened in April 1950. *(Continental, Inc.)*

The tree-lined, scholastic serenity of **Seventeenth Avenue Northeast** makes you want to start singing, *"Gaudeamus igitur, juvenes dum sumus,"* or at least hum a few bars of Brahms' Academic Festival Overture. The Olmsteds planned this street as "University Boulevard," but everbody else calls it **Frat Row.** Notable fraternity and sorority houses include **Sigma Nu** (Ellwsorth Storey, 1916), 1616 Northeast Forty-seventh; **Alpha Tau Omega** (Lionel Pries, 1929), 1800 Northeast Forty-seventh; and **Phi Gamma Delta** (Mellor, Meigs & Howe, with J. Lister, 1927), 5404 Seventeenth Northeast.

## OTHER POINTS OF INTEREST IN NORTHEAST SEATTLE

**Magnuson Park,** Sand Point Way Northeast at Northeast Seventy-fifth Street. This level bulge into Lake Washington was the site of Seattle's first real aerodrome. In the first aerial circumnavigation of the globe, four Navy Douglas Air Cruisers left here on April 6, 1924, and three returned on September 28. After an intense and protracted lobbying campaign, the Navy took over the base in 1928 (and civil aviation shifted to Boeing Field). A portion of the base was surplused in the 1970s and converted into a National Oceanographic and Atmospheric Administration (NOAA) center and park honoring U.S. Senator Warren G. Magnuson. The rest of the base was recently turned over to the City of Seattle.

**Northgate Shopping Center,** Northeast Northgate Way at Fifth Avenue Northeast. Designed by John Graham Jr., the original complex opened in April 1950 and was one of America's first suburban shopping centers. It has since expanded many times.

# 6

# Southeast
# Seattle

## GEORGETOWN AND BOEING FIELD

### Orientation

Seattle's main industrial district begins south of Pioneer Square and occupies the Duwamish Valley between West Seattle and Beacon Hill. Georgetown stands on the north end of Boeing Field, at the Albro Street exit from Interstate 5. For detailed directions, see the suggested tour that follows.

### History of Georgetown

The east bank of the Duwamish River in Georgetown could lay legitimate claim to being Seattle's "real" birthplace. John Holgate canoed up the river from Olympia and staked the very first claim within the future city limits in the fall of 1850, but he neglected to record the correct papers. A year later, Luther Collins filed a proper claim on the same tract of fertile bottomland. He was joined by Henry Van Asselt and Joseph and Samuel Maple, whose September 14, 1851, claims coincided with the arrival of the Denny party scouts at Alki Point.

Unlike the would-be city builders led by Arthur Denny, these Duwamish settlers were farmers drawn to the meandering river's bounty of rich soil and level fields. The Seattle area's first race track was also established here in

Opposite: Franklin High School's dramatic Classical Revival facade has been restored. *(Paul Dorpat)*

These boaters were part of a *Seattle Post-Intelligencer* expedition that tried to row from Lake Washington to the Duwamish via the Black River in 1906. They gave up when night fell, which left them roughly in the middle of what is today a McDonald's parking lot in Renton.

1869 and operated by John Pennell, a famous scoundrel, and the area later became a center for "adult entertainment" of many varieties. Mother Joseph and her Sisters of Providence arrived in 1877, despite this, took over the county's "poor farm," and established their first hospital in the area.

In 1883, John Clausen and Edward Sweeny established the first of the town's three breweries. These merged in 1893 to form the Seattle Brewing and Malting Company, and output from the 5 acre complex was built up by Emil Sick for Rainier Beer and other brands until Georgetown was the world's sixth largest brewery. This may account for the town's large influx of German immigrants and the fact that brewing foreman Frank Mueller later served as its mayor.

Breweries such as this made Georgetown the world's sixth-largest beer maker in the early 1900s.
*(Rainier Beer)*

Much of the land was owned by Julius Horton (brother of Seafirst Bank founder Dexter Horton), who had purchased the Collins homestead in 1871. He incorporated the district in 1890 and named it Georgetown after his son, a surgeon who actually spent little time within its increasingly notorious precincts. The new city was linked to its northern neighbor by the region's first interurban streetcar line in 1893, and Stone & Webster extended the line to Tacoma in 1902. In addition to passangers, the interurban often carried produce grown by the German, Italian, and Japanese truck farmers who tilled the fertile Duwamish Valley.

Stone & Webster fired up the Georgetown Steamplant in 1906 to power its electric railroad and nearby breweries and factories. By then, Georgetown's population topped 4,000, but Seattle now surrounded it on three sides. Facing the inevitable, Georgetown's citizens voted for annexation on March 29, 1910.

By then, work was well advanced in filling the Duwamish mud flats to create Harbor Island. Dredging began in 1913 to straighten the kinks in the meandering river and continued over several decades, creating today's modern industrial district. The rich soil that had first lured John Holgate to the valley and sustained generations of farmers was soon buried beneath acres of concrete and vast rail yards.

## History of Boeing Field

As Georgetown voters debated annexation, the age of flight arrived a mile south of town. On March 11, 1910, a young daredevil named Charles K. Hamilton sped down the lawn of the Meadows Race Track in a spindly Curtiss biplane and soared into the air over a crowd of amazed spectators. William E. Boeing may have been among them, for he had already caught the flying bug at a 1910 air race in Los Angeles. Just two weeks earlier, Boeing had purchased the Heath Shipyard, where his personal yacht was under construction, on an oxbow of the Duwamish not far to the east of Hamilton's improvised airfield.

Boeing built his first airplanes on Lake Union (see Lake Union section). When the United States entered World War I in 1917, he shifted production to the main shed of his Duwamish shipyard, which became known as the Red Barn. At first Boeing chiefly built seaplanes, so a muddy field near his plant was adequate as a landing strip. His winning bid for a major airmail contract in 1926 demanded a larger field for both production and operation of what became United Airlines.

Boeing announced that he would move his company to Los Angeles if he could not find a suitable field in the area (the region's main airstrip at Sand Point on Lake Washington had been sold to the Navy). Since Boeing was already the area's largest employer, the county got the hint and built "Boeing Field" south of the Meadows Track. When it was dedicated on July 26, 1928, Bill Boeing gushed, "This day is just about the happiest of my life." A few weeks

Scores of new B-17G Flying Fortresses line up on the tarmac of Boeing Field late in World War II. Boeing's Plant 2 turned out 16 giant bombers each day at the peak of production. *(Boeing Airplane Co.)*

later he rolled out his first airliner onto the field, the Model 80 tri-motor, and started construction of "Boeing Plant 2" (the Red Barn being number 1).

Boeing Field went on to launch some of the world's most famous aircraft: the 247, the first modern airliner; the B-17 Flying Fortress; the B-29 Superfortress; the B-47 Stratojet; the B-52 Stratofortress; and the 707 jet airliner. Military use of Boeing Field became so intense during World War II that some production (chiefly B-29s) shifted to Renton and the Port of Seattle developed Seattle-Tacoma International Airport, but it did not start regular civilian operations until 1947.

Although scheduled airline activity at Boeing Field ended in the 1950s, it remains a busy hub for general aviation, cargo lines, and charters, as well as for Boeing testing and production. A few cranky bureaucrats insist on calling the strip King County International Airport, but for everyone else it will always be plain old "Boeing Field."

## Points of Interest

For a "scenic" tour of industrial Seattle from downtown, take First Avenue or Highway 99 South to East Marginal Way. Just beyond the Museum of Flight at the south end of Boeing Field, turn left (east) on Boeing Access Road South and turn again on Airport Way South to return north through Georgetown.

**Starbucks Coffee World Headquarters,** First Avenue South at South Lander Street. This colossal Sears & Roebuck store and mail-order center was designed by James E. Blackwell and Frank L. Baker in 1913 and expanded two years later. The retailer departed in the 1980s and the building was con-

A Seattle-Tacoma interurban train pauses in front of the former Sears and Roebuck store in the 1920s. The building now houses the corporate headquarters of Starbucks Coffee. *(Lawton Gowey)*

The abandoned Hat 'n' Boots service station remains one of Seattle's most distinctive examples of highway vernacular architecture.

verted into the "SoDo" (South of the Dome) Center. Starbucks Coffee took over the facility in 1997 for its corporate headquarters.

**Hat 'n' Boots,** 6800 East Marginal Way. This service station was designed by Allen Poe and Lewis Naismith and built in 1955. A 1,000-gallon Stetson covered the office, and boots contained

the restrooms. The station closed in 1988 and the state acquired the property. Locals hope to have the site designated as a city landmark.

**Museum of Flight,** 9204 East Marginal Way. Boeing's original Red Barn was floated down the Duwamish and trucked to its present site in 1975, near the spot of C. K. Hamilton's 1910

Boeing's original "Red Barn" plant is shown here during World War I. It was moved across the Duwamish and restored at the Museum of Flight. *(Boeing Airplane Co.)*

flight. The Museum of Flight lovingly restored the structure and opened its first displays in 1983, and completion of Ibsen Nelson's spectacular "Grand Gallery" followed in 1987. The museum's permanent exhibits include Boeing's Model 80-A trimotor biplane, P-26 (replica), 247D, B-17F, B-29, B-47E, B-52G, "Air Force One" 707, and the very first 747. Since the museum is an independent, nonprofit facility, it also displays many non-Boeing aircraft such as a DC-3, F-4 Phantom, MiG-21, F-18, Apollo and Mercury space capsules, a functioning replica of an air control tower, and the only A-12/SR-71 "Blackbird" with D-21 drone you'll ever see anywhere.

**Georgetown Steam Plant,** north end of Boeing Field. Built in 1906 by Stone & Webster, the power plant was acquired by Seattle City Light in 1951 when voters approved purchase of the last private utility services within the city limits. The plant, which operated until 1977, is now a National Landmark.

**Seattle Brewing & Malting Co.,** 6000 Airport Way South. The existing building dates from 1900, but Rainier Beer was first brewed here in 1883 by Edward Francis Sweeney. Prohibition ended production on January 1, 1916, and the building was converted to cold storage. Emil Sick resumed production of Rainier at the nearby Bayview Brewery in 1938, four years after the repeal of Prohibition.

**Georgetown City Hall,** 6202 Thirteenth Avenue South. Georgetown's third and last city hall was designed by Frederick Sexton. It opened in 1909, eight months before the city ceased to exist.

Georgetown's City Hall lost its spire since this photo was taken in the late 1940s. *(Seattle Public Library)*

**Jules Maes Restaurant,** 5919 Airport Way South. Originally called "the Brick Store," this building dates from 1897, and the Maes family has run an eatery here since 1937.

**The Castle,** 6420 Carlton Avenue South. Peter Gessner built this Victorian mansion in 1902 to house a gambling saloon and bordello, but before it was finished, he committed suicide in its back room when he discovered that his wife was pregnant by his business partner.

**Grover Cleveland High School,** 511 Fifteenth Avenue South. The western slope of Beacon Hill above Georgetown is crowned by the Georgian Revival mass of Cleveland High School. In service since 1927, Cleveland was designed by Floyd Naramore.

# RAINIER VALLEY AND COLUMBIA CITY

## Orientation

Rainier Valley extends from Jackson Street south to Renton, with Rainier Avenue South as its centerline. Columbia City is clustered at the intersection of Rainier and South Ferdinand Street. Note that this area includes some pockets of high crime and gang violence.

## History

Like the early Duwamish, Rainier Valley was a magnet for farmers of many nationalities, particularly Japanese and Italians. The presence of the latter earned the area the nickname "Garlic Gulch," and this community produced some remarkable leaders such as former governor Albert Rosellini and his cousin Victor Rosellini, a legendary restaurateur, and writer/professor Angelo Pellegrini.

J. K. Edmiston established the valley's primary arterial when he inaugurated service on the Rainier Avenue Electric Railway in 1891, and service was later extended to Rainier Beach, south of Seward Park. The railway helped to establish the little mill town of Columbia City, which supplied much of the lumber for rebuilding Seattle after the great fire of 1889.

Developer C. D. Hillman used the transit system to recruit home buyers to the valley. A bustling business district developed at the intersection of Rainier Avenue and South Ferdinand Street, and Columbia City incorporated in 1893.

Frank Osgood took over the streetcar line in 1895 and pushed south to Renton the following year. In 1903 he renamed the route the Renton and Southern Railway to reflect its new, truly interurban service. Local entrepreneurs also drew plans to dredge a nearby slough on Lake Washington and transform Columbia City into a "seaport" with the opening of the Ship Canal.

This 1904 view of the Rainier Beach station of the Renton & Southern Railway gives a sense of Lake Washington's former rustic character. *(Webster & Stevens, Photographers; Lawton Gowey)*

Rainier Avenue is still new in this early 1900s view of Columbia City. The Columbia Hotel *(center)* was built in 1893 and still stands. (MOHAI)

Despite these ambitions, Columbia City joined the rest of Southeast Seattle in voting to annex to Seattle in 1907. A decade later the Ship Canal had the reverse effect on local maritime ambitions by dropping the level of the lake nine feet, but through the years the town prospered on farming and steady residential growth. Meanwhile, on the north end of the valley Sick's Stadium regularly attracted thousands, who cheered on the Seattle Rainiers and such Pacific Coast League stars as Fred Hutchinson.

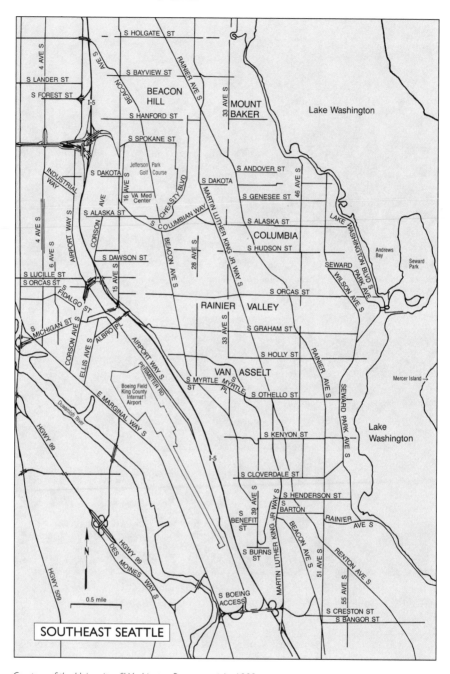

Courtesy of the University of Washington Press, copyright 1992.

The World War II internment of its Japanese farmers undermined the valley's agricultural base, and low-cost homes were thrown up to house defense workers in projects such as Holly Park. Industry began to spread south from Seattle, paving over farms and intruding on once-peaceful neighborhoods. Sick Stadium, rendered redundant by the Kingdome in 1976, was demolished.

The valley fell on harder times with declining incomes and rising crime while trying to accommodate thousands of new Southeast Asian immigrants. In an effort to reverse these trends, the Columbia City Historic District was established in 1978, and a new Regional Transit Authority rapid rail line is now being planned for the area. Thus, an interurban streetcar may once again ride to the rescue of Rainier Valley.

## POINTS OF INTEREST

**Columbia Hotel,** Rainier Avenue South at South Ferdinand Street. The town's first brick building was built in 1892, a year before incorporation.

**Columbia Branch Library,** 4721 Rainier Avenue South : This handsome little Carnegie Library was designed by W. Marbury Somervell and Harlan Thomas and opened in 1915. It occupies a small park donated in 1892.

**Kubota Gardens,** 9727 Renton Avenue South. First planted in the 1920s as a nursery by Japanese gardener Fujitaro Kubota, the Gardens fell into neglect during his World War II internment. Kubota and his family returned, but they could not afford to maintain them properly. The Gardens were purchased by the city in 1987 and have been restored as a public park.

Volunteers and Seattle Parks and Recreation staff have lovingly restored much of Fujitoro Kubota's original nursery, now Kubota Park. *(Paul Dorpat)*

# MOUNT BAKER AND LAKE WASHINGTON BOULEVARD SOUTH

## Orientation

Mount Baker occupies a ridge separating Rainier Valley from Lake Washington and is best reached via South McClellan Street. This stretch of Lake Washington Boulevard runs north from Seward Park along the lake, then winds uphill through Colman Park, crosses over the I-90 Floating Bridge lid, and then returns to the lakeshore at Leschi. (The stretch of roadway between Colman Park and Leschi is Lakeside Avenue South.)

## History

First owned by David Denny and then by the Seattle & Walla Walla Railroad, Mount Baker was acquired by Dan Jones in 1907. His Hunter Tract Development Company hired the Olmsted brothers to plat the community to take full advantage of its spectacular Lake Washington views, and coordinated development of the new "Mount Baker Park District" with nearby tracts

Motorists parade along the new Olmsted-designed Lake Washington Boulevard, which opened in 1909. *(Webster & Stevens, Photographers; Old Seattle Paper Works)*

owned by Charles Dose and George M. Taggert. Ellsworth Storey and other architects then went to work filling the neighborhood with some of the city's most beautiful homes.

Lake Washington Boulevard was completed in 1909. John C. Olmsted also designed the area's two major parks, Colman and Mount Baker, in 1910 and went to work on Seward Park's 278 acres when the city bought it in 1912.

Mount Baker survived construction of the first Lake Washington Floating Bridge in 1940 with little intrusion, but later plans for I-90's expansion were a different matter. At the same time, young professionals began rediscovering inner-city living in the 1970s, and they used new environmental laws to force the state to scale back its plan from 18 lanes to 8 and secured mitigating amenities such as the lid that covers much of the route.

## Points of Interest in Mount Baker

For a quick loop, take Rainier Avenue South to South McClellan Street Boulevard and turn (left) east. Turn right (south) on Mount Rainier Drive. Turn left (east) on South Ferris, then left (north) on Cascadia Avenue South. Follow this down and around until you find yourself back at McClellan. You have the choice of returning to Rainier Avenue via scenic Mount Baker Boulevard or taking a hairpin right (north) and heading down Lake Park Drive South to Lake Washington Boulevard.

**Franklin High School,** 3013 South Mount Baker Boulevard. The first wing of this impressive Renaissance structure was designed by Edgar Blair with a low-pitched, Grecian temple roof in 1912; it was expanded in 1925 and again in the late 1950s. District plans for Franklin's demolition were defeated by the neighborhood, and Bassetti Norton Meltner architects guided a complete renovation in 1989.

**Mount Baker Commercial Center,** 2803–2809 Mount Baker Drive South. This neighborhood retail complex was designed by John Graham Sr. and completed in 1928.

**Mount Baker Community Club House,** 2811 Mount Baker Drive South. Variously attributed to Ellsworth Storey and Charles Haynes, the best source says this spacious community center was designed by Charles C. Dose, the son of developer Charles P. Dose. It was completed in 1914 to house the activities of one of the city's first community councils.

**R.C. Force House,** 2810 Cascadia South. This was one of the district's first homes, designed by Charles Saunders and his second partner, George W. Lawton. During Prohibition it was suspected to be a covert center for rumrunners.

**Dr. Bouffler House,** 3036 Cascadia South. W. Marbury Somervell designed this home in 1925 with his Canadian partner, John L. Putnam.

**Peterson House,** 3303 Hunter Boulevard South. This flamboyant Craftsman-stick-style structure was built in 1913 to house its architect, A. Peterson, who is believed to have also designed its neighbors at 3317 and 3319 Hunter.

Spectators gather in Mount Baker to witness the opening of the first Lake Washington Floating Bridge on July 2, 1940. *(Washington State Department of Transportation)*

**Bowles House,** 2520 Shoreland Drive South. Arthur Loveless designed this sprawling Tudor mansion in 1925.

**Dyer House,** 2704 Thirty-fourth Avenue South. Located a few blocks west of the formal Mount Baker district, this chalet-style residence dates from 1922 and was one of Ellsworth Storey's later works. A Prairie-style bungalow by Storey (1926) can be found on the southwest corner of South McClellan and Thirty-third South.

## POINTS OF INTEREST ON AND NEAR LAKE WASHINGTON BOULEVARD SOUTH

**Lake Washington Floating Bridge Overlook.** The idea for a floating concrete bridge across Lake Washington was first proposed in the late 1920s, and it took State Highway Director Lacey V. Murrow (the brother of journalist Edward R. Murrow) a while to convince both engineers and legislators that it was feasible. His vision was vindicated on July 2, 1940, when Governor Clarence Martin led the first autos across the floating marvel. The bridge sank 50 years later, not long after its new twin span opened; repair workers had breached its floatation chambers and they filled with water during a sudden, violent storm. The replacement span was completed in 1993.

**Dose Terrace Steps.** This stairway at the foot of South Dose Terrace was built in 1906 and now leads down to the Mount Baker Rowing and Sailing Center. A 1915 residence by Ellsworth Storey stands on the southwest corner of Dose and Thirty-third South.

Stan Sayre's revolutionary Slo-Mo-Shun kicks up a rooster tail during a 1949 test on Lake Washington. *(Mary Randlett)*

**Thompson/La Turner House,** 3119 South Day Street. Dating from 1897, this is one of the area's last surviving Queen Anne mansions.

**Storey Cottages,** 1706-1816 Lake Washington Boulevard South and 1725-1729 Thirty-sixth Avenue South: Ellsworth Storey designed these charming little residential clusters "to be nice, low-cost rental homes in a good neighborhood."

**Stan Sayre's Memorial Hydroplane Pits.** This facility has been the site of motor boat races since the 1940s. It was later named for Stan Sayres, whose "Slo-Mo-Shun" hydroplane revolutionized the sport in 1950.

**Seward Park,** Lake Washington Boulevard South at Seward Park Avenue South. This park started out as an island owned by and named for the family of former congressman and lieutenant governor Joel Pritchard. The city acquired "Pritchard Island" in 1912, and the Olmsteds transformed it into a 278-acre park. It became a peninsula in 1917 when the new Ship Canal lowered Lake Washington by 9 feet and a new road linked it to Lake Washington Boulevard.

# 7

# West Seattle

## Orientation

Seattle's birthplace feels like a small town separated from its giant neighbor by more than just Elliott Bay and the Duwamish River. The West Seattle peninsula seems to occupy a different place and time altogether, yet it can be reached from downtown Seattle in only a few minutes via direct ramps linking Interstate 5 and Highway 99 to the Spokane Street Viaduct and the soaring West Seattle Freeway Bridge.

## History

Seattle takes November 13, 1851, as its official birthday, and Alki Point as its official birthplace. On that date, the schooner *Exact* anchored off the point and Arthur Denny led the rest of his party of a dozen adults and a dozen children ashore.

They were greeted by a drizzly rain and a very grateful David Denny, Arthur's younger brother. He and John Low had left their fellow Oregon Trail survivors in Portland the previous summer to scout a township on distant Puget Sound. In Olympia they linked up with Lee Terry and sailed up the

Opposite: The West Seattle ferry docks on Harbor Avenue c. 1900. Most of the shallows in the distance have been filled for Harbor Island and the Duwamish Waterway. *(Museum of History and Industry)*

Sound in a small boat bound for Elliott Bay to trade for salmon caught by its Duwamish natives.

They landed on September 25 and were warmly welcomed by Chief Seattle and his Duwamish tribesmen in the crude Chinook patois coined by Hudson's Bay Company trappers. Terry and Low then set out on foot to scout the area. They later encountered Luther Collins, who had already staked a claim on rich valley land near the mouth of the Duwamish River.

Denny, Low, and Terry were not interested in farming, so they went in search of an area suitable for a future port city. On September 28 they found their promised land on the exposed northwest shore of Alki Point, which juts into Puget Sound and was called "sbuh-kwah-buks" by the natives. Lee Terry suggested a new name in honor of his hometown, New York. The native word *Alki* (pronounced Al-*kee* by purists), meaning "by and by,". was appended; thus, New York-Alki was named. The natives, who had the good sense to camp out of the weather, looked on with amusement as their new white neighbors laid claim to the beach.

Denny scribbled a note to his brother: "We have examined the valley of the Duwamish River and find it a fine country. There is plenty of room for one thousand settlers. Come at once." This was entrusted to John Low, who commissioned Denny and Terry to build a cabin for him near the beach while he returned to Portland.

John Low's cabin, the first structure built in Seattle, is shown here in about 1900, before it was destroyed. It didn't look much better when the Denny Party arrived at Alki Point on November 13, 1851. *(West Seattle Historical Society)*

The walls were completed in October, but the two men lacked a froe, an L-shaped axe needed to cut shingles for the roof, so Terry set off to borrow one from any settlers he might find in the neighborhood. Denny remained behind in the unfinished cabin under a steady rain. A few days later, he cut himself while chopping wood. Then a band of skunks invaded his camp and made off with his provisions. Finally, he fell into a fever and began to wonder if he would live to see his 20th birthday.

David Denny was therefore greatly relieved when, at eight o'clock on the morning of November 13, the schooner *Exact* dropped anchor off Alki and put Arthur Denny and his party of ten adults and a dozen children ashore. They huddled in the roofless cabin, pelted by a bitter, wintry rain, and the women wept. Theirs were not tears of joy.

Fortunately, Arthur Denny had brought his own froe, for Lee Terry returned empty-handed soon after the *Exact's* arrival. Low's cabin was quickly finished and others begun when, in December, the brig *Leonesa* called at Alki and contracted for a load of timber piles. New York-Alki was in business. Meanwhile, Carson Boren, William Bell, and Arthur Denny explored Elliott Bay. On February 15, 1852, they decided that the little beach and island below present-day South Washington Street was a much better location on which to realize their dream of a great metropolis to come.

Charles Terry, who had joined the Denny Party on the *Exact* by a remarkable coincidence, was unconvinced and established a "New York Store." His younger brother, Lee, wearied of frontier life and returned to the real New York in April 1852. Soon after, physician and merchant David "Doc" Maynard traveled up from Olympia and established a claim and a store in the village of "Duwamps," which he successfully argued should be renamed Seattle to honor its host chief. A few months later, Henry Yesler chose Seattle for the Sound's first steam-powered sawmill, giving it a major economic boost over its friendly rival on Alki Point.

Charles Terry responded by persuading William Renton to build a mill in his town, leaving opinion divided over which settlement would win out in the long run. In July 1856, seven months after a brief native rebellion shook confidence in Seattle's future, Doc Maynard traded his 260 acres in present-day Pioneer Square to Charles Terry for $3,300 and 320 acres on Alki Point. In retrospect, Maynard's move was probably the dumbest land transaction in local history.

Both villages grew slowly during the 1860s. A new town of Freeport sprang up on the Elliott Bay side of the West Seattle peninsula with a mill and shipyard, and farmers began to clear patches of the interior. Relative fortunes changed in the early 1880s, however, when it became clear that Seattle would finally be linked to the Northern Pacific Railroad terminus in Tacoma, and West Seattle became a de facto suburb of the town on the east shore of Elliott Bay.

This was not completely bad news for developers such as Colonel Thomas Ewing, who formed the West Seattle Land and Improvement Company (WSLIC) in July 1888 and platted much of the area's northern plateau for new residences. On Christmas Day, 1888, the company launched service on its new steam ferry, *City of Seattle,* from the foot of Cherry Street to a point north of the present-day Seacrest Marina. Two years later, WSLIC began building its own cable railway to carry prospective home buyers from the ferry landing to lots on the plateau above.

The company's plans stalled after the Panic of '93, and few sales or improvements were made. The Klondike gold rush jolted Seattle out of the doldrums in 1897, but West Seattle's economic coma persisted. On April 21, 1902, West Seattle's few dozen residents took matters in their own hands by incorporating the peninsula's northern tip as an independent city. In 1904 the new city government replaced the long-closed cable railway with electric streetcars and, thereby, became the first municipality in the United States to own and operate its own street railway (Seattle would not take over its private transit system until 1918). Despite this innovation, the city government lacked the tax base to develop other needed improvements and utilities.

On May 25, 1907, the little city's southern neighbors voted to annex to it. That same day, a petition with 360 signatures requested that Seattle absorb its expanded western neighbor, now measuring nearly 20 square miles in area. A direct streetcar line was built from Seattle, and a new ferry boat, *West Seattle,* entered service early in 1907. On June 27 of that year, Luna Park— "the Coney Island of the West"—opened on Alki Beach. Two days later the Seattle annexation measure passed by 323 votes to 8, and the City of West Seattle ceased to exist.

Despite this political affiliation, West Seattle's development continued to trail other areas of Seattle. New rail and streetcar lines, bridges, and industrial expansion along the Duwamish failed to trigger the kind of fast growth envisioned by early developers and entrepreneurs. Instead, West Seattle slowly matured into a pleasant middle-class residential community and came to value its cultural independence from the rest of the city.

Yet West Seattle residents fought tenaciously for better bridges across the Duwamish and threatened to secede if their needs were not met. Their prayers were answered early on the morning of June 11, 1978, when Rolf Neslund, pilot of the freighter *Antonio Chavez,* misjudged the gap between the piers of the Spokane Street bascule bridge and steered the giant ship into the north draw-span, jamming it open. The accident also opened federal coffers for a new "high span" bridge, previously approved by voters but stalled by scandals and inadequate funds. (Meanwhile, Rolf Neslund disappeared, and his wife was convicted of doing him in and, possibly, mixing his ground-up remains in the cement of her new driveway.)

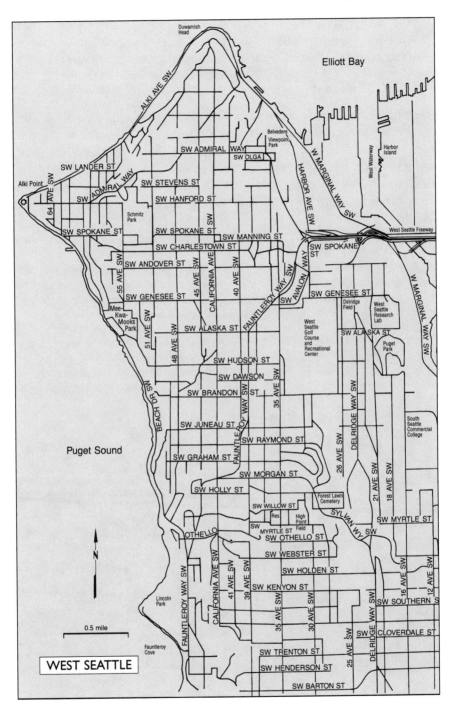

WEST SEATTLE

*Courtesy of the University of Washington Press, copyright 1992.*

The new high bridge was dedicated on July 14, 1984, and a new Spokane Street bascule followed a few years later. Ironically, another movement has been launched in West Seattle to secede from its big sister.

## Points of Interest

The West Seattle Bridge offers drivers three options for touring the district: the Harbor Avenue Southwest exit puts you on the lower beachfront; Admiral Way Southwest takes you up and across the plateau and down to Alki Point; and staying on the highway gives you the choice of taking Fauntleroy Way Southwest to Lincoln Park and the Vashon Island ferry dock, or entering the main business district at "the Junction" of Southwest Alaska Street and California Avenue Southwest.

Take the exit to Harbor Avenue and turn right for the following mini-tour.

**Harbor Avenue Southwest.** This scenic road takes you along the western shoreline of Elliott Bay. The old West Seattle ferry used to land just north of the present-day Seacrest Marina. Luna Park, "the Coney Island of the West," opened below the promontory of Duwamish Head on June 27, 1907, and offered visitors rides on a giant roller coaster and other amusements for the next six years. A natatorium survived until it was consumed by a devastating fire on April 14, 1931. Harbor Avenue becomes Alki Avenue Southwest as it rounds the northern tip of West Seattle.

**Alki Beach.** This long strand has been a popular swimming beach since Seattle's earliest days, despite Puget

Luna Park at Duwamish Head billed itself as the "Coney Island of the West" between 1907 and 1913, when it closed. *(Oregon Historical Society)*

Pioneers and newcomers gathered on November 13, 1905, to dedicate a monument marking the birthplace of Seattle on Alki Beach. *(West Seattle Historical Society)*

Sound's bitterly cold waters. A private natatorium was built here in 1905, and the city established a public bathing beach four years later. Developers built a new, glass-enclosed natatorium in 1934, which the Parks Department took over in 1942 and operated until 1953, when persistent and expensive vandalism forced its closure and removal. The miniature replica of the Statue of Liberty, which stands near the natatorium's former site, was donated by the Boy Scouts in 1952.

**The Alki Pylon,** foot of Sixty-third Avenue Southwest on Alki Avenue Southwest. This small obelisk marks the "Birthplace of Seattle" and bears the names of the Denny party's 24 adults and children who assembled here on the rainy morning of November 13, 1851. A gift of Lenora Denny, the pylon was originally installed on the south side of Alki in front of the former Stockade Hotel. It was unveiled on November 13, 1905, in a ceremony attended by founding father Carson Boren and numerous descendants of the first settlers of "New York-Alki."

The pylon was moved to its present location in 1926, and the first motorcar caravan to cross the northern states delivered a piece of Plymouth Rock for placement in the monument's new base. On the occasion of Seattle's centennial in 1951, General Douglas MacArthur presided over the burial of a time capsule just north of the pylon, which is to be opened in 2051.

**Alki Homestead Restaurant and Log House Museum,** 2717 and 3003 Sixty-first Avenue Southwest. The Homestead is located a block south of the pylon and was built by Fred L. Fehren for soap maker William Bernard and his wife Gladys during the winter of 1903–04. The Bernards vacated their "Fir Lodge" three years later, and it was taken over by the Auto Club and later tenants. In 1950, the Alki Homestead began its present career as a restaurant. The nearby Log House Museum is believed to have belonged to the original Bernard estate and is now operated by the West Seattle Historical Society.

**Alki Point Light Station.** The present lighthouse was built by the Coast Guard in 1913 according to standard plans. The Olmsteds argued for a park covering most of the Point, but the city tarried too long and private owners developed the site. At this point, you have a choice of ascending Admiral Way or taking the following side trip.

### ■ Side Trip on Beach Drive Southwest.

This scenic residential arterial follows the shoreline to **Lincoln Park** at Williams Point. A park on this 120-acre patch of woods and beach was first proposed by the Olmsteds in 1903, although West Seattle lay outside the existing city limits, and finally established in 1923. Its large saltwater swimming pool opened in 1941 and honors West Seattle philan-thropist Laurence Colman.

The **Fauntleroy-Vashon Ferry Dock** lies a few blocks south of Lincoln Park. Ferry service to Vashon Island was established from here in 1925 by the Kitsap County Transportation Company, and taken over by the state in 1951. Fauntleroy Cove was named by Captain George Davidson, the homesick leader of an 1850 coastal survey, for his Indiana sweetheart, Ellinor Fauntleroy.

To resume the tour, head back north on Beach Drive.

### ■ Ascending Admiral Way Southwest.

At Alki Point, turn inland on Admiral Way Southwest. The arterial crosses the northwest tip of **Schmitz Park,** a 50-acre wooded ravine containing the last stand of virgin timber remaining within the Seattle city limits. "Forest Park" was recommended for acquisition by the Olmsteds' 1903 report and

In this 1996 view from West Seattle's Belvedere Park, the Denny party's dream of building a "New York, by and by" seems to have been realized. *(Paul Dorpat)*

donated to Seattle five years later by Ferdinand and Emma Schmitz.

**Admiral Way at California Avenue Southwest.** This compact business district has changed little since 1941, when the **Admiral Theater** opened at 2343 California Southwest. It was designed by B. Marcus Priteca in a maritime Moderne style and originally featured a tall ship's mast. The theater was later "twinned," but by the early 1990s it faced the same fate that had befallen so many other neighborhood movie houses. Fortunately, residents manned the historic preservation pumps in 1993 and saved the Admiral from being scuttled.

**Belvedere Viewpoint Park,** Admiral at Thirty-seventh Avenue Southwest. The city established the original viewpoint in 1912, the same year that voters rejected Virgil Bogue's proposed comprehensive plan and his idea for a giant monument on nearby Duwamish Head. West Seattle made do with a totem pole carved by Bella Coola Indians in 1901 and donated by the owner of Ye Olde Curiosity Shop. It was replaced in 1966 with a replica carved at no charge by Boeing engineers Michael Morgan and Robert Fleischman. From here, Admiral Way descends the bluff and returns you to the West Seattle Freeway and downtown.

# 8

# Nearby
# Historical Destinations
# on Puget Sound

*The following is a sampling of the historical attractions to be found within an hour or two's travel of downtown Seattle (non-rush-hour travel times are estimated).*

## East of Seattle

**Kirkland.** Take I-5 to the State Route 520 Evergreen Point Floating Bridge and follow the signs; allow 30 minutes. Established on Moss Bay in the 1870s, Kirkland was later named by and for Peter Kirk, who dreamed of fueling the "Pittsburgh of the West" here with local iron ore and coal deposits. The dream melted in the turmoil of the Panic of '93, but not before several charming homes and and buildings were erected. Some survive, and the town now rings an attractive public beach and marina. The MV *Kirkland,* a converted Columbia river ferry, docks here and offers tours that recall the days when similar craft were Lake Washington's only "floating bridges."

**Marymoor Park,** 6036 West Lake Sammamish Parkway Northeast, Redmond. Take State Route 520 and follow signs to Redmond; allow 30 minutes. This large county park was designed by Richard Haag and encloses the Clise Mansion, dating from 1904, which houses the Marymoor Museum

Opposite: The *Virginia V* is the last "Mosquito Fleet" steamship still operating on Puget Sound. *(Frank Shaw)*

The Seattle Lake Shore & Eastern Railroad linked the young city to Eastside coal fields in the 1890s.
*(Greg Lang)*

(425-885-3684) and exhibits tracing the history of Lake Washington's "Eastside". The nearby campus of the Microsoft Corporation is making future history, but it is not open to visitors.

**Spirit of Washington Dinner Train.** Enjoy dinner and a scenic tour of the east shore of Lake Washington from downtown Renton to the Columbia Winery in Woodinville. Call 800-876-RAIL for information.

**Snoqualmie.** Take I-90 east and follow the signs; allow 40 minutes. This timber town on the main pass through the Cascade Mountains dates from 1865, when Seattle citizens hacked a wagon trail from the crest to their town. The Northwest's first and oldest operating hydroelectric plant was constructed in 1899 to harness Snoqualmie Falls, from which water plummets 268 feet—100 feet longer than Niagara Falls. The original wing of the nearby Salish Lodge was built in 1916 and may be familiar to fans of the bizarre TV drama *Twin Peaks*. The nearby town features a lovingly restored railroad station built by the Seattle Lake Shore and Eastern in 1890. It houses the Northwest Railway Museum (425-888-0373), which operates a steam-powered excursion train from April through September. Roslyn, which lies off I-90 on the east side of the Cascades crest, was cast as the fictional Alaskan village of Cicely in the TV series *Northern Exposure*.

## West of Seattle

**Tillicum Village,** Blake Island. Take the excursion boat from Pier 55-56. This resort features dances and a salmon dinner based on Northwest native themes (206-443-1244).

**Bremerton and Puget Sound Shipyards.** Take the Bremerton Ferry from Colman Dock; allow 40 minutes. Bremerton is named for Seattle developer Willam Bremer, who persuaded locals to sell land for the Navy's Puget Sound shipyard in 1891. The USS *Missouri* will soon depart for Pearl Harbor, but there are many other operating and mothballed naval vessels on view. Historical displays may be found at the Bremerton Naval Museum, 130 Washington Avenue, Bremerton (360-479-7447) and the Naval Undersea Museum, Garnett Way, in Keyport (360-396-4148).

**Suguamish Museum,** 15838 Sand Hook Road, Suquamish Indian Reservation. Take the Bremerton Ferry from Colman Dock, then Highway 305 to Poulsbo and follow the signs; allow 1 hour. This tribal museum features award-winning displays telling the story of Puget Sound's original residents, and its grounds shelter Chief Seattle's grave (360-598-3311).

**Port Townsend.** Take the Bainbridge Island ferry from Colman Dock to Winslow, follow Highway 305 to Highway 104, turn north on Highway 19 to Highway 20, and follow the signs; allow 2.5 hours. This port city on the northeast tip of the Olympic Peninsula was briefly the Puget Sound city that many deemed "most likely to succeed." Founded a few months before Seattle, Port Townsend's strategic position at the junction of Puget Sound and the Strait of Juan de Fuca and its proximity to Vancouver Island, British Columbia, gave it an early advantage. The city's boosters counted on a direct railroad link to the Columbia River to secure its dominance, but this never came to pass. Port Townsend's handsome commercial buildings and imposing Victorian homes

Coastal schooners such as the *Wawona* plied Puget Sound until the 1950s. *(NW Seaport)*

were trapped in the amber of unfulfilled expectations, and most are now preserved within a National Historic District. For more information, contact the Port Townsend Visitor Center, 2437 East Sims Way, Port Townsend, WA 98368 (360-385-2722).

## North of Seattle

**Everett.** Take I-5 north and follow the signs to city's center; allow 40 minutes. This city's harbor on Port Gardiner Bay and the nearby iron deposits attracted investment from John D. Rockefeller and other Eastern capitalists, and James J. Hill stoked the speculative fire by suggesting that his Great Northern Railroad might terminate here rather than pushing on to Seattle. The bubble burst in the Panic of 1893, but the city recovered with construction of major lumber and paper mills. This also set the stage for bloody confrontations with early labor unions, including the "Wobblies" of the Industrial Workers of the World. More recently, Everett rebounded from a long economic slump with construction of Boeing's huge plant at Paine Field (home of the 747 and the 777) and the Navy's new base for the North Pacific fleet. For more information, contact or visit the the Snohomish County Museum, 2817 Rockefeller Avenue, Everett, WA 98201 (425-259-2022).

**Whidbey Island.** Take I-5 north to Mukilteo and then take the ferry to Clinton; allow 1 hour. This slender, 40-mile-long island offers a number of attractions, including the historic towns of Langley, Freeland, and Coupeville (situated within Ebey's Landing National Historic Reserve) and the abandoned coastal gun battery at Fort Casey. The island is linked with Port Townsend via ferry service (follow the signs from Highway 525), and its north end is joined to the mainland by a spectacular bridge over Deception Pass.

**La Conner.** Take I-5 north and follow the signs; allow one hour. The main street of this popular if over-prettified fishing village gives some hint of the North Sound's early rustic character. The town's name is a romantic artifice created by merchant J. S. Conner to honor his wife, Louisa Ann Conner.

**Anacortes and the San Juan Islands.** Take I-5 north and turn west on Highway 20; allow two hours to reach Anacortes. This area marks the southernmost penetration of Washington waters by early Spanish explorers, who named many of the area's islands and channels. Anacortes (a corruption of the name of founder Amos Bowman's wife, Anna Curtis) is a pleasant coastal town built on timber and fishing, and its state ferry terminal provides service to all of the major San Juan islands. Of historical interest are the American and English camps, artifacts from the brief 1859 "Pig War" boundary dispute between the United States and Great Britain, and the Roche Harbor resort and nearby Lime Kiln Park on San Juan Island; and Robert Moran's "Rosario" mansion and resort on Orcas Island.

**Bellingham and Fairhaven.** Take I-5 north and follow the signs; allow 2.5 hours. Lying only 18 miles south of British Columbia, Bellingham was a tiny fishing and logging village until the Fraser River gold rush of 1858. Development followed in fits and starts, often driven by unrealized dreams of transcontinental rail service and Pacific Rim commerce. The present city encompasses several distinct districts, the best preserved of which is Fairhaven, now home of the Alaska ferry terminal. The Victorian pile of Bellingham's Old City Hall (1892) at 121 Prospect Street houses the Whatcom Museum of History and Art (360-676-6981).

## South of Seattle

**Renton.** Take I-5 south and follow the signs to the city's center; allow 20 minutes. Renton was settled in 1853, but the town did not take off until 20 years later when coal was discovered. In 1877, the Seattle & Walla Walla railroad arrived from Seattle and helped to spur the growth of nearby mining towns with names such as Newcastle and Black Diamond. Their town cemeteries document the hard toil and short lives of hundreds of miners of all races and nationalities. The Renton Historical Society operates a museum at 235 Mill Street South (206-255-2330).

**Tacoma.** Take I-5 south and follow the signs to Pacific Avenue and the city's center; allow 40 minutes. Tacoma was a village of only a few hundred souls in 1873 when the Northern Pacific Railroad selected it as the western

The new Washington State Historical Museum's huge arches echo the entrance to Tacoma's Union Station. (Joel Polsky, Washington State Historical Museum)

terminus for the region's first transcontinental railroad and set off a long rivalry with Seattle. Thanks to its vast harbor on Commencement Bay, Northern Pacific capital, and the harvesting of its land grant timber, Tacoma grew quickly at first, but its dependence on a single company proved to be a two-edged sword during the wild financial swings of the 1880s and 1890s. The city survived, and in the early 1900s it bloomed, creating a rich architectural legacy. Notable downtown structures include the Old City Hall, Tacoma Elks, Northern Pacific headquarters, Pantages Theater, Stadium High School, numerous fine homes, and Reed & Stem's dramatic Beaux Arts Union Station (1911) on Pacific Avenue. The latter's oversized Roman arches are repeated in Charles Moore and Arthur Anderson's elegant design for the nearby Washington State History Museum's new home at 1911 Pacific Avenue, whose innovative exhibits are a must-see (888-238-4373). Nearby warehouses have been converted to house the new Tacoma campus of the University of Washington. The Tacoma Architectural Foundation also offers tours of the city's historical attractions (253-593-3305).

**Paradise Inn, Mount Rainier.** Take I-5 south and follow the signs; allow 2 hours. Mount Rainier and vicinity were dedicated as the United States' fifth national park in 1899. The mountain was named by George Vancouver a century earlier to honor his patron, Admiral Peter Rainier, but Tacoma residents preferred the original Nisqually name, Mount Tahoma. Heath & Gove designed the original, hand-crafted Paradise Inn guest lodge in 1917. For information, call 360-569-2275. In the nearby town of Elbe (on Highway 7), the Mount Rainier Scenic Railway operates a steam-powered excursion train during summer months (360-569-2588).

**Olympia.** Take I-5 south to the Capitol exit; allow 70 minutes. This south Sound village grew up near the original Hudson's Bay Company's Fort Nisqually (now DuPont). Olympia became the Territorial Capital when Washington was divided from Oregon in 1853 and retained the seat of government with statehood in 1889. Willis Ritchie designed the original County Courthouse, which served as the "Old Capitol" until 1928 and now houses the Office of the State Superintendent of Public Instruction. New York architects Wilder & White were selected in 1911 to design a new capitol campus, but money woes delayed completion of the first buildings until 1920. The Olmsted brothers laid out the grounds, and Bebb and Gould assisted in the design of the domed Doric temple that now houses the legislature and the governor's office. The nearby C. J. Lord House, 211 Twenty-first Avenue West, now houses the State Capitol Museum (360-753-2580).

# Appendix A

## HISTORICAL MUSEUMS AND PERMANENT EXHIBITS IN SEATTLE

**Burke Museum of Natural History and Culture** (science and historical exhibits near north gate, University of Washington campus), 17th Avenue Northeast at Northeast Forty-fifth Street, Seattle, WA 98195 (206-543-5590)

**Center for Wooden Boats** (displays, demonstrations, and rentals at south end of Lake Union), 1010 Valley Street, Seattle, WA 98109 (206-382-2628)

**Chittenden Locks Visitor Center** (Ballard), 3015 Northwest 54th Street, Seattle, WA 98107 (206-783-7059)

**U.S. Coast Guard Museum Northwest** (displays on Pier 36, downtown waterfront), 1519 Alaskan Way South, Seattle, WA 98154 (206-286-9608)

**Klondike Gold Rush National Historic Park** (Pioneer Square), 117 South Main Street, Seattle, WA 98104 (206-553-7220)

**Museum of Flight** (historic aircraft at south end of Boeing Field), 9404 East Marginal Way South, Seattle, WA 98108-4097 (206-764-5700)

**Museum of History and Industry** (diverse exhibits and programs, near north end of the Arboretum and Montlake Bridge), 2700 24th Avenue East, Seattle, WA 98112 (206-324-1126)

**Nordic Heritage Museum** (Ballard), 3014 Northwest 67th Street, Seattle, WA 98117 (206-789-5707)

**Northwest Seaport** (historic vessels *Wawona, Relief,* and *Arthur Foss,* moored at south end of Lake Union), 1002 Valley Street, Seattle, WA 98109 (206-447-9800)

**Odyssey Maritime Discovery Center** (may open 1998, Bell Street Pier, downtown waterfront), Planning Office 318 First Avenue South, Seattle, WA 98104 (206-623-2120)

**The Olmsted Legacy** (display), Volunteer Park Water Tower, Seattle

**U.S. Postal Service Museum** (display in Pioneer Square Branch), 91 South Jackson Street, Seattle, WA 98104 (206-623-1908)

**Puget Sound Maritime Museum** (exhibits displayed at Museum of History and Industry), P.O. Box 9731, Seattle, WA 98109-9731

A Boeing Model 80-A and other vintage aircraft occupy the Museum of Flight's "Grand Gallery" in Seattle. *(Museum of Flight)*

**Rainier Square Concourse** (historic photos and artifacts of downtown Seattle development, Boeing, and Eddie Bauer), beneath 5th Avenue between University and Union Streets

**Seattle Architectural Foundation** (permanent display on Level 3, Rainier Square, downtown Seattle; also conducts "Viewpoint" historical tours), 1333 Fifth Avenue, Seattle, WA 98101 (206-667-9184; tours, 206-667-9186)

**Seattle Art Museum** (notable Northwest native art collection, downtown Seattle), 100 University Street, Seattle, WA 98101 (206-654-3100)

**Seattle Public Library Central Branch** ("Seattle Room" document collection, downtown Seattle), Fourth Avenue at Madison Street, Seattle, WA 98101 (206-386-4636)

**Underground Tour** (within and beneath Pioneer Square), 610 First Avenue, Seattle, WA 98104 (206-682-4646)

***Virginia V* Foundation** (last operating "Mosquito Fleet" steamship, to be available for charters and tours following repairs in mid-1998), P.O. Box 24805, Seattle WA 98124-0805 (206-624-9119)

**Waterfront Streetcar** (vintage streetcar service on downtown waterfront); Metro Transit Rider Info: 206-553-3000

**Wing Luke Asian Museum** (Asian-American history, Chinatown/International District), 407 Seventh Avenue South, Seattle, WA 98104 (206-623-5124)

# Appendix B

## HISTORIC PRESERVATION
## AGENCIES AND ORGANIZATIONS

**Allied Arts of Seattle,** 105 South Main Street, Seattle, WA 98104 (206-624-0432)

**American Institute of Architects, Seattle Chapter,** 1911 First Avenue, Seattle, WA 98101 (206-448-4938)

**Association of King County Historical Organizations,** P.O. Box 3257, Seattle, WA 98114

**City of Seattle Urban Conservation Division** (Fourth Floor, Arctic Building), Third Avenue at Cherry Street, Seattle, WA 98104 (206-684-0228)

**Historic Seattle Preservation and Development Authority, Inc.,** 1117 Minor Avenue, Seattle, WA 98101 (206-622-6952)

**King County Office of Cultural Resources** (11th Floor, Smith Tower), 506 Second Avenue, Room 1115, Seattle, WA 98104 (206-296-7580)

**Seattle Architectural Foundation** (Level 3, Rainier Square), 1333 Fifth Avenue, Seattle WA 98101 (206-667-9184)

**Washington State Office of Archeology and Historic Preservation,** P.O. Box 48343, Olympia, WA 98504-8343 (360-753-5010)

**Washington Trust for Historic Preservation,** 204 First Avenue South, Seattle, WA 98104 (206-753-4011)

# Appendix C

## ROSTER OF OFFICIAL SEATTLE LANDMARKS (AUGUST 1997)

(Key: **S**—City of Seattle Designated Landmark; **N**—National Register of Historic Places and Washington Heritage Register; **W**—Washington State Heritage Register only; **NL**—National Historic Landmark)

### DOWNTOWN SEATTLE

#### In or Near Pioneer Square Historic District

Battle of Seattle site, Third Avenue at Jefferson Street (W)
Grand Central Building, 214 First Avenue South (N)
Old Public Safety Building, Fourth Avenue at Terrace Street (N)
Pioneer Building, First Avenue at Yesler Place (NL)
Pioneer Place Totem and Pergola, First Avenue at Yesler Way (NL)
Smith Tower (L. C. Smith Building), 506 Second Avenue (S)
Triangle Hotel and Bar (Flatiron Building), 551 First Avenue South (S, N)
Washington Street Public Boat Landing (Harbormaster Station, site of hospital ship *Idaho*), Alaskan Way at South Washington Street (W, N)
Yesler Wharf site, Alaskan Way and Yesler Way (W)

#### In or Near Chinatown-International District Historic District

Chinese Baptist Church, 925 South King Street (N)
Chinese Community Bulletin Board, 511 Seventh Avenue South (S)
Eastern Hotel, 506½ Maynard Avenue South (S)
King Street Station, Third Avenue South at South King Street (N)
Nihon Go Gakko, 1414 South Weller Street (N)
Nippon Kan Theater, 622 South Washington Street (N)
Old Main Street School, 307 Sixth Avenue South (S)
Seattle Buddhist Church, 1427 South Main Street (S)
Union Station, Fourth Avenue at South Jackson Street (N)
U.S. Immigration Building and Assay House, 815 Airport Way South (N)
Victorian Apartments, 1234–1238 South King Street (N)
Yesler Terrace Public Housing Project, 903 Yesler Way (N)

#### On or Near the Central Waterfront

Beebe Building, 1013 First Avenue (S, N)
Colman Building, 801–821 First Avenue (S, N)
Colman Dock Site, Pier 52 (W)
Colonial Hotel, 1110–1123 First Avenue (S, N)
First Post Office site (A. A. Denny House), First Avenue at Marion Street (W)

Globe Building, 1001–1011 First Avenue (S, N)
Grand Pacific Hotel, 1115–1117 First Avenue (S, N)
Hoge Building, 705 Second Avenue (S, N)
Holyoke Building, 107 Spring Street (S, N)
Hotel Cecil, 1019–1023 First Avenue (S, N)
National Building, 1006–1024 Western Avenue (S, N)
Olympic Warehouse and Cold Storage Building, 1203–1207 Western Avenue (S)
Pier 42, former shipyards (W)
Pier 56, *Miike Maru* arrival site (W)
Pier 64, "Great White Fleet" disembarkation site, (W)
U.S. Immigration Building, 84 Union Street (S, N)
Waterfront Park, S.S. *Portland* landing site (W)
West Seattle Ferry site, Alaskan Way at Madison Street (W)

## In or Near Pike Place Market Historic District

Alaska Trade Building, 1915–19 First Avenue (N)
Butterworth Building, 1921 First Avenue (N)
Terminal Sales Building, 1932 First Avenue (S)

## Central Business District

1411 Fourth Avenue Building, 1411 Fourth Avenue (S, N)
Arctic Building, 306 Cherry Street (S, N)
Bon Marche, 300 Pine Street (S)
Central School site (first public school), Third Avenue at Madison Street (W)
Cobb Building, 1301–1309 Fourth Avenue (N)
Carson Boren Home Site, Second Avenue at Cherry Street (W)
Brooklyn Building, 1222 Second Avenue (S)
Coliseum Theater, Fifth Avenue at Pike Street (S, N)
Decatur Building, 1521 Sixth Avenue (S)
Arthur Denny Home site, Second Avenue at Union Street (W)
Dexter Horton Building, 710 Second Avenue (S)
Doyle Building (J. S. Graham Store), 119 Pine Street (S, N)
Eagles Temple Building, 1416 Seventh Avenue (S, N)
Exchange Building, 821 Second Avenue (S)
Federal Office Building (and site of the great Seattle fire of 1889),
    909 First Avenue (N)
Four Seasons Olympic Hotel (and Territorial University site),
    1200 Fourth Avenue (N)
Great Northern Building, 1404 Fourth Avenue (S)
Key Bank (Bank of California), 815 Second Avenue (S)
Leamington/Pacific Hotel & Apartments, 317 Marion Street (S, N)
Liggett/Fourth and Pike Building, 1424 Fourth Avenue (S)
Lyon Building, 607 Third Avenue (S, N)
Mann Building, 1411 Third Avenue (S)
McGraw Place, Westlake Avenue at Stewart Street (S)
Olympic Tower (United Shopping Tower), 217 Pine Street (S, N)
Paramount Theater and Building, 901 Pine Street (S, N)
Rainier Club, 810 Fourth Avenue (S, N)
Seaboard Building (Northern Bank and Trust), 1506 Westlake Avenue (S)
Seattle (Northern Life) Tower, 1212 Third Avenue (N)
Skinner Building and Fifth Avenue Theater, 1300–1334 Fifth Avenue (N)
Sixth and Pine Building (Shafer Building), 515 Pine Street (S)

Times Square Building, 414 Olive Way (S, N)
U.S. Courthouse (and Sisters of Providence Hospital site),
   1010 Fifth Avenue (N)
YMCA Central Branch, South Building, 909 Fourth Avenue (S)

*Pending City Designations*

Frederick & Nelson Building, 500-524 Pine Street
Joshua Green Building, 1425 Fourth Avenue
Seattle Tower, 1212 Third Avenue

## Belltown and Denny Regrade

Barnes Building, 2320 First Avenue (S, N)
Austin Bell Building, 2326 First Avenue (S)
Fire Station No. 2, 2318 Fourth Avenue (S)
Guiry Hotel, 2101–2105½ First Avenue (S, N)
Hull Building, 2401–2405 First Avenue (S, N)
Josephinum (New Washington Hotel), 1902 Second Avenue (S, N)
Moore Theater and Hotel Building, 1932 Second Avenue (S, N)
New Pacific Apartment Building, 2600–2604 First Avenue (S)
Schillestad Building, 2111 First Avenue (S, N)
Tillicum Place and Chief Seattle statue, Fifth Avenue at Denny Way
   and Cedar Street (S, N)
William Volker Building, 1000 Lenora Street (N)

## EAST OF DOWNTOWN:

## First Hill

Northwest School (Summit School), 1415 Summit Avenue (S, N)
Old Firehouse No. 3, 301 Terry Avenue (S)
Old Firehouse No. 25, 1400 Harvard Avenue (S)
William Phillips House, 711–712 East Union Street (N)
Judge James T. Ronald House, 703 Eighth Avenue (N)
St. James Cathedral, rectory and Site, Ninth Avenue and Marion Street (S)
Seattle First Baptist Church, 1121 Harvard Avenue (S)
Stimson/Green House, 1204 Minor Avenue (S, N)
Trinity Parish Episcopal Church, 609 Eighth Avenue (S, N)
U.S. Assay Office/German House, 613 Ninth Avenue (S, N)
Wintonia Hotel, 1431 Minor Avenue (S)

## Central Area and Beacon Hill

Twelfth Avenue Bridge, Dearborn Street (N)
Twenty-Third Avenue Houses Group, 812–828 Twenty-Third Avenue (S, W)
Beacon Hill First Baptist Church, 1607 South Forest Street (S)
Black Property, 1319 Twelfth Avenue South (S)
Immaculate Conception Church, 820 Eighteenth Avenue (S)
Fire Station No. 23, Eigthteenth Avenue at Columbia Street (S, N)
First Methodist Protestant Church of Seattle, 128 Sixteenth Avenue East (N)
Langston Hughes Cultural Arts Center (Bikur Holim Synagogue),
   104 Seventeenth Avenue South (S)
Pacific Medical Center (U.S. Marine Hospital), 1200 Twelfth Avenue South (S, N)
Raymond/Ogden Mansion, 702 Thirty-Fifth Avenue (N)

Rederlsheimer/Ostrander House, 200 Fortieth Avenue East (N)
Row houses, 806–828 Twenty-Third Avenue (N)
Victorian house, 1414 South Washington Street (S)
Victorian Row Apartment Building, 1236–1238 South King Street (S)
James W. Washington, Jr., home and studio, 1816 Twenty-Sixth Avenue (S)

## Capitol Hill

Anhalt Apartment Buildings, 1005 and 1014 East Roy Street (S)
Bower/Bystrom House, 1022 Summit Avenue East (S)
Capitol Hill United Methodist Church, 128 Sixteenth Avenue East (S)
Cornish College of the Arts, 710 East Roy Street (N)
East Republican Street stairway, between Melrose Avenue East &
    Bellevue Avenue East (S)
P. P. Ferry House/Old Deanery of St. Mark's Cathedral, 1531 Tenth Avenue East
    (S, N))
Fire Station No. 7, 402 Fifteenth  Avenue East (W)
Fire Station No. 25, 1400 Harvard Avenue (N)
First African Methodist Episcopal Church, 1522 Fourteenth Avenue (S)
First Church of Christ Scientist, 1519 East Denny Way (S)
Harvard-Belmont Historic District (S, N)
Harvard Mansion, 2706 Harvard Avenue East (S)
Samuel Hill House, 814 East Highland Drive (N)
Hillcrest Apartment Building, 1616 East Howell Street (S, W)
Caroline Kline Galland House, 1605 Seventeenth Avenue (N)
Eliza Ferry Leary House, 1551 Tenth Avenue East (N)
Maryland Apartments, 626 Thirteenth Avenue East (S)
R. D. Merrill House, 919 Harvard Avenue East (N)
Moore Mansion, 811 Fourteenth Avenue East (S)
Parker/Fersen House, 1409 East Prospect (S)
William Parsons House, 2706 Harvard Avenue East (N)
St. Nicholas/Lakeside School, 1501 Tenth Avenue East (S)
St. Nicholas Russian Orthodox Cathedral, 1714 Thirteenth Avenue (S)
San Remo Apartment Building, 606 East Thomas Street (S)
Isaac Stevens School, 1242 Eighteenth Avenue East (S)
Volunteer Park (N)
Ward House, 520 East Denny Way (S, N)

*Pending City Designations*

St. Joseph's Church, 732 Eighteenth Avenue East
Seattle Art Museum at Volunteer Park, 1400 East Prospect

## Leschi, Madrona, Madison Park, and Montlake

Arboretum Aqueduct, Lake Washington Boulevard (S, N)
Richard A. Ballinger House, 1733 Thirty-ninth Avenue (N)
Brehm Brothers Houses, 219 and 221 Thirty-sixth Avenue East (S)
Charles Bussell House (Eastman/Jacobsen), 1630 Thirty-sixth Avenue (S, W)
Boyer/Lambert House, 1617 Boyer Avenue East (S)
Epiphany Chapel, 3719 East Denny Way (S)
Hebrew Academy (Forest Ridge Convent), 1617 Interlake Drive East (S)
Samuel Hyde House, 3726 East Madison Street (S, N)
Montlake Bridge and Montlake Cut (S, N)
Myron Ogden House, 702 Thirty-fifth Avenue (S)

Pioneer Hall, 1642 Forty-third Avenue East (N)
Ellsworth Storey Houses, 260 and 270 Dorffel Drive (S, N)

*Pending City Designations*

Lake Washington Bicycle Path, Interlaken Boulevard between
  Delmar Drive East and Twenty-fourth Avenue East

## NORTH OF DOWNTOWN

### Cascade and Eastlake

Denny Park, Denny Way at Dexter Avenue North (W)
Fisher/Howell House, 2819 Franklin Avenue East (S)
Immanuel Lutheran Church, 1215 Thomas Street (S, N)
Jensen Block, 601–611 Eastlake Avenue East (S)
Lake Union Steam Plant and Hydro House, 1179 Eastlake Avenue East (S)
Nelson/Steinbrueck House, 2622 Franklin Avenue East (S)
Parks Department building, 301 Terry Avenue (N)
St. Spiridon Russian Orthodox Cathedral, 400 Yale Avenue North (S)
Seattle Times Building, 1120 John Street (S)
Seward School, 2515 Boylston Avenue East (N, S pending)
Troy Laundry Building, 311-329 Fairview Avenue North (S)
Wagner Houseboat, 2770 Westlake Avenue North (N)

*Pending City Designations*

Old Norway Hall, 2015 Boren Avenue

### Queen Anne Hill and Magnolia

Fourteenth Avenue West Group, 2000–2016 Fourteenth Avenue West (S)
Alexander Hall, Seattle Pacific University (W)
Ballard/Howe House, 22 West Highland Drive (S, N)
Bethany Presbyterian Church, 1818 Queen Anne Avenue North (S)
Bowen/Huston Bungalow, 715 West Prospect Street (S)
Brace/Moriarty House, 170 Prospect Street (S)
C. H. Black House and Gardens, 615 West Lee Street (S)
Chelsea Apartment Building, 620 West Olympic Place (S, N)
Cotterill House, 2501 Westview Drive West (S)
Delamar Apartment Building, 115 West Olympic Place (S, N)
Fort Lawton (N)
Handschy/Kistler House, 2433 Ninth Avenue West (S)
McFee/Klockzien House, 524 West Highland Drive (S)
North Queen Anne Drive Bridge, over Wolf Creek Canyon (S, N)
Parsons House, 618 West Highland Drive (S)
Parsons Memorial Garden, immediately west of 618 West Highland Drive (S)
Queen Anne Branch Library, 400 West Garfield Street (N)
Queen Anne Club, 1530 Queen Anne Avenue North (N)
Queen Anne High School, 215 Galer Street (S, N)
Stimson-Griffith House, 405 West Highland Drive (N)
Stuart/Balcom House, 619 West Comstock Street (S, N)
West Point Light Station, Discovery Park (N)
West Queen Anne Elementary School, 515 West Galer Street (S, N)

West Queen Anne Walls, west side Eighth Avenue West and
    Seventh Avenue West (S)
Wilke Farm House, 1920 Second Avenue North (N)

*Pending City Designations*

Hay School, 2100 Fourth Avenue North
Queen Anne Boulevard, certain streets on Queen Anne Hill

## Northwest Seattle

Aurora (George Washington Memorial) Bridge (S, N)
Ballard Avenue Historic District (S, N)
Ballard Bridge (N)
Ballard Carnegie Library, 2026 Northwest Market Street (N)
Chittenden Locks and Lake Washington Ship Canal Historic District (N)
Drake House, 6414 Twenty-second Avenue Northwest (S)
Dunn Gardens, 13533 Northshire Road Northwest (N)
Fire Station No. 18, 5427 Russell Avenue Northwest (N)
Fremont Branch Library, 731 North Thirty-fifth Street (N)
Fremont Bridge (S, N)
Fremont Building, 3419 Fremont Avenue North (N)
Fremont Hotel, 3421–3429 Fremont Avenue North (S)
Green Lake Branch Library, 7364 East Green Lake Drive North (N)
Home of the Good Shepherd, 4647 Sunnyside Avenue North (S, N)
Louisa Building, 5220 Twentieth Avenue Northwest (S)
New Age Christian Church, 1763 Northwest Sixty-second Street(S)
Norvell House, 3306 Northwest Seventy-first Street (S)
Old Fire Station No. 18, 5427 Russell Avenue Northwest (S)
Red Hook Ale Brewery (Fremont Trolley Barn), 3400 Phinney Avenue North (S)
Salmon Bay Railroad Bridge (S, N)
Wallingford Center (Interlake Elementary School), 4416 Wallingford Street
    North (N, S pending)
Wallingford Fire and Police Station, 1629 North Forty-fifth Street (S, N)

*Pending City Designations*

B. F. Day School, 3921 Linden Avenue North
Latona School (portion), 401 Northeast Forty-second Street

## Northeast Seattle

Twentieth Avenue Northeast Bridge over Ravenna Park ravine (S)
Brooklyn Square (University Methodist-Episcopal Church),
    4142 Brooklyn Avenue Northeast (W)
Church of the Blessed Sacrament and rectory, 5041 Ninth Avenue
    Northeast (S, N)
Cowen Park Bridge, Fifteenth Avenue Northeast (S, N)
Ramsing House, 540 Northeast Eightieth Street (S)
Ravenna Park Bridge, Twentieth Avenue Northeast (N)
Sand Point Naval Air Station (1924 U.S. Army Air Corps global
    circumnavigation site) (W)
University Methodist Episcopal Church and parsonage (Brooklyn Square),
    4142 Brooklyn Avenue Northeast (S)
University Branch Library, 5009 Roosevelt Way Northeast (N)

University Bridge (N)
University Presbyterian Church "Inn," 4555 Sixteenth Avenue Northeast (S)
Ye College Inn, 4000 University Way Northeast (N)

*Pending City Designations*

Nathan Eckstein Junior High School, 3003 Northeast Seventy-fifth Street
University Heights Elementary School, 5031 University Way Northeast

## University of Washington Campus

Architecture Hall (W)
Clark Hall (W)
Denny Hall (W)
Lewis Hall (W)
Naval Military Hangar and Shell House (N)
Observatory (W)
Parrington Hall (W)
Territorial University Columns (W)

## Southeast Seattle

Fourteenth Avenue Bridge, Duwamish River (N)
Black Manufacturing Building, 1130 Rainier Avenue South (S)
Boeing Plant 1 ("Red Barn"), Museum of Flight (N)
Jesse C. Bowless House, 2540 Shoreland Drive South (N)
Columbia City Historic District (S, N)
Duwamish Archeological Site No. 1, Duwamish River (N)
Firehouse No. 33, 10235 Sixty-second Avenue South (S)
Georgetown City Hall, 6202 Thirteenth Avenue South (S, N)
Georgetown Steam Plant, northeast corner of Boeing Field (S, NL)
Kraus/Andersson House, 2812 South Mount St. Helen's Place (S, N)
Maple Donation Claim (Boeing Field), Airport Way South (W)
Lacey V. Murrow Bridge and East Portals of the Mount Baker Tunnels (S, N)
Rainier Cold Storage and Ice (Seattle Brewing and Malting Company),
    6000–6004 Airport Way South (S)
Seattle's first gas station site, Holgate Street at Alaskan Way (W)
Sick's Stadium site, Rainier Avenue South at South McClellan Street (S)
Ellsworth Storey Historic Cottages Group, 1706–1816 Lake Washington
    Boulevard South, and 1725–1729 Thirty-sixth Avenue South (S, N)
Thompson/LaTurner House, 3119 South Day Street (S)
Turner/Koepf House, 2336 Fifteenth Avenue South (N)

*Pending City Designations*

Cleveland High School, 5511 Fifteenth Avenue South
Franklin High School, 3013 South Mount Baker Boulevard
Kubota Gardens, 9727 Renton Avenue South

## West Seattle

Admiral Theater, 2343 California Avenue Southwest (S)
Alki Beach Park (W)
Akli Point Light Station (N)
Fauntleroy Community Church and YMCA, 9260 California Avenue
    Southwest (S)
Fir Lodge/Alki Homestead Restaurant, 2727 Sixty-first Avenue Southwest (S)

Hainsworth/Gordon House, 2657 Thirty-seventh Avenue Southwest (S)
Log House Museum Building, 3003 Sixty-first Avenue Southwest (S)
Schmitz Park Bridge, Admiral Way over Schmitz Park Ravine (S, N)
Hiawatha Playfield, 2700 California Avenue Southwest (S)
Satterlee House, 4866 Beach Drive Southwest (S)
Tracy House, 18971 Edgecliff Drive Southwest (N)
West Seattle Branch Library, 2306 Forty-second Avenue Southwest (N)

*Pending City Designations*

Duwamish Railroad Bridge over Duwamish Waterway
Gatewood School, 4320 Southwest Myrtle Street
West Seattle High School, 4075 Southwest Stevens Street

## Historic Districts

Ballard Avenue, Northwest Seattle (S, N)
Chinatown-International District (King Street), Downtown (S, N)
Chittenden Locks and Lake Washington Ship Canal, Northwest Seattle (N)
Columbia City, Southeast Seattle (S, N)
Harvard-Belmont, Capitol Hill (S, N)
Pike Place Market, Downtown (S, N)
Pioneer Square, Downtown (S, N)

## Vessels and Vehicles

*Adventuress*, schooner (NL)
*Arthur Foss*, tugboat (S, NL)
Brill Trolley No. 798 (S)
*Duwamish*, fireboat (S, NL)
*Fir*, Coast Guard cutter (NL)
*Kirkland*, ferry/excursion boat (W)
*W.T. Preston*, snagboat (S)
*Relief*, lightship (S, NL)
*San Mateo*, ferry (S, N)
*Virginia V*, "Mosquito Fleet" steamer (S, NL)
*Wawona*, schooner (S, NL)
*Zodiac*, schooner (N)

## Street Clocks

Benton's Jewelers, 3216 Northeast Forty-fifth Street (S)
Ben Bridge Jewelers, 409 Pike Street (S)
Carroll's Jewelers, 1427 Fourth Avenue (S)
Century Square, 1529 Fourth Avenue (S)
Dexter Horton Building, 720 Second Avenue (S)
Greenwood Jewelers, 129 North Eighty-fifth Street (S)
Meyers Music, 1206 First Avenue (S)
Restaurant, 3119 Eastlake Avenue East (S)
West Earth Co., 406 Dexter Avenue North (S)

# Sources and Suggested Reading

Lydia Aldredge et al. *Impressions of Imagination: Terra-Cotta Seattle.*
Seattle: Allied Arts of Seattle, 1986.

Clarence B. Bagley. *History of Seattle from the Earliest Settlement to the Present Time.*
Chicago: S. J. Clarke Publishing Co., 1916.

Richard C. Berman. *Seattle in the Twentieth Century,* Vols. 1 and 2.
Seattle: Charles Press, 1991, 1992.

Leslie Blanchard. *The Street Railway Era in Seattle.* Forty Fort, Pa.: Harold E. Cox, 1968.

T. William Booth and William H. Wilson. *Carl F. Gould: A Life in Architecture and Art.*
Seattle: University of Washington Press, 1995.

David Buerge. *Seattle in the 1880s.* Seattle: Historic Society of Seattle and King County, 1986.

David Buerge and Junius Rochester. *Roots and Branches, The Religious Heritage of
Washington State.* Seattle: Church Council of Greater Seattle, 1988.

Daniel Jack Chasan. *The Water Link, A History of Puget Sound as a Resource.*
Seattle: University of Washington Press/Washington Sea Grant Program, 1981.

Ron Chew, ed. *Reflections of Seattle's Chinese Americans: The First 100 Years.*
Seattle: University of Washington Press/Wing Luke Asian Museum, 1994.

Walt Crowley. *The Compleat Browser's Guide to Pioneer Square.*
Seattle: Pioneer Square Merchants Committee, 1981.

————. *Seattle University, A Century of Jesuit Education.* Seattle: Seattle University, 1991.

————. *Routes: A Brief History of Public Transportation in Metropolitan Seattle.*
Seattle: Metro Transit, 1993.

————. *Rites of Passage: A Memoir of the Sixties in Seattle.*
Seattle: University of Washington, 1995.

————. *The Woodland Park Zoo Guide.* Seattle: Woodland Park Zoo Society, 1995.

————. *To Serve the Greatest Number, A History of Group Health Cooperative of Puget
Sound.* Seattle: University of Washington/Group Health Cooperative, 1996.

Paul Dorpat. *Seattle Now & Then,* Vols. 1, 2, and 3.
Seattle: Tartu Press, 1984, 1988, and 1989.

————. *Seattle Chronicle, A Chronology of Seattle's Early History.*
Seattle: Tartu Publications, 1992. Videocassette.

Don Duncan. *Meet Me at the Fair: The Story of Seattle Center.*
Seattle: Seattle Center Foundation, 1992.

*The Duwamish Diary.* Seattle: Cleveland High School, 1946, 1996.

Clay Eals et al. *West Side Story.* Seattle: West Seattle Herald, 1987.

Patricia C. Erigero et al. *Seattle Public Schools Historic Building Survey.*
Seattle: Historic Seattle Preservation and Development Authority, 1989.

Jim Faber. *Steamer's Wake: Voyaging Down the Old Marine Highways of Puget Sound,
British Columbia, and the Columbia River.* Seattle: Enetai Press, 1985.

Robert L. Ferguson. *The Pioneers of Lake View: A Guide to Seattle's Early Settlers and
Their Cemetery.* Seattle: Thistle Press, 1995.

Charles M. Gates. *The First Century of the University of Washington, 1861–1961.*
Seattle: University of Washington Press, 1961.

Neal O. Hines. *Denny's Knoll: A History of the Metropolitan Tract of the University of
Washington.* Seattle: University of Washington Press, 1980.

*King County Survey of Historic Places.* Seattle: King County Department of Planning and
Community Development, 1979.

Ruth Kirk and Carmela Alexander. *Exploring Washington's Past: A Road Guide to History.*
Seattle: University of Washington Press, 1990, 1995.

M. S. Kline and G. A. Bayless. *Ferryboats: A Legend on Puget Sound.*
Seattle: Bayless Books, 1983.

Lawrence Kreisman. *Apartments by Anhalt.* Seattle: City Office of Urban Conservation, 1978.

———. *Art Deco Seattle.* Seattle: Allied Arts of Seattle, 1979.

———. *Historic Preservation in Seattle.* Seattle: Historic Seattle Preservation and Development Authority, 1985.

———. *The Stimson Legacy: Architecture in the Urban West.*
Seattle: Willows Press/University of Washington Press, 1992.

Cal McCune. *From Romance to Riot: A Seattle Memoir.* Seattle: C. M. McCune, 1996.

Murray Morgan. *Skid Road.* New York: Viking, 1951.

———. *Puget's Sound: A Narrative of Early Tacoma and the Southern Sound.*
Seattle: University of Washington Press, 1979.

Esther Hall Mumford. *Seattle's Black Victorians, 1852–1901.* Seattle: Ananse Press, 1980

———. *Calabash: A Guide to the History, Culture and Art of African Americans in Seattle and King County, Washington.* Seattle: Ananse Press, 1993.

Bryce E. Nelson. *Good Schools: The Seattle Public School System, 1901–1930.*
Seattle: University of Washington Press, 1988.

Robert C. Nesbit. *He Built Seattle: A Biography of Judge Thomas Burke.*
Seattle: University of Washington Press, 1961.

Roy Nielsen. *UniverCity: The Story of the University District in Seattle.*
Seattle: University Lions Foundation, 1986.

Jeffrey K. Ochsner, ed. *Shaping Seattle: A Historical Guide to Architects.*
Seattle: University of Washington Press, 1994.

Myra Phelps. *Public Works in Seattle: A Narrative History of the (Seattle) Engineering Department, 1875-1975.* Seattle: City of Seattle, 1978.

Kay Francis Reinartz et al. *Passport to Ballard: The Centennial Story.*
Seattle: Ballard Tribune, 1988.

———. *Queen Anne, Community on the Hill.* Seattle: Queen Anne Historical Society, 1993.

Robert H. Ruby and John A. Brown. *A Guide to the Indian Tribes of the Pacific Northwest.*
Norman: University of Oklahoma Press, 1986, 1992.

James M. Rupp and Mary Randlett. *Art in Seattle's Public Places: An Illustrated Guide.*
Seattle: University of Washington Press, 1992.

Roger Sale. *Seattle, Past to Present.* Seattle: University of Washington Press, 1976.

Roger Sale and Mary Randlett. *Seeing Seattle.* Seattle: University of Washington Press, 1994.

Archie Satterfield. *The Seattle GuideBook.* Chester, Conn.: The Globe Pequot Press, 1989.

J. Willis Sayre. *This City of Ours.* Seattle: Seattle School District No. 1, 1936.

Carlos Schwantes. *Railroad Signatures Across the Pacific Northwest.*
Seattle: University of Washington Press, 1993.

Diane Shamash and Steven Huss, eds. *A Field Guide to Seattle's Public Art.*
Seattle: City of Seattle Arts Commission, 1991.

Alice Shorett and Murray Morgan. *The Pike Place Market: People, Politics and Produce.*
Seattle: Pacific Search Press, 1985.

Robert Spector. *More Than a Store: Frederick & Nelson, 1890 to 1990.*
Bellevue, Wash.: Documentary Books, 1990.

Bill Speidel. *Sons of the Profits, The Seattle Story, 1851-1901.*
Seattle: Nettle Creek Publishing, 1967.

———. *Doc Maynard: The Man Who Invented Seattle.* Seattle: Nettle Creek Publishing, 1978.

Victor Steinbrueck. *Seattle Cityscape.* Seattle: University of Washington Press, 1962.

——— *Market Sketchbook.* Seattle: University of Washington Press, 1968, 1997.

Quintard Taylor. *The Forging of a Black Community: Seattle's Central District from 1870 Through the Civil Rights Era.* Seattle: University of Washington Press, 1994.

Caroline Tobin. *Downtown Seattle Walking Tours.* Seattle: City of Seattle, 1985.

James R. Warren, *King County and its Emerald City: Seattle.* Seattle: Museum of History and Industry and American Historical Press, 1997.

Warren W. Wing. *To Seattle by Trolley.* Edmonds, Wash.: Pacific Fast Mail Press, 1988.

———. *To Tacoma by Trolley.* Edmonds, Wash.: Pacific Fast Mail Press, 1996.

Sally B. Woodridge and Roger Montgomery. *A Guide to Architecture in Washington State.*
Seattle: University of Washington Press, 1980.

# Index